THE HASKELL LECTURES IN COMPARATIVE RELIGION

MODERN JAPAN
AND SHINTO NATIONALISM

MODERN JAPAN AND SHINTO NATIONALISM

A STUDY OF PRESENT-DAY TRENDS IN JAPANESE RELIGIONS

Revised Edition

Third Impression

By D. C. HOLTOM

PARAGON BOOK REPRINT CORP.

New York

1963

FOREWORD TO REVISED EDITION

JAPAN'S religion of conquest was brought to an end on December 15, 1945. On this date State Shinto was disestablished and reduced to the position of a privately supported sect. Although deprived of special legal privileges and endowments, the national faith of Japan still continued to exist, with latent possibilities for good or evil to the world. This important fact gave rise to two considerations in the revision of this book: one, the value of preserving the record of what State Shinto was prior to the close of World War II and, the other, the need of trying to outline the main direction of change since that event. Without the former, the latter could not be understood.

This revised edition, therefore, gives the first six chapters as originally published in 1943, when the United Nations were engaged in a bitter struggle with their aggressive Pacific enemy. They endeavor to set forth the significance of Japan's state religion in that struggle. To this, two new chapters have been added, one dealing with the vastly altered status of the national cultus in the new regime, the other with its possible value as a cultural resource either to Japan or to the world.

D. C. Holtom

SAN GABRIEL, CALIFORNIA
May 3, 1947

TABLE OF CONTENTS

CHAPTER I

THE RELIGIOUS FOUNDATIONS OF THE JAPANESE STATE

IMBEDDED in our Western culture the student of history can find many survivals out of our ancient religious past. We may see them in our Christmas trees, our Santa Claus beliefs, our memories of witches and warlocks, fairies and elves, our names for the days of the week, our unorthodox saints, our ill-adjusted beliefs in atonement and purification by scapegoats and substitutes, our faith in luck, and even in our essentially sound conviction that religion ought somehow to have a more vital adjustment to contemporary social life than that reached through dogma and theology. In these and many other ways we preserve the cultural fragments of the communal folk religions that our ancestors once wholeheartedly and unreflectingly espoused. But as living systems of ritual and belief they are gone to us forever. Our old sacred world with its sanctions in the oversight of ancient tribal gods has been broken up and scattered by our new knowledge, or, what is even more fateful for the destruction of the primitive way of life, its inner bonds have been dissolved in the new loyalties of an uncompromising and at the same time universalizing monotheism. Even when the racial rededication of a totalitarianism seeks spiritual renewal by lighting again its purification fires on the mountaintops and singing once more the old songs of blood and soil, the "homecoming" seems strained and pathetic, like that of the children of a new generation who have tried to go back and live with the outmoded furnishings of an ancestral home that has long lain in ruins.

The old communal form of religion that was normal in

the West two thousand years ago exists in Japan today as a powerful social and religious force. Into this religion the Japanese individual is born; loyalty to its belief and practice is his first qualification as a "good Japanese." It is not his by election; even when he chooses to attach himself to a universal religion like Buddhism or Christianity, the old is ever there as a vital, all-pervading influence, fundamentally conditioning his mentality and conduct and supplying a pattern to which all else must be accommodated. It permeates his home life, his agriculture, his business, his industry, his education, even his sports, and, above all, his conception of the state and his duty to it.

Problems arising out of conflict and adjustment in this area furnish many of the chief issues of the clash of cultures in the Far East today. The protection and deepening of the loyalties of this old religious life in the presence of new knowledge and new forms of conduct constitute the major concern of the state education of modern Japan. The old is deliberately and almost desperately revived as the means of guaranteeing the survival of a distinctive national character during the process of assimilating certain indispensable elements of the new.

This means that anyone who would seek to discover the dominant trends of the religious world of Japan today must find his most important clue in the remarkable enhancement of the fortunes of State Shinto that has been going on since the beginning of the modern period in 1867. This development has seen increasing acceleration in the fifty years that have elapsed since the promulgation of the Imperial Rescript on Education in 1890. In the decade that has just closed it has been stimulated to a new and previously unknown intensity. We can go beyond what has just been said to the statement that one who would make plain to himself the most characteristic aspects of the entire social and political, as well as religious, life of contemporary Japan must look for them in this same area, that is, in the study of the religious foundations of the Japanese state. We must never let ourselves lose sight of that characteristic of Japanese culture pointed out above: in this land community life and religion still are one. We must remember also that here the highest form of the community life is the merging of personal destiny in the greater destiny of the nation and that this great personal dedication is fostered by what is neither more nor less than a vital religious belief. We can make no adequate study of the existing Japanese national life apart from a thoroughgoing recognition of the fundamental position of the national faith which is the means by which the Japanese community is unified. Conversely, we can understand neither the national faith nor other religions in isolation from their relations to the almighty state. This persistent and challenging fact underlies the entire cultural life of Japan today and must be taken into careful consideration in any attempt at an appraisal of the forces that are working toward the creation of "a new order in East Asia." It has far-reaching implications not only for the Far East but also for the world at large. Trends in other religions, if they are to be founded on realism, must be oriented with respect to Shinto and the increasingly nationalistic Japanese state.

When we speak of the religious foundations of the Japanese state, we are not using the word "religious" in a merely figurative sense. It is not a reference to something which in its hold on sentiment or in its challenge to loyalties resembles or takes the place of religion. It is rather a carefully organized religious cultus with its pantheon of deities, its thousands of priests, its tens of thousands of sacred places, its elaborate ceremonies, its dogmas and sacred texts, and, most significant of all for the peoples of other nations, especially for those of the Far East who are rapidly coming under the sway of Japanese domination and influence, its sense of divinely ordained mission. This is State Shinto.

A further introductory remark should be stressed: it is essential to recognize as a primary datum the fact that major trends in Japan today arise from the necessity that is laid on all subjects of the realm, whatever their religious affiliations, to accommodate themselves in such wise to a Shinto-motivated nationalism as to furnish evidence that they are trustworthy members of the community. The main task of the studies that follow will be the attempt to identify and interpret the principal problems that have arisen out of this situation.

Japanese sources commonly make use of a special term to indicate the close relationship that exists between the affairs of government and those of national Shinto. This is *saisei itchi*. *Sai* here means ceremony or ritual; *sei* refers to governmental or political administration; *itchi* means unity. The whole, therefore, may be translated "the unity of rites and politics," or "the unity of government and Shinto ceremonies," or "the unity of government and religion," depending on the quality, religious or otherwise, which we attach to the rites. Inasmuch, however, as it seems necessary to yield to the overwhelming weight of evidence favoring the interpretation that the rites are essentially religious, we may accept the translation, "the unity of government and religion."

These words carry us back to the days of Old Shinto when the affairs of the state and religion were avowedly one, when the chief officers of administration in political affairs were likewise the high priests of the national religion, and when the first concern of the government was to know and do the will of the gods. As we shall soon see, these same characteristics are identifiable to a remarkable extent in the Japanese state life of today. Contemporary Japan is witnessing a vigorous revival of the ancient unity expressed in *saisei itchi*. State Shinto is today so intimately associated with communal solidarity that participation in the former is regarded as the measure of loyalty to the latter.

The modern Japanese state was deliberately established on a foundation which unified government and religion. In 1868 Shinto was made the state religion and has remained so ever since, in spite of strong statements to the contrary made largely on the basis of political necessity.

Saisei itchi has been a consciously formulated objective of the directors of the Japanese national life right through the modern period. A major purpose—we might almost say the major purpose—of successive governments from the opening of the Meiji era in 1868 to the immediate present has been to furnish the state life with a standardized ritual, centering in a faith in the traditional gods, to the end that the national psychology shall be safeguarded against the dangers of foreign contacts and unified in the support of vital national polity. The evidence for these statements is very substantial. We may at least direct our attention to enough of it to make the presentation definite.

An imperial edict promulgated in the first year of Meiji (1868) reads:

The worship of the gods and regard for ceremonies [Shinto] are the great proprieties of the Empire and the fundamental principles of national polity and education. . . . . On this occasion of the restoration [of direct imperial rule], Tokyo has been made the new capital and the Emperor shall reign in person. First of all rituals shall be initiated and the administration of law and order shall be established. Thus the Way of the unity of religion and government (*saisei itchi*) shall be revived.[1]*

Two years later (1870) saw the promulgation of another imperial rescript which refers to the great antiquity of the system of the unification of religion and the state in Japanese history and, by implication, its primary importance in the national structure.

From the very beginning of the establishment of the affairs of government by the Great Ancestress [Amaterasu Omikami], she worshiped the

* Footnotes are at ends of respective chapters.

gods and cherished the people with tender affection. The origin of the
unity of religion and the state (*saisei itchi*) is long ago.[2]

On the same day another edict was promulgated which
sets forth the same conception of the state in even greater
detail:

> We solemnly announce: The Heavenly Deities and the Great An-
> cestress [Amaterasu Omikami] established the throne and made the suc-
> cession secure. The line of Emperors in unbroken succession entered
> into possession thereof and handed it on. Religious ceremonies and gov-
> ernment were one and the same (*saisei itchi*) and the innumerable sub-
> jects were united. Government and education were clear to those above,
> while below them the manners and customs of the people were beautiful.
> Beginning with the Middle Ages, however, there were sometimes sea-
> sons of decay alternating with seasons of progress. Sometimes the Way
> was plain, sometimes, darkened; and the period in which government
> and education failed to flourish was long.
> Now in the cycle of fate all things have become new. Polity and edu-
> cation must be made clear to the nation and the Great Way of obedi-
> ence to the gods must be promulgated. Therefore we newly appoint
> propagandists to proclaim this to the nation. Do you our subjects keep
> this commandment in mind.[3]

In spite of minor fluctuations in the fortunes of State
Shinto in the years that have passed since these documents were issued, accompanied by a small amount of
change in the functions of the national cult, they may be
taken as typical of the entire modern period. The doctrine
of the unity of government and religion has recently received new emphasis in the state educational system.

In 1937 the Department of Education of the central
government in Tokyo issued a remarkable book called
Kokutai no Hongi ("The Fundamental Principles of the
National Structure"). It is a study of the Japanese state in
what may be called its spiritual foundations. It is a classical revelation on the part of the government itself of the
religious foundations of Japanese nationalism. It goes even
further than the documents that we have just noted and
sets up a threefold relationship between religious ceremonies, government, and education. In this matter it
says:

The Emperor by means of religious ceremonies (*saishi*) becomes one with the divine imperial ancestors, and through participation in the spirit of the imperial ancestors, He is able to educate the subjects of the state ever more and more and promote their prosperity. In this way the spirit wherewith the Emperor rules the country is imparted. For this reason the worship of the gods on the part of the Emperor and His administration of government are in their fundamental aspects one and the same thing. Furthermore the Emperor is the custodian and executor of the testaments of the ancestors and with these He makes clear the great principles on which the nation was founded and the Great Way in which the subjects should walk. In these consist the great essentials of our education. Thus, education in its fundamental aspects is unified with religious ceremonies and government. That is to say, although religious ceremonies and government and education have each their own separate operations, yet in the last analysis they are one and the same.[4]

Examination of the precise manner in which this union of government, education, and religion finds expression in Japanese institutions and psychology carries us into the heart of the study of the religious foundations of the state. One can frequently find contemporary Japanese writers making the declaration that the essential basis of their nationalism lies in the historical fact of the divine origin of the dynasty of emperors reigning in an unbroken line forever, in the eternal guardianship which the spirits of the deified ancestors extend to the state and its subjects, and in the consciousness of a sacred mission laid on the Japanese people to share their peerless national life with the rest of mankind and thus contribute to the salvation of the world. All these propositions require examination from the side of their religious associations.

We consider first the dogma of unbroken divine imperial sovereignty. This is the primary dictum of all Japanese education and the foundation on which the entire state is erected. The first article of the written constitution of the empire, promulgated in 1889, reads: "The Empire of Japan shall be reigned over and governed by a line of Emperors unbroken for ages eternal." The third article reads: "The Emperor is sacred and inviolable."

There is no officially established statement that exactly defines the sacredness or divinity of the emperor. In this respect the state leaves itself free to benefit by whatever sentiments of awe and reverence exist in the national mind. Interpretations range through various stages, from a view which assigns omniscience to the emperor and would make him the chief object of religious worship in the homes and at the public ceremonies of the Shinto shrines and elsewhere, to a politico-humanistic view which lodges the divinity of the sovereign in an inviolable legal headship, entailing a corresponding obedience on the part of the people. There are no shrines where a reigning monarch is officially worshiped during his lifetime on earth. Only the spirit of a deceased emperor is accorded this kind of apotheosis. An important recent trend appears, however, in the fact that the politico-humanistic form of interpretation, just mentioned, has been largely suppressed, while over against this the growth of military totalitarianism has been accompanied by an increased emphasis on the dogma of the mystical divinity of the emperor.

To speak more specifically, the divinity of the ruler is not found merely in his exercise of final and absolute authority in the state or, again, in his moral character. It lies not in mere power, neither in virtue in and of itself, although as the idealized center of the national life these qualities are naturally believed to manifest themselves to an unparalleled degree in the person of the sovereign. Divinity lies rather in the blood connections of the emperor with the great *kami*[5] ancestors of the past. It is biological and historical, a divinity and sacredness preserved in the germ plasm. Hence the indispensability of the doctrine of an unbroken lineage reaching back to the very beginning of the foundation of the state. The emperor is divine because he is the living extension in time of the very bodies and souls of the great divine ancestors of the past and, in particular, of the physical and spiritual attributes of the sun-goddess, Amaterasu Omikami, by whose will and wisdom the state was originally founded. This divine ancestress is the chief of the contemporary, politically inspired pantheon of Shinto deities, and her great shrine at Ise is the center of the devotion and worship of the entire nation. It is obvious that, when we reach this kind of interpretation of imperial divinity, we have transcended the limits of logic and history and find ourselves in the presence of assertions of religious faith that represent sentimental attachments to traditional survivals out of ancient folkways and mythology. The existence of these ancient sentiments and the national capacities for belief which support them open to the Japanese state an extraordinary field for political cultivation and equip it with an emotional integration that cannot be duplicated the world over.

Although the subject deserves a whole book rather than the few paragraphs that are possible here, there follow in supplementation of the above remarks a few examples of the forms of exposition which Japanese authorities themselves give to the dogma of divine imperial sovereignty.

Prince Itō, who was chiefly responsible for the drafting of the written constitution under which modern Japan is governed, says in his *Commentaries on the Constitution*, published in 1889:

The Sacred Throne was established at the time when the heavens and the earth became separated. The Emperor is Heaven descended, divine and sacred; He is preeminent above all his subjects. He must be reverenced and is inviolable. He has indeed to pay due respect to the law, but the law has no power to hold him accountable to it. Not only shall there be no irreverence for the Emperor's person, but also He shall not be made a topic of derogatory comment nor one of discussion.[6]

The late Kunitake Kume, formerly a professor in the Imperial University of Tokyo, writing on Shinto in a volume called *Fifty Years of New Japan*, says:

He [the Emperor] is regarded as a living *kami*, loved and revered by the nation above all things on earth, and himself loving and protecting the nation, who are deemed sons of *Kami-nagara* ["the gods them-

selves"] and are entrusted to his care by the *kami*. . . . . Thus, Shintō
(doctrine of the *kami*) is *kundō* (doctrine of the Emperor), for Shintoism
is Mikadoism; "the *kami*'s will is the Emperor's will" is a maxim inscribed on the heart of every Japanese. Herein one may see the fountain-head of our patriotic spirit, whose marvelous activity has served
to raise Japan in these fifty years to the level of the first-rate Powers of
the world.[7]

The depth and uniformity with which this primary
"maxim" of the state is "inscribed on the heart of every
Japanese" are complete evidence of the thoroughness of
the nationalistic educational process. The following statement of a cabinet official only repeats what every school-
boy is taught:

The protection and advancement of the country are in the care of the
ancestral spirits and their power resides in the Emperor. The use of that
power is the work of the Imperial Throne. . . . . The central idea of the
Japanese state is the belief that the spirits of the Imperial ancestors continue to rule through their living representatives, and from this belief
springs the singular national spirit of the Japanese people.[8]

Uyehara, writing in *The Political Development of Japan*,
says:

He [the Emperor] is to the Japanese mind the Supreme Being in the
Cosmos of Japan, as God is in the universe of the pantheistic phi-
losopher. From him everything emanates, in him everything subsists.
. . . . He is supreme in all temporal affairs of the state as well as in all
spiritual matters.[9]

The relation of all this to individual personality and initiative is well expressed by the late Dr. Shinkichi Uesugi,
at one time a professor in the law department of the Imperial University of Tokyo, when he says:

Subjects have no mind apart from the will of the Emperor. Their individual selves are merged with the Emperor. If they act according to
the mind of the Emperor, they can realize their true nature and attain
the moral ideal. This is the fundamental relationship existing between
the Japanese people and their Emperor who is the descendant and extension in time of the Great Deity [Amaterasu Omikami]. The organizing will resides inherently in the Emperor and apart from the Imperial
mind there exists no organizing will.[10]

When we pass on to very recent years, we find a wealth
of similar utterances that bear testimony to the dominance

in the thought of the nation of the conviction that the unique stability of their state lies in the fact that its ultimate authorizations come from divine sanctions communicated through the throne. In fact, the tempo of this belief has accelerated extraordinarily during the past decade in proportion as crisis has accentuated in the consciousness of ruling groups the necessity of increasing totalitarian regimentation and widespread military control over the domestic life. The army is the chief mediating agency of the divine imperial will. While serving as minister of education in 1938, General Sadao Araki wrote:

The Japanese conception of political origin lies in the very law of nature in conformity with Divine Will. According to our belief, Japan was founded by the Sun Goddess, Amaterasu-Ōmikami, who is revered by the entire nation for her all-pervading virtues, and from whom our Imperial House is descended. We, therefore, are proud to look upon our Emperor as the fountain-head of our national life. In this respect our Empire rests upon the foundation of blood relationship which far transcends mere morality, and our Ruler is viewed in the light of a super-moral Being. . . . . .

The *Tennō*,[11] by which name our Sovereign is known, embodies in Himself the spirit of the deities of the primordial universe, as well as the guiding spirit of government, manifested by His divine ancestress, Amaterasu-Ōmikami. His august virtues thus pervade both time and space, and He reigns over His people with love and benevolence.[12]

Writing in *Contemporary Japan* for March, 1940, Dr. Shinichi Fujii, professor at Waseda University, director of the Institute for the Study of National Policies in Asia, and author of numerous books on political science and law, speaks of "the innate sacredness of the *Tennō*, whom his subjects look up to as a divine Sovereign." The author then continues:

The subjects' faith lies in the fact that their *Tennō*, being a descendant of the Sun Goddess, that is, a living God, therefore practices the Way of *Tennō*, or the Way of the Sun Goddess. It is stated in Article III of the Constitution that "The *Tennō* is sacred and inviolable." One may say that there are similar provisions in every country's constitution, but I wonder if there is any other country where these words are as endearing as they are to the Japanese. These two attributes of the *Tennō* [sacredness and inviolability] are not only revealed in the historical fact of government by one unbroken line of Rulers, but also testified by many other pieces of historical evidence. One of them is the fact that the Imperial Family has no family name, contrary to the sovereign houses of Europe. This phenomenon is explained by the fact that, whereas in other countries rulers sprang from the people, in Japan the divine descendants of the Sun Goddess (that is, living Gods) have each in succession possessed the Three Sacred Treasures [i.e., the regalia emblems, consisting of a sword, a mirror, and a stone necklace] bequeathed from the preceding *Tennō* as the very symbol of the foundation of the country by the Great Imperial Ancestress [Amaterasu Omikami].[13]

The best-known interpreter of the modern Shinto revival is Dr. Genchi Katō, formerly professor of Shinto in the Imperial University of Tokyo and now on the staff of the Shinto College of the same city (Kokugakuin Daigaku). Dr. Katō writes: "The position occupied by *Ten* and *Jōtei* among the Chinese or by Jehovah among the Jews has been held in Japan from ancient days by the Emperor."[14] Again he says: "From ancient times the Emperor has been called by such titles as *Aki tsu Kami* (Manifest Deity), *Ara-hito Kami* (Incarnate Deity), and *Ara Mikami* (Incarnate Great-deity)."[15]

According to this author, Shinto reaches its highest form of manifestation in worship of the emperor. On this point he says:

Shintō .... has culminated in Mikadoism or the worship of the Mikado or Japanese Emperor as a divinity, during his lifetime as well as after his death. .... Herein lies even at the present day, in my opinion, the essence or life of Shintō, inseparably connected with the national ideals of the Japanese people. Japanese patriotism or loyalty, as you might call it, really is not simple patriotism or mere loyalty as understood in the ordinary sense of the word, that is, in the mere ethical sense of the term. It is more—it is the lofty self-denying enthusiastic sentiment of the Japanese people towards their august Ruler, believed to be something divine, rendering them capable of offering up anything and everything, all dearest to them, willingly, that is, of their own free will; of sacrificing not only their wealth or property, but their own life itself, for the sake of their divinely gracious Sovereign. .... All this is nothing but the actual manifestation of the religious consciousness of the Japanese people.[16]

There is good evidence that these sentiments are shared by the chief authorities of the national government today.

Mr. Kan Kikuchi, writing in *Shūhō* ("Weekly Gazette"), the official publication of the Department of Home Affairs, in his capacity as councilor to the intelligence bureau of this department, on the subject of "Aspects of Two Thousand Six Hundred Years of Japanese History," summarizes an account of the exploits of the first ruler, Jimmu Tennō, with the words:

Our Japanese race thus passed through a great testing in the time of Jimmu Tennō. Thereby were fostered a spiritual stability that never yields no matter what the hardships, a strong racial capacity for unification, and a reverential and worshipful faith in the Emperor, exalted to a religious character. These have come down through two thousand six hundred years as the very core of the Japanese national spirit.[17]

We shall have to leave to later discussion the relation of the doctrine of the divinity of the emperor to organized religious groups. The data just introduced may be taken as sufficient to the purpose of setting forth the form that this doctrine takes in the national educational scheme.

In approaching the second dogma of modern Japanese nationalism in its religious aspects, we are confronted with a deep and widespread belief in a special guardianship extended to the land and its people by the ancestral deities. Japan is "the Land of the Gods." This is the name that patriots throughout a long history have liked to give to their homeland. It does not mean merely that the gods are many, that unseen spirits haunt the mountains and valleys, the streams and woodlands. More than this, it means that the very islands themselves, the people, their racial characteristics, and the unique form of their national life are something more than the resultants of ordinary geographical and historical forces. From the beginning they have received the impress of the creative wills of divine ancestors who foresaw the far-distant future and gave to land and race and institutions an initial divine character that must be forever theirs. It means that these ancestral deities are eternally living in the spirit world from which they mold the destiny of the present according to their unchanging purposes. The existence of such superlative benefits, manifested in the form of sacred historical absolutes and immediate superhuman guidance, entails corresponding responsibility and loyalty on the part of the living.

In 1881, in an imperial rescript notifying the nation of an intention to establish a parliamentary form of government, the Emperor Meiji declared: "Our ancestors in Heaven watch our acts, and We recognize Our responsibility to them for the faithful discharge of Our high duties, in accordance with the principles and the perpetual increase of the glory they have bequeathed to Us."[18]

The belief set forth in these words underlies the entire social and political life. The very soil is uniquely divine. The early Japanese cosmogony is developed about this theme. The center of the world is the Eight Great Islands of the Japanese archipelago. The lands that they loved and knew constituted the real universe to the early mythmakers. The islands were brought into being by the creative purposes of the gods and are the direct offspring of the union of Izanagi and Izanami, the sky-father and the earth-mother. Hirata Atsutane, the early nineteenth-century theologian of Shinto, merely gave expression to a typical conception when he declared that the Japanese islands were produced first by the greatest of the ancestral *kami* and that the inferiority of the rest of the world was indicated by the fact that it was produced later out of sea-foam and mud.

Educated Japanese of today are, of course, not ignorant of the fact that this kind of primitive cosmogony can be duplicated elsewhere at appropriate levels of culture, but they nevertheless find special significance in the fact that throughout the entire sweep of their national history the sentiments of religion have been fused to the land. This is not merely an aesthetic response to the beauty of nature that has been extended to Japan in lavish measure; it is also a sense of patriotic responsibility to a sacredness that resides even in the soil.

When we come to the interpretation of the psychological characteristics of the race, we find the same thing even more intensely sensed and asserted. There is probably no nation on earth today more conscious of itself, its psychological and institutional characteristics, its problems and tensions, than is the Japanese. The fact of a strong and isolated ethnocentrism brought sharply and suddenly into conflict with the bewildering culture of the West has accentuated pre-existing tendencies to introspection and has thrown Japan into an introverted psychosis of national proportions as a means of trying to save her own soul. Japanese moral and historical discussions abound in lengthy disquisitions on the possession of unique and superior racial qualities. To enumerate these qualities, count them over and over, analyze and describe them, and proclaim them as the basis of unparalleled achievement has become almost a national obsession. Some would find four, others five, some ten or more of these primary national psychological qualities. A general list of those that are emphasized in present-day discussions would have to include a unique loyalty and patriotism, a special endowment of assimilative power which can take in the best of foreign culture and yet remain forever Japanese, unusual powers of organization, an unrivaled capacity for expansion and achievement, reverence for ancestors and regard for family name, a this-worldly and practical nature, love of natural beauty, an artistic and refined skill (particularly manual skill), candor and openheartedness, optimism, unique regard for purity and cleanliness, propriety and orderliness, and, finally, a gentle and forbearing disposition.

It is no part of the purpose of the present discussion to attempt the critical examination of this extraordinary galaxy of virtues. We are here interested in the fact that they are commonly referred for origin to a divine impress on the

Japanese character. They are in the national soul because the gods put them there. They have a mystical, religious basis. One hundred years ago Hirata Atsutane, the Shinto theologian mentioned above, wrote:

We [i.e., the members of the Japanese race] who have been brought into existence through the creative spirits of the sacred ancestral *kami* are, each and every one, in spontaneous possession of the Way of the Gods. This means that we are equipped by nature with the virtues of reverence for the gods, for rulers and parents, with kindness toward wife and children, with the moral qualities which in Confucianism are called the five great ethical relationships (*gorin*) [i.e., those of ruler and subjects, parent and child, husband and wife, older and younger brothers, and friend with friend] and also with the five virtues (*gojō*) [i.e., benevolence, justice, propriety, wisdom, and faith], and to follow this nature just as it is, without bending or turning aside, is to conform to the teaching of the *kami*.[19]

Contemporary writers and educators constantly reiterate these same ideas. *Yamato*[20]-*damashii* ("the Yamato soul"), or, to use the expression that is widely current today, *Nippon Seishin* ("the Japanese Spirit"), is the peerless and divinely contributed endowment of the race that gives characteristic form to everything it touches. One of the most influential of the modern Shinto teachers has said, in words that are reminiscent of the famous statement of Hirata's just quoted:

We are recipients from the *kami*, by direct descent through the ancestors, of a specific endowment of tendencies and capacities, and if we permit this innate disposition to find normal expression, we achieve spontaneously filial piety, loyalty and love of fellow-men. There is here no conflict of individualism and no placing of the gods outside of the world of men. As a race we are one with our ancestors, a part of divine nature. It is thus involved in the natural unfolding of the Way of the Gods within us that we should be prudent regarding self, that we should contribute to national progress and anticipate the future peace of the whole world.[21]

The possession of these divinely implanted qualities gives unique form and stability to the state. The sanctity of the state is guaranteed in the belief that it was founded by the ancestral gods. For the eternal protection and development of the state, rulers and people alike are responsible to the gods. The Japanese national structure (*koku-tai*) is not the result of the interplay of the ordinary factors that are found in the evolution of other countries. At heart it is the expression of the purposes of the ancestral *kami* who founded the state in the far-distant past. It has as its inner, unique, and most characteristic feature a divine, immutable, and eternal quality. In its essential nature it has never changed in the past, and it will not change in all the future. There is no room for the conception of genuine historical evolution in the officially sponsored theory of state prevalent in Japan today; the people have always lived in a golden age under the manifestation of a mighty historical absolute. Its form is divinely foreordained and final.

This sacred absolute has its classical formulation in a text that appears in the *Nihongi* as the command of the sun-goddess to her grandson when she sent him down from heaven (Takama-ga-Hara) to take dominion over the territory that was, by divine intention, to form the nucleus of the future Japanese state. The command reads:

This Reed-plain Land of Fifteen Thousand Autumns of Fair Rice-ears is the country over which my descendants shall be lords. Do thou, my August Grandchild, proceed thither and rule over it. Go! and may prosperity attend thy dynasty, and it shall, like Heaven and Earth, endure forever.[22]

Japanese historians and educators have always found in these words an edict from the highest personage of the Shinto god-world, whereby the state was founded. They have been pronounced the fundamental faith of the nation and the motivating force of all its activities. The "National History for Ordinary Primary Schools" issued by the Department of Education says of this event: "The foundations of our national structure with its single line of emperors, unbroken through the centuries, which shall not be moved throughout all ages, were in truth laid at this time."[23] The corresponding text of the "Teacher's Manual" says:

Thus the antiquity of the establishment of our state is seen to be greater than that of all other countries. . . . .

When we consider the history of all other lands, we find that in all foreign countries for the most part the people have prior existence and the rulers are subsequently elected. On this account revolutions are frequent and rulers are constantly being raised up and put down, and practically none of these countries preserves its original national structure. When we make comparison with this, we perceive the reason why our national structure is supreme among all the nations of the world. Kitabatake Chikafusa [1293–1354] at one time wrote *The Account of the Righteous Reigns of the Divine Emperors (Jinnō Shōtōki)* in which he extolled our superior national structure and said, "Great Japan is the Land of the Gods. Here the Deity of the Sun has handed on her eternal rule. This is true only of our country and there is nothing like it in any other land." We, the people of the nation, must realize the nature of the splendor of our national structure and must be increasingly zealous in the manifestation of loyalty and must exert ourselves in the patriotic protection of the state.[24]

These assertions are typical of all Japanese state education. Here again the immediate purposes of our investigation do not carry us into the historical criticism of the material before us. Our interest lies in noting the form and depth of the conviction that the foundations of the state are religious. In summary of this section of the discussion, then, the national gods have given to Japan a divine land, a divine racial psychology, and a divinely established structure in the state. Corresponding to this conviction of a unique and sacred endowment from the ancestral *kami* is a sense of responsibility to the unseen spirit world. Recent years in Japan have produced a rather bewildering succession of premiers, but, however much these men have differed among themselves, they have been one in making known to the nation their sense of responsibility to the gods.

No one has been more ardent in this matter than Baron Hiranuma, who in the course of his brief tenure of office in the early part of 1939 repeatedly emphasized the religious aspects of civil administration. He declared:

The carrying-out of the will of the gods is true politics, and to enshrine the gods and pray to them is to establish communion with the will of the gods.[25]

To pray to the gods is the fundamental principle of politics.[26]

The objective of Japan's guiding political principles is the realization of the justice of Heaven and the expression of the Divine Will.[27]

Japan is secure from the invasion of ideas (from abroad) because it has its own Imperial Way.[28]

In his address to the seventy-fifth session of the imperial diet, delivered on February 1, 1940, the newly appointed prime minister, Admiral Mitsumasa Yonai, said:

History shows that whenever an emergency arises, our national spirit is most emphatically manifested to advance the prestige and fortune of the nation. It is incumbent upon us to leave no stone unturned in order to promote loyalty and bravery on the home front as well, and to replenish and demonstrate our nation's powers, for which are required the inculcation of the spirit of reverence for deities and respect for ancestors, the renovation of national education and the improvement of the people's physical strength.[29]

Assertions like these reveal one of the essential characteristics of the Japanese conception of the sources of national stability. The depth of the conviction of responsibility to the ancestral deities is the index of the feeling of dependence on superhuman direction for the realization of national purpose and is the measure of the extent to which the entire structure of the state rests on religious foundations.

The third and final phase of the discussion introduces us to the dogma of benevolent destiny. At the root of Japan's dedication to what she calls her "holy war" in East Asia lies the conviction that she is sent to be the savior of the world. Hand in hand with her deep economic need goes the belief that she is ordained by the divine forces that work through her history to share with less fortunate nations the blessings of her peerless institutions. Indeed, the doctrine that her state structure is the strongest and most excellent of all the world must have as its corollary the idea that non-Japanese peoples can benefit only by being brought under its sway. It would be a misreading of the facts if we should be content to account for the vigor and steadfastness with which this conviction of mission is asserted, merely as a search for compensation in the presence of frustration and insecurity, or as a pious verbiage that cloaks desperate economic need, on the one hand, and bitterly inconsistent severity toward conquered peoples, on the other.

The great eighteenth-century scholar, Motoori Norinaga, held that Shinto was a divine way expressed in the classical literature. The sanctions of nationalism may be found in ancient texts that are given the authority of holy scripture. Modern Japanese theory of state has been much influenced by this idea. Nowhere does it appear more clearly than in the doctrine of benevolent destiny. The Japanese people are taught that their state has developed out of the distant past under the formative influence of a special divine commission to expand sovereignty and righteousness over ever widening territories. This commission finds authorization in two imperial edicts which the *Nihongi* places in the mouth of the semilegendary first emperor, Jimmu Tennō. The first was spoken just before this ruler set out from Kyushu to conquer the districts of the east that eventually were to become the seat of the flourishing Yamato culture. Speaking of these unconquered places, the Mikado is made to say: "I think that this land will undoubtedly be suitable for the extension of the Heavenly task [i.e., for the further development of the Imperial power], so that its glory should fill the universe. It is, doubtless, the center of the world."[30]

Aston, after translating in these words, introduces the necessary caution into the acceptance of their historical validity by pointing out that the entire speech from which the passage is taken is copied from a Chinese original. If any present-day Japanese historians share this information, the light of their knowledge is effectively darkened beneath the heavy political and military coercion that now covers them. Historical veracity cannot be permitted to dim the purpose of the directors of the national life to use the text as an inspired revelation to world expansion. Army authorities have declared that it sets forth an eternal categorical imperative. It has been interpreted to mean that Japan is ordained by the will of the ancestral gods for the limitless extension of the imperial dominion and for ruling the entire world.

The next scriptural authorization of this conviction of benevolent destiny is used even more widely than the first in support and vindication of national expansion. Aston, in connection with his translation of the text which we are to consider, calls attention to the fact that Hirata once justified Hideyoshi's invasion of Korea on the grounds that the sovereigns of Japan were the *de jure* lords of the whole earth. This second commission was issued, according to the *Nihongi*, which is again our source, on the occasion of the first accession to the imperial throne in 660 B.C., after six years of struggle against rebellious tribes within Japan. The edict promulgated at that time says in part:

> In regard to matters that are above, We shall respond to the good-ness of the Heavenly Powers in granting us the Kingdom. In regard to matters that are below, We shall foster righteousness and extend the line of the imperial descendants. Thus, hereafter, the capital [i.e., the imperial rule] shall be extended so as to embrace all the six quarters [north, south, east, west, zenith, and nadir, that is, the entire world] and the universe [*ame no shita*, written "eight cords"—*hakkō*—in the original] shall be covered so as to form a (single) roof [i.e., one family].³¹

From these words has been derived the slogan, "The Whole World under One Roof" (*hakkō ichi-u*), which Japanese authorities have pronounced the revelation of the great timeless mission of the nation, the keystone of Japanese diplomacy, and the declaration of the great ideals of the Yamato race. Important documents of state, as well as responsible public utterances of all sorts, constantly re-iterate the slogan as a rallying cry to "mobilize the national spirit" and inspire loyalty with an idealism commensurate with the sacrifices demanded of it. The consummation of the Three-Power Pact between Germany,

Italy, and Japan was made known to the Japanese nation by an imperial edict, issued on September 27, 1940. The opening words declare: "To enhance justice on earth and make of the world one household is the great injunction, bequeathed by Our Imperial Ancestors, which We lay to heart day and night."[32]

Earlier in the same year Admiral Yonai, speaking as newly appointed premier, had said: "The principle of the whole world under one roof embodies the spirit in which the Empire was founded by Jimmu Tennō. My understanding is that this is the spirit of making the boundless virtues of the Emperor prevail throughout the whole world."[33]

Later in the same year Prince Konoye began his statement of the fundamental policy of his government with the words: "The basic aim of Japan's national policy lies in the firm establishment of world peace in accordance with the lofty spirit of *Hakkō Ichi-u,* in which the country was founded."[34]

A minister of war has recently declared: "Since the foundation of the Japanese Empire it has been the yearning of all Japanese to unite all the races of the world into a happy society. We regard this as the great mission of the Japanese people. We strive also to clear away from the earth injustice and inequality and to bring everlasting happiness to mankind."[35]

These few illustrations will prepare us for the assertion that Japan's national educational program gives large place to the inculcation of her particular brand of ecumenicity. Earlier in the discussion the Department of Education publication entitled "The Fundamental Principles of the National Structure" was introduced. The importance of this textbook in the existing educational scheme justifies calling it the bible of contemporary Japanese nationalism. One of the widely used commentaries on this textbook enters into a detailed exposition of the content of the *hakkō ichi-u* doctrine; it may be taken as typical of all discussions of the subject. The phrase "the whole world under one roof" does not mean bald aggression and military exploitation, as those affected by the materialism and individualism of Europe and America might easily misunderstand it to mean. It means the establishment in the earth of peace and righteousness, aiming to cover the whole world with the illuminating rays of charity, love, virtue, truth, and justice. When each nation and race has opportunity to fulfil its rightful destiny, take its place in the sun, express its will and own special characteristics of culture and racial soul, and thus make its unique contribution to the general good, then the doctrine will be realized. All the peoples of the world, with mutual assistance and good will, will then live together as one great family. At the same time the leadership of Japan in this benevolent reconstruction of the world must be recognized. The *hakkō ichi-u* teaching involves the purpose to extend to the four seas the imperial glory which now fills Japan herself and thereby bring in the universal reign of peace. This in turn involves the use of military power, but history shows that the military might of Japan is always that of a "divine soldiery that is sent to bring life to all things."[36]

We come around then to the conclusion that the principal agency for the fulfilment of Japan's mission of benevolent destiny is her army. At this point we confront a might to which all else in the nation must be subordinated and which operates in complete independence of the ordinary offices of civil government. The army is established on the unique and impregnable foundation of sole and immediate responsibility to the sacred throne. In such manner there is imparted to military command the quality of inviolability that attaches to the divine emperor himself. We may say without hesitation that the entire educational process that goes on in the schools and the entire theory and practice of the army are set up so as to secure a corre-

sponding absolute obedience on the part of the subjects of
the state. This is the fundamental virtue of modern Japan.
Whatever the soldier does in the extension of the power
and glory of Japan throughout the world, and in obedience
to the commands of superior officers, has behind it the authority of an absolute divine initiative. It possesses the
quality of religious finality; it is as coming from God.
There is no room here for either thought or conduct that is
motivated by the dictates of individual conscience or even
by the promptings of individual intelligence. There is no
place whatsoever for any standard of judgment set over
against the absolute military authority of the state. Since
the army is the custodian of the mediation of the imperial
will, merely to raise the question of rights of personal criticism is to be guilty of lèse majesté, punishable as a violation of the sacred national structure. A statement made
by General Hisauchi Terauchi when he was minister of
war is a candid avowal of the position of the army in this
respect: "All kinds of liberalism based on individualism
must be set aside."[37] We get here more than a glimpse of
what is involved in the extension of the glory of Japanese
institutions throughout the earth and making the whole
world one loving family.

We have examined in some of its major aspects a situation that introduces us to the pattern according to which
the Japanese mind is molded from the cradle to the grave
and to forms of nationalistic dogma that are so successfully imbued through constant reiteration in the schools, in
the newspapers, in magazines, in books, over the radio, in
all the manifold agencies of propaganda of an all-powerful
state, and which are so inextricably merged with the sanctions of religion that rejection of the stereotype becomes an
indignity offered to deity and criticism a form of treason.
The rare university professor who dares to turn the light of
scientific historical research into the amazing mixture of
mythology, rationalization, and historical fact that makes

up the texture of the Japanese state structure and its official interpretation finds his writings confiscated, himself apprehended by the police and prosecuted in the courts of law, and his family subjected to social censure. There was a time when the mythological elements in the traditional picture of the sun-goddess Amaterasu Omikami or the impossible idealization of history that places the first accession to the throne at 660 B.C. could be brought up for open discussion. To raise the questions now would involve serious consequences. Japanese scholarship is in the hands of a modern inquisition.

The situation which we have just examined must be taken into primary consideration in any attempt to know Japan either in her domestic operations or in her foreign relations. To fail to do this is not only to fail fundamentally in our comprehension of Japan but also to fail to take the initial and indispensable measures whereby we, as Western peoples, may adjust ourselves intelligently to entering into adequately reciprocal relations with the Japanese people and their government. We find, then, that, in order to understand modern Japan and her significant trends, we must deal first and foremost with a highly successful, rigorously centralized, religiously founded educational program whereby the national mentality is fixed in terms of forms that are governmentally expedient and necessary to military control. But these forms are not arbitrarily manufactured out of makeshift materials in the social and political life. They have come down out of an ancient past, they are erected on literary foundations that have the sanctity of holy scripture, and they survive as almost instinctive elements in the folkways. In all this we come to recognize that the center of that ethical certitude that stands so firmly in the midst of the storm of Far Eastern politics is lodged in the conviction of the possession as a race of unique divine attributes, of a peerless national structure, and of a sacred commission to save the world.

NOTES

1. An imperial rescript promulgated November 30, 1868, on the occasion of the visit of the emperor to the Hikawa Shrine (Shōzō Kōno, *Jingishi Gaiyō* ["An Outline of Shinto History"] [Tokyo, 1927], p. 143).

2. Imperial rescript of February 3, 1870 (*ibid.*, p. 144).

3. *Ibid.*, p. 149.

4. *Kokutai no Hongi* ("The Fundamental Principles of the National Structure") (Tokyo: Japanese Department of Education, 1937), p. 26.

5. Commonly translated "god," "the gods," or "deity," but also used in the wider sense of "sacred" or "holy." *Kami* may be either singular or plural, masculine or feminine. It is probably similar in origin to the term *mana*.

6. Hirobumi Itō, *Commentaries on the Constitution* (Eng. ed.; Tokyo, 1889), p. 6.

7. Kunitake Kume, "Shintō," in *Fifty Years of New Japan*, II (London, 1910), 30.

8. *Japan Advertiser*, November 3, 1916.

9. G. Etsujirō Uyehara, *The Political Development of Japan, 1867–1909* (New York, 1910), p. 23.

10. Shinkichi Uesugi, *Kokutai Seika no Hatsuyō* ("Exalting the Essence o f the National Structure") (Tokyo, 1919), p. 58.

11. "Heavenly Sovereign."

12. Sadao Araki, "State and Education," *Contemporary Japan*, VII, No. 3 (December, 1938), 422.

13. Shinichi Fujii, "Characteristics of the Japanese Constitution," *Contemporary Japan*, IX, No. 3 (March, 1940), 162–63.

14. Genchi Katō, *Waga Kokutai to Shintō* ("Our National Structure and Shinto") (Tokyo, 1919), p. 4.

15. *Ibid.*

16. Genchi Katō, *A Study of Shintō: The Religion of the Japanese Nation* (Tokyo, 1926), pp. 206–7.

17. Kan Kikuchi, "Nisen Roppyaku Nen Shishō ("Aspects of Two Thousand Six Hundred Years of Japanese History"), *Shūhō* ("Weekly Gazette"), February 7, 1940, p. 46. Published by the Department of Home Affairs.

18. *Japan Weekly Mail*, 1881, p. 1199.

19. Atsutane Hirata, *Zoku Shindō Taii* ("The Great Principles of Shinto"); text in *Shintō Daijiten* ("The Shinto Encyclopaedia"), I (Tokyo, 1937), 399.

20. Yamato is an archaic name for Japan preferred by modern Japanese writers because of its historical and literary associations. The name is found in both the *Kojiki* and the *Nihongi*. W. G. Aston says in explanation: "Yamato means probably mountain-gate. It is the genuine ancient name for the province which contained Nara and many of the other capitals of Japan for centuries, and it was also used for the whole country. Several of the Mikados called themselves Yamato-neko. It is mentioned by the historian of the Later Han dynasty of China (A.D. 25–220) as the seat of rule in Japan at that time" (*Nihongi* [London, 1924], I, 13, n. 3).

21. Kazusaku Kanzaki, "Shintō Honkyoku no Kyōri" ("The Doctrines of Shinto Honkyoku"), in *Uchū* ("The Universe"), January, 1930, pp. 13–15.

22. See Aston, *op. cit.*, I, 77. The *Nihongi* was published in A.D. 720. The wording I have used is slightly different from Aston's.

23. *Jinjō Shōgaku Kokushi* ("National History for Ordinary Primary Schools"), I (Tokyo, 1927), 3.

24. *Shōgaku Kokushi Kyōshi Yōsho* ("Teacher's Manual of National History for Primary Schools"), V (Tokyo, 1931), 1–12.

25. *Japan Advertiser*, January 17, 1939.

26. *Ibid.*

27. *Ibid.*, May 19, 1939.

28. *Ibid.*

29. *International Gleanings from Japan* (monthly publication of the International Association of Japan), February 15, 1940, p. 2.

30. Aston, *op. cit.*, I, 111.

31. *Ibid.*, p. 131. In a footnote to his translation of the text in which this passage appears Aston remarks: "This whole speech is thoroughly Chinese in every respect, and it is preposterous to put it in the mouth of an Emperor who is supposed to have lived more than a thousand years before the introduction of Chinese learning into Japan. The strange thing is that it is necessary to make this remark. Yet there are still writers who regard this part of the *Nihongi* as historical." Were Aston living today he might find occasion to comment on the fate of the Japanese writer who does not find these words historical.

32. *International Gleanings from Japan*, XVI, No. 10 (October 15, 1940), 1.

33. *Japan Advertiser*, February 25, 1940.

34. *International Gleanings from Japan*, XVI, No. 8 (August 15, 1940), 3.

35. Cited in *Seimei no Idzumi* ("The Fountain of Life") (Tokyo, 1939), p. 2.

36. Magota and Hara, *Kokutai no Hongi Kaisetsu Taisei* ("A Commentary on the Fundamental Principles of the National Structure") (Tokyo, 1940), p. 100.

In the spring of 1940 a monument to the spirit of "the whole world under one roof" was erected in the city of Miyazaki, Kyushu, at a cost of some six hundred thousand yen. It stands on Hakko Hill in the form of a great tower of ferroconcrete, overlooking the Hyuga Straits and rising to a height of more than a hundred feet. In outline it suggests the shape of a Shinto *gohei*, the zigzag purification device in common use at the shrines. On each of the four sides of the pillar is set a representation of a human figure, symbolizing the four primary agencies wherewith Japan attains the realization of her mission in the world— commerce and industry, fishing, agriculture, and war.

37. *Japan Advertiser*, March 23, 1940.

CHAPTER II

SHINTO AND JAPANESE NATIONALISM

THE national character which we have previously examined finds institutional expression in an organized cultus, that is, in State Shinto, and any movement of religion or thought, any program of moral reinforcement or social melioration, that expects to make headway in Japan today must first of all work out a basis of accommodation with this powerful system.

As already indicated, the most significant trend in the religious life of present-day Japan is to be found in the process of nationalistic unification that is now being consummated through the agency of a state religion. To accomplish this end, the authorities have had to deal with problems within Shinto itself.

One of these problems is the elimination of nonofficial interpretations and institutions. Shinto as we find it today flows in two great currents. The one has carefully defined official relation to the national life and is protected in a special status because of its value to the state. The other is dependent entirely on the voluntary support of adherents for institutional maintenance. The former is generally called State Shinto (*Kokka Shintō*), sometimes Shrine Shinto (*Jinja Shintō*); the latter is called Sectarian Shinto (*Shūha Shintō*). Both branches have received influences from the parent-stream of an ancient and indigenous religion, the former more directly and on the whole in more unmixed character than the latter. In fact, modern interpreters of the state system are generally quick to assert that the ceremonies and beliefs connected with the shrines represent the true and uncontaminated line of pure Shinto, while the sectarian forms have been more or less

28

modified through foreign corruptions and the contributions of their founders and other teachers.

Certain it is that some of the sects, notably Tenri Kyō and Konkō Kyō, are a far cry from the classical model of the earliest Shinto literature. Over against this, however, we can find apologists for the sects who maintain that they alone preserve the true and original Shinto and that the official cultus may not inexactly be regarded as merely another sect, officially sponsored and demanding in the name of patriotism a nation-wide allegiance.

The main features that distinguish Sectarian Shinto from State Shinto should be carefully noted, since the two are often confused. It must be frankly recognized, however, that some of the confusion exists in actual fact and could be resolved only by a more rigorous delineation of function on the part of the authorities.

Sectarian Shinto, the Shinto of the people, exists in the form of thirteen sects and numerous subsects. It is for the most part the result of the labors of historical founders, organizers, and teachers who have systematized special forms of doctrine and ceremony and have propagated these for the purpose of creating followings and thereby bringing benefit to individuals and communities. This statement is not exclusively true, since at least three of the thirteen sects insist that they merely perpetuate and expound the orthodox Shinto inheritance. Although all the sects are officially classified as Shinto, in certain cases this is nothing more than the convenience of governmental control. There is wide difference in the details of doctrine and ritual between the different sects. Taken as a whole, and recognizing the dangers of overgeneralization, we can note the dominant characteristics of the sects as: popular folklore and magic; colorful imaginings of simple peasant-minded founders mixed with many wholesome ethical precepts and spiritual insights; elaborate regard for purification ceremonies, ranging from magical rituals that drive away demonic defilement to inner prayer that cleanses the heart; mountain worship; and faith-healing—all intermingled with and supported by the beliefs and ceremonies of the traditional Shinto sanctuaries. Most of the sects represent movements that have come into existence since the beginning of the Meiji era in 1868; in certain cases, however, we must go back to earlier periods to find the beginnings.

The state system which we must differentiate from all this began its modern existence also in 1868. At that time a classical revival which had been going on vigorously in the latter part of the Tokugawa era bore fruit in the establishment of so-called "pure Shinto" as the state religion. The special legal and ceremonial relationship with the national life which was consummated then has been maintained ever since. It was not long, however, before a sharper delineation of function as over against popular movements became imperative. Beginning with the opening of the Meiji era and culminating in the eighties of the last century the government took various steps to make clearly drawn distinctions between the rapidly growing popular sects and the official system centering in the shrines. Regulations were set up under which all the recognized institutions of the state, whether national or local, large or small, were to reserve to themselves the title of *jinja,* meaning "god-house," or "dwelling-place of the *kami* (deity)," while in contradistinction the institutions of the sects were to be called *kyōkai,* or "churches," and accorded the same legal classification and treatment as other religions like Buddhism and Christianity.

Japanese writers have frequently attempted to elucidate the distinctions between the two branches of Shinto thus authorized. The most conspicuous example of this is in a statement made by the National Association of Shinto Priests published in the monthly magazine of the Shinto College of Tokyo for July, 1932. The statement refers to the work of a commission on the investigation of the shrines of State Shinto appointed by the national government and remarks that, among all the problems studied by this commission, none is more important than the clarification of the proper distinction between the activities of the shrines of the state system and those of Sectarian Shinto. The document then goes on to say:

There are many points of similarity between the shrines [of State Shinto] and Sectarian Shinto. In popular opinion these two are frequently confused and the real differences are often unknown. There are even cases in which writers have given erroneous expositions of the supposed differences. It is highly important to the strengthening of the institutions of the shrines that the real differences between State Shinto and Sectarian Shinto be made plain.

It is true that in the matter of the worship of the national deities the shrines and Sectarian Shinto have much in common. It is true also that when we go back to historical origins we find situations in which it is not easy to distinguish between them. In the processes of development through which they have passed and in actual present-day manifestations, however, it is possible to make clear distinctions between them. The fundamental differences are as follows:

I. DOCTRINES

The existence of certain specified doctrine is essential to Sectarian Shinto. In the case of the shrines this condition does not obtain. All the branches of Sectarian Shinto without exception possess certain special religious affirmations which serve as their sectarian standards; in other words, they possess doctrines. As a matter of fact these are a fundamental condition of the origin of Sectarian Shinto and apart from the attempt to induce people to believe these doctrines and to lead them accordingly it would have been impossible for Sectarian Shinto to have come into existence. To be sure, among these teachings which we have called doctrines there are some that are not systematized in any particular literary document or sacred scripture. Certain teachings exist merely as moral exhortations or by mutual consent. This matter, however, simply concerns difference in degree. It remains true that the primary condition for the existence of all the branches of Sectarian Shinto is the acceptance, application, and propagation of certain special doctrines.

II. FOUNDERS

The Sectarian Shinto which promulgates these doctrines also naturally possesses individual sect founders. That is to say, all the branches of Sectarian Shinto go back to certain persons who at first themselves believed the teachings which constituted the basis of organization, and who proclaimed these teachings and induced others to believe and propagate them. That is, there exist of necessity sect-fathers, founders, and organizers.

In the case of the shrines, however, nothing resembling this exists.

III. RELIGIOUS ORGANIZATIONS

Inasmuch as the existence of Sectarian Shinto depends on the possession and propagation of doctrines, it is essential that the necessary organizations be provided for the dissemination of the teachings. This makes a clear point of distinction between the shrines and Sectarian Shinto which establishes agencies of propaganda and organizes into a single body the adherents who believe particular doctrines. As has been already pointed out, since the shrines do not propagate doctrines and have no founders, it is not necessary that they have the religious organizations that accompany these. The various societies and organizations that are connected with the shrines are not established on the basis of the acceptance of some special doctrines, and for this reason it is not inconsistent for one and the same person to have membership in two or more of these shrine societies.[1]

How much credence can be given this analysis? It is true that the priests of the state shrines are prohibited from attempting to indoctrinate parishioners with any particular tenets of belief. Their chief functions are supposed to be those of ritualists who perform ceremonies that protect the state and symbolize and dramatize its greatness. It is true also that no formal credal subscriptions are required of worshipers at the shrines as the condition of participation. Private beliefs may be held in reservation as long as the ritualistic acts are complete. Over against this, however, stands the all-important fact that definite doctrinal beliefs underlie the state ceremonies. The dogmas of nationalistic Shinto that we have already examined may be adduced as supporting evidence here. What is more, they are dogmas that are established and propagated by the unique power of the state itself. If any difference between Sectarian Shinto and State Shinto is to be drawn at this point, it is that the acceptance of the doctrines of the former is left to voluntary choice, while those of the latter are required by national authority as the essence of loyalty.

The observations of the National Association of Shinto Priests regarding the contributions of founders to Sectarian Shinto are largely valid, but here again the distinction is not entirely clear cut. As has already been pointed out, some of the sects maintain that their teachings and ceremonies have never been modified through the activities of sect fathers and organizers. According to their own statements, they are now, and always have been, the "pure Shinto" of the Age of the Gods. In addition to all this, the important fact remains that historical Shinto as manifested in the shrines and their ceremonies has been very much influenced in the past by individual organizers and interpreters. Furthermore, the Japanese state itself with its elaborate offices of control over the national cultus must be regarded as a powerful manifestation of organizing interest.

In so far as agencies of propaganda are concerned, every school in the empire is a center of the dissemination of Shinto dogma and correct views regarding the gods. The whole nation takes on the aspect of a Shinto church organized for purposes of propaganda and belief. With these remarks before us we may pass on to the consideration of further details in the comparison of the organization and activities of Sectarian Shinto with those of the cult of the state.

The popular sects, like all recognized religious bodies, maintain their own independent organizations and possess legal properties that are almost exclusively distinct from those of the shrines. In general, they are not permitted to make use of the latter as meeting places for sectarian purposes. On the other hand, the shrines receive supervision and a measure of financial support from village, municipal, prefectural, or national governments, depending on the grade of the particular shrine concerned. Other and more extensive sources of shrine income are revenues from shrine properties, voluntary offerings and subscriptions, earnings from the sale of charms and talismans, and fees for divination and exorcism.

State Shinto in the matter of legal control and co-ordination of activities is placed under the jurisdiction of a bureau of shrines in the Department of Home Affairs. Special enactments and administrative orders issued in this ministry regulate the affairs of the shrines in matters of organization, priesthood, and ceremonies. A major interest of the bureau of shrines is so to direct the ceremonies and beliefs of the national faith as to overcome local superstition and heterogeneity in the interest of ceremonies that foster community and national solidarity. The shrines and their rituals are united into a hierarchy that is a projection into the god-world of the vital interests and patterns of the political life. We will return to this matter later.

Over against this, the affairs of Sectarian Shinto are looked after by a bureau of religions in the Department of Education. Thus Sectarian Shinto is afforded the same legal treatment as Buddhism and Christianity and, while subject to careful official supervision and discipline under a recently enacted "Law Governing Religious Organizations," is nevertheless thrown completely on its own resources in matters of places of worship, finances, internal management, doctrines, etc. The Shinto sects carry on voluntary, nonofficial religious propaganda and employ their own teachers, preachers, and priests, in addition to a vast number of unpaid instructors of all sorts. They maintain churches, schools, kindergartens, social welfare activities, various kinds of organizations for young people and adults, as well as extensive agencies for literary propaganda. In all this they are left to their own initiative and direction in so far as they do not violate the interests of public peace and order and in so far as their programs and doctrines meet the approval of local governors and competent ministers of state, under the operation of the new law for the control of religious organizations which went into effect on April 1, 1940.

State Shinto, in turn, is supposed to have its chief function in the celebration of rites that are considered appropriate to the deepening of national sentiment. The visitor to any one of the larger shrines will commonly fall in with bands of children from the primary schools led by their teachers, groups of students from higher schools, squads of soldiers from their barracks, groups of civilians from various walks of life, coming and going along with multitudes of individual worshipers. After a ceremonial purification, accomplished sometimes by the magical power of a wand-like device waved over the heads of the worshipers by a priest, but more often by alternately pouring water over the hands and rinsing the mouth, the bands draw up in the shrine inclosure before the altars of the oratory (*Haiden*) and at a command from their leader make profound obeisance and then quietly go their way. That is all. It is very simple, very dignified, and soon over. The members of the groups have obeyed the commands of their superiors and thereby have done their duty as patriotic subjects of the emperor. They have paid homage to the ancestors and the souls of the dead, given public witness to their gratitude for benefits that have come down to them out of the mysterious past, confessed their dependence on the unseen spirit world, and once again, by a ritualistic act, have renewed their pledge of unqualified allegiance to the state. We can understand how, with the interpretation of the meaning of the shrines here given, participation in their ceremonies through the simple devotional act of obeisance is taken as a primary test of loyalty. But this is far from being all that the shrines stand for in the national and the individual life. Indeed, this is not their chief function. Their main part is to provide places of communion with the spirits of the god-world, where thanksgiving may be expressed and petitions offered for protection in the individual life, in homes, in business, and in the wider relations of community and nation.

The devotional acts of individual worshipers may be

somewhat more complicated than those just stated for the group, although for the most part they follow the same pattern. The individual may ring a bell to announce his presence, cast in a small coin offering, bow low in reverence, clap his hands in salutation, and withdraw. Here and there one appears who bows longer than the others, sometimes kneels on the altar stairs, while the many come and go, and makes a prayer. The prayer may be a repetition of the words which the state ritualists use in their great ceremonies; it may be the spontaneous and impromptu utterance of the needs of the heart. The actual historical character of the deity supplicated is a relatively unimportant element. Japanese writers often say that it is the faith that counts. The deity may be a primitive nature *kami* or a personification of thunder, lightning, or rain or of the mysterious powers of generation and growth; it may even have begun life as a phallic god; it may be a wayside fox-god or the spirit of tree or mountain. Or, to pass to the dignified realm of some of the great national shrines, the prayer may be to the deified spirits of authentic rulers or to national heroes or to warriors who have died for their country. The god-world is rich and diverse; but, although Japan is the Land of the Gods, those who really know the histories of the gods are not many. They are limited to a few scholars and fewer priests; and the present is not an opportune time for those who know to speak forth frankly and truly what they know, especially since the all-powerful state itself has said that the deities whose worship it sponsors are the spirits of genuine ancestors. One does not argue with the state in Japan.

The stream of ordinary worshipers may now and then be broken and held back to make place for the prayers of an important official of the state—perhaps a cabinet minister from Tokyo or an ambassador or high commissioner just about to leave the country or just returning from a foreign post. Such an official will read before the enshrined spirits an announcement of his commission, a statement of thanks, and a prayer for protection and success. No journey, whether undertaken by prime minister or by humble peasant, is safe unless it is first announced before either the local tutelary deities or the great national *kami*, and the special protection of the spirit world secured. The return from a journey calls for like recognition of the goodness and power of the national gods. Every important event in the national life—the beginning of war, success in arms, conclusion of peace, births in the royal family, changes in the government, everything of significance in either domestic or foreign affairs—must be duly announced before the gods, their favors acknowledged, and their blessings invoked.

One of the major activities of the Shinto shrines, as it is also of most Buddhist temples, is the sale and distribution of charms and talismans. In the smaller sizes these are worn on the person; larger ones are placed on the godshelves of private homes, pasted on the lintel, or erected in other positions of advantage in the home or business establishment. They drive away demons, protect women in childbirth, secure offspring for the impotent, unite lovers and secure happy marriages, promote health and prosperity in flock and family and field, bring a good turn to business ventures, function as burglar protection and as fire and earthquake insurance, and attach the mystical influence of the home deity to the persons of travelers who have temporarily passed outside the geographical range of the local shrine—in fact, they meet all the thousand and one crises that are likely to arise in the course of complicated life in this world below. They are sold by all shrines from the highest to the lowest, and, although generally obtainable in return for a small coin, they are distributed in such large numbers that they bring in a reasonably good income to the shrine treasury. In spite of obvious magical associations, they have been defended by governmental officials on the ground of their utility in attaching the persons and homes of the nation directly to the interests of the shrines and thus broadening and deepening national unification through the state cult.

In addition to all this, practically all the shrines, with the exception of a small number of the very largest, serve individuals and local groups and families in ways that are not essentially different from what we find in connection with the Shinto sects. In fact, it is not an unknown thing for the same priests and ritualists to minister to local groups in both the churches of the sects and the shrines of the state. The priests of the local state shrines perform marriage ceremonies in vast numbers and conduct funerals and prayer services for soldiers called to war or for other parishioners in special need. They dedicate new building sites and purify new projects of all sorts. They hold various other community gatherings for the edification and instruction of parishioners (*ujiko*). They direct ordinary communion rites between the worshipers and the gods in prayers (*norito*) read by the attendant priests.

It will be recalled that in the pronouncement from the National Association of Shinto Priests the statement was made that in the matter of the deities honored the two great branches of Shinto have much in common. This is an important fact that should be kept in mind in any attempt to try to reach an understanding of the religious situation of modern Japan. Taking the sects as a whole, it may be said that they have included in their god-world the entire pantheon of the state shrines and have added certain deifications of their own, notably the spirits of founders.

According to the latest available statistics, Sectarian Shinto reports 16,238 churches, 124,877 teachers, preachers, and priests, and 17,607,605 adherents. State Shinto reports 15,801 priests and 110,239 shrines. The official cult publishes no statistics of adherents. The explanation may be found in the fact that, theoretically speaking, all Japanese are properly considered as legitimate parish-

ioners of the state shrines. The statistics of adherents of
State Shinto would thus have to include the total population of the empire.

Since the time of the promulgation of the written constitution in 1889, containing an article guaranteeing freedom of religious faith to all subjects within limits not
prejudicial to the maintenance of peace and order and not
damaging to the duty of subjects of the state, officials of
the government, supported by various scholars and writers, have been particularly emphatic in asserting that the
state cultus is not a religion, notwithstanding the fact that
another group, including Japanese Shinto scholars of the
first order and even some of the members of the priesthood
of the state system, have been equally emphatic in insisting that State Shinto is *de facto*, if not *de jure*, a genuine religion. The main cause of the difference of opinion is undoubtedly the exigencies of governmental supervision in
the matter of classification. This in turn is determined by
political expediency, not by any regard for the historical
nature of Shinto. One of the most influential of the contemporary Japanese authorities on Shinto has declared
that a nonreligious status was claimed for the state cult
by the Meiji statesmen in order to avoid a head-on colli-
sion with Christianity, which at the time had the support
of Western nations that Japan could not afford to offend.
There is no law or ordinance that says in so many words
that State Shinto is not a religion and that Sectarian
Shinto is. Governmental agents, however, speaking in
their official capacities, have frequently interpreted existing
legal arrangements to mean that State Shinto is not a religion, since under the national law it does not receive the
treatment accorded to ordinary religions. As far as governmental administration is concerned, Shinto as a religion
appears only in the popular sectarian groups. Japanese
scholars and writers have found it to their advantage to
follow suit.

The problem of safeguarding the interests of nationalistic centralization through a state religion was not solved for the civil authorities when they had successfully cut connections with Sectarian Shinto and established a favored legal status for the state cultus distinct from all other religions. An even more difficult problem remained —that of overcoming the heterogeneity of the local shrines. The existence of this problem has already been suggested. It must now be examined somewhat in detail.

National Shinto, in its inner beliefs and ceremonies, its god-world and festivals, has never in the past presented a unified and consistent whole. It does not do so in the present, in spite of the persistent efforts of the government to overcome its diversities and integrate its various parts. It is a manifold of complex and sometimes contradictory elements. One of the most prominent of living Japanese authorities on the religion of his country, a man who has probably done more than any other writer to present the knowledge of the cultural life of his native land to the people of the West, has found justification for repudiating the conclusion that Shinto may properly be designated the national religion of Japan on the ground that it has never been organized into a homogeneous whole.[2]

Investigation of the actual situation, however, will show that the Japanese government has already succeeded in introducing sufficient uniformity into the activities of the shrines to make it possible to say that, while we must recognize the existence of many exceptions and inconsistencies, yet their major significance is national. On the whole, State Shinto, thanks to a systematic governmental supervision and reinterpretation, now appears as a unified system of belief and practice relative to sacred things, thereby satisfying the conditions of a well-known definition of religion. Furthermore, this national standardization is going on apace.

In speaking thus, we cannot overlook the existence of important factors that make for diversity. Heterogeneity exists in the nature of the historical elements that have entered into the creation of the shrines, their supporting beliefs, their ceremonies, and their architecture. Some of these have come from the South Pacific and southeastern Asia. Some show Mongolian and shamanistic affinities; for example, the ceremonial treatment of the horse. Other aspects of Shinto suggest Ainu penetration. A large group of elements, which Japanese scholars would almost unanimously pronounce the most distinctive, owe their origin and development to the influence of environment and social experiences within Japan proper. Confucianism, Taoism, Buddhism, and even Christianity have all left their marks on Shinto. These last-named factors have made for much diversity, especially in doctrinal areas.

Extraordinary variety exists in the god-world. State Shinto supports a polytheism of great magnitude and complexity. Shinto texts frequently speak of the *Yao-yorodzu-no-Kami*, the eight hundred myriads of deities of the classical faith. This tremendous number is merely poetic and figurative, however, indicating a belief in a vast and indefinite host. Authentic gods and goddesses recognized in the ceremonies of the local shrines, both past and present, excluding the spirits of the warrior dead enshrined in the national sanctuary in Tokyo, have been estimated at not more than a few thousand. If we limit our observations to the larger shrines where deities of most significance to the state are worshiped and again omit the modern deifications of the spirits of those who have died in military service, then the number falls to slightly over two hundred. Even so the diversity is considerable.

Local rites and ceremonies present a richly variegated picture, depending on varying manners and customs, stages of development, and needs and characteristics of different geographical areas. Rites that summon ancient storm-gods to mountaintops, others that induce god-possession, ceremonies that drive away defilement from individuals and groups, that exorcise evil spirits, that expel insects from crops or protect them from wind and storm, ceremonies for the presentation of first-fruits, planting rites, harvest rites, services for the dedication of children, and here and there in remote rural districts even a lingering phallicism—all this and vastly more exists within the great diversity of the Shinto complex. Above all this rises the edifice of elaborate ceremonies that celebrate the significant events of the wider national community and support the chief interests of the state. The adequate exploration of this field would call for the writing of the encyclopedia of Shinto, a task that Japanese writers themselves have only just begun.

Yet in spite of all this diversity it is possible to claim State Shinto as a unified system. This leads us to the consideration of the means whereby heterogeneity is being overcome in support of ends that are truly national in scope.

It is being overcome and systematized by the progressive elimination of small inferior shrines and their amalgamation with larger ones, by the elevation of pre-existing lower-grade shrines to national status, and by the steady construction of new shrines that have a national importance. Shrines are divided into twelve grades, ranging from certain lesser sanctuaries that are classified as being "without rank" (*mukakusha*), through those of village, town, city, district, prefectural, and central governments, on up to the Grand Imperial Shrine of Ise, which, corresponding to the position of the emperor in the state, is outside and above all. The effectiveness of this policy of national unification as applied to the shrines of Shinto is clearly indicated in the statistics. In the year 1900 the grand total for all shrines stood at the impressive figure of 196,357. This was the peak. Since then there has been a steady decrease, amounting altogether, in the course of four decades, to a shrinkage of over 86,000 shrines. It should be noted carefully, however, that this reduction has been entirely within the areas of small ungraded and village shrines. For all shrines of higher grade there has been a constant increase. In 1900 the total for all shrines above the ranks of village and ungraded classes was 4,026. The latest available statistics show approximately five thousand. Since the beginning of the present century State Shinto has increased its number of large and important shrines by nearly one thousand institutions. This is a highly significant achievement—one that furnishes statistical evidence of a noteworthy trend in nationalistic unification.

Further impetus in the same direction is furnished by providing uniform regulations made out under ordinances of law superintended by the bureau of shrines of the Department of Home Affairs, establishing standard ceremonies for all shrines of whatever grade to be used on the occasions of all national festivals and other state occasions. By this means local communities are made aware of their national relationships, and the activities of the shrines are arranged in the perspective of a great hierarchy that culminates in the imperial throne.

The problem of overcoming the diversity of polytheism remains and still presents serious difficulties, especially to those who have a conscience in regard to historical accuracy. The official interpretation boldly sets aside all embarrassments by affirming a legitimate ancestral significance for all the chief deities honored in the state shrines. The Japanese government has recently declared that all new shrines established on the Asiatic mainland or elsewhere overseas shall honor only the sun-goddess, Amaterasu Omikami, and the spirit of Emperor Meiji.

At the same time the need of emotional unification is emphasized. An example of the form which discussion assumes at this point is furnished in an article which appeared in the *Yomiuri Shimbun* for May 26, 1940. It bears the title, "A Policy for the Unification of the National Faith." The universal nature of the sentiment of reverence for the imperial throne is appealed to as the basis of correlation in the multiform god-world. The article says:

At some of the shrines of our country the ancestors of the Imperial Family are worshiped; at others, the spirits of loyal subjects who have contributed meritorious service to the state; and at still others, manifestations of nature, such as mountains, rivers, plants, and animals. The enshrined objects are exceedingly complex and diversified. Much thought has been given to the problem of how to co-ordinate and standardize these many deities so as to bring unity to the national faith. No matter how sound the historical origins or how exalted the personages of the enshrined deities may be, if the attitudes and motives of the people who worship them are impure and sordid and scattered in many directions, the unification of the national faith is hardly to be expected. On the other hand, if the attitudes and beliefs of the people who revere and worship these many deities are pure and noble and systematized, then the national faith attains spontaneous unification.

For example, if when we worship before the sanctuaries where the ancestors of the Imperial Family are enshrined, we bear in mind that the sacred spirits of the great ancestors are even now living in the mighty will of the Emperor, then mediated through these shrines, we do reverence to the Emperor's will. If, again, when we worship at the shrines dedicated to national heroes, we bear in mind that the great work of the Emperor in ruling over the state is exalted by these heroes, then in the same way, mediated through these shrines, we are revering the will of the Emperor. And if, again, when we worship before the shrines dedicated to the manifestations of the natural world such as mountains, rivers, animals, and plants, we bear in mind that these various manifestations of nature offer up their manifold powers and thereby sustain the imperial destiny, then in the same way, mediated through these shrines, we worship the will of the Emperor.

In this manner, no matter what may be the nature of the enshrined deity, if mediated through them all in a single line, the great heart of the Emperor and that alone is revered, then the faith of the nation is completely unified and the greater the number of deities worshiped, the more does this single faith attain depth and loftiness.[3]

The best indication of the unifying trends of State Shinto in the national life is derived from the examination of the functional activities of the shrines themselves. Acquaintance with the meaning of these sacred places—problems included—studied one by one, is the primary requisite to reaching an understanding of what State Shinto really is. Investigation in anything even remotely approximating such terms is, however, manifestly impossible here. We are obliged to limit the examination to the two greatest shrines of the national cult. We take up first the deification of the war dead of the nation.

Standing on Kudan Hill in the Kojimachi district of Tokyo and overlooking the entire Kanda Valley is the great memorial sanctuary known as the Yasukuni Jinja, or "The Nation-protecting Shrine." It is probably safe to say that, with the exception of the shrine to the sun-goddess at Ise, no other spot in the entire country is so magnified in the national life or so closely bound up with the deepest sentiments of the people. It is here that the war dead of the nation have been enshrined and deified throughout the entire modern period of Japanese history. Yet, as compared with the great majority of Shinto shrines, the Yasukuni Jinja is a new creation. It represents a modern trend in Japanese politico-religious affairs. It was founded on its present site in the year 1869 shortly after the seat of the newly restored imperial government had been transferred from Kyoto to Tokyo.

During the year prior to this, while civil war was still in progress between the forces of the throne and those of the dying Tokugawa shogunate, ceremonies for the deification of the spirits of those who had recently died in the military service of the restored imperial power were conducted in Kyoto. At this time the residence of the emperor was still in this city. The deifications included all who had died for the imperial cause since 1853. All those who had died in the service of the shogunate were, of course, regarded as traitors and not rewarded. No enshrinements were made at the Yasukuni Jinja before the date just given. After the throne had been transferred to Tokyo in the second year of Meiji (1869) and the new hero shrine on Kudan Hill dedicated, all these former Kyoto enshrinements were reinstalled in the Tokyo sanctuary. It is quite important, in view of interpretations of the nature of the Yasukuni ceremonies sometimes met with, especially those intended for reading by extra-Japanese constituencies, to give attention to the official motives that gave rise to the original enshrinements. These did not lie primarily in the mere desire to commemorate in national rite and institution the final sacrifice of brave men for their country. This is not to say that the memorial idea was not present, but it was not primary. The real and underlying motive lay in the purpose to give a just reward to the spirits of those who had undergone great hardship, resulting in death, and to strengthen dynastic interests by a proper recognition of those who had been loyal to the newly established government. There is the best of evidence for these assertions.

In the spring of 1868, while the seat of the government was still in Kyoto, an imperial message had been issued defining the official interpretation of the deification of war dead. I cite from an English translation of the imperial statement promulgated at this time, as published in 1938 by Momoki Kamo, the chief priest of the Yasukuni Shrine.

Not a few patriotic subjects both of good social standing and of lowly origin, taking lead of the national movement, were put to death for no established serious offence, subsequently to the sixth year of Kaei (1853). They lost their lives because of their faithfulness to the principle of loyalty and patriotism and also because of their leadership in the movement started for the cause of Tennō. They had no energy left to spare for the cause of their parents, they deserted their homes, relinquishing their feudal fiefs, they found themselves refugees in strange corners of this land, they were homeless wanderers throughout this land where they once had homes, they underwent hardships of all descriptions. This was their life. They were aggrieved at the maladministration of the Shogunate Feudal Government. They made vehement appeals to the feudal authorities, at the risk of their personal safety, drawing their attention to the widespread suffering of the people, they tried hard to persuade the court nobles to rise to the occasion, they earnestly remonstrated with their feudal lords on their conduct relative to national affairs. Personal ease was of no concern to them. They were all patriotic workers, always ready to sacrifice themselves for the good of the people. They did this only to bring every member of the nation to the knowledge of those noble principles of which they should be consistently observant. They were actuated by their earnest sincerity to undertake the restoration of the Throne to its old prestige, dignity, and sovereign power. They must be accorded justice with due honour; their noble achievements should be properly repaid. Those who rendered valuable services with silent efforts and whose achievements constituted a cause of the increase of national prosperity and the enhancement of the Imperial fortunes, must not be left to remain in obscurity.[4]

This rescue from obscurity was accomplished not so much by rehabilitation in the memories of the living as it was by providing the dead with a spirit-house whose magnificence was considered something like adequate compensation for the sufferings which they had endured in a noble cause. The idea of the state of the dead that is implied here will come up for consideration again later in the discussion. In passing, however, it may be pointed out that the legitimacy of the interpretation just made is given a measure of support by the fact that the original name of the war-dead shrine was *Shō-kon-sha*, from *shō*, "to summon," *kon*, "spirit," and *sha*, "god-house." It was a god-house into which the spirits of the dead were summoned to take up residence, or into which they could be called under the mystic spell of appropriate ceremonies. This name was changed in 1879 to the present designation of Yasukuni Jinja.

An important question that has recently attained prominence with the recent notable increase in the enshrinement of the war dead of the nation at the Yasukuni Shrine concerns the legitimacy of speaking of them as deifications at all. Is it really believed, and do the official rites themselves assume, that the spirits of the warrior dead who are immortalized in the ceremonies are exalted to the ranks of the *kami* and regarded as actually living denizens of the spirit world? Or is it correct to say, as some do, that the rites have mainly, if not purely, a memorial significance in which the last great sacrifice of brave men for the state is glorified? The question broadens out into the query: "What kind of ideas are entertained regarding the nature of the deities of State Shinto in general and what are the presuppositions that underlie the official rites of the shrines as a whole?"

In a book published during 1938 Dr. Masaharu Anesaki wrote regarding this matter:

At the present time, the Shinto sanctuary is mainly a public institution for a "state cult," and this character is quite justified as regards most of these *jinja* which have been established under the new regime. For example, such famous modern sanctuaries as the Yasukuni Jinja, instituted in honor of those who have died for their country, or the Meiji Jingū, set up in honor of the great Emperor Meiji, and other similar *jingū* (which word means "divine palace") are undoubtedly state institutions. Foreigners would not be wide of the mark if they found an analogy to these *jingū* in the Lincoln Memorial at Washington or the Pantheon at Paris, while for the Yasukuni Jinja they might well take the tomb of the Unknown Soldier at the Etoile or the Cenotaph in Whitehall.[5]

A reading of the above passage leaves one wondering if, in spite of the knowledge of Japanese religions possessed by its distinguished author, it really does justice either to the intimacy of feeling and the religious warmth of the Japanese people in their faith in the divine beings of these great shrines or, again, to the ideas concerning the state of the dead that underlie the official rites themselves. To make the position clearer, let us take another quotation, this also from a Japanese writer who is a well-known authority on the folkways of his own people and a close student of their religious life. In his account of the autumn festivals of the Yasukuni Shrine for the year 1938, Mr. Setsuo Uenoda says:

The significance and solemnity of the occasion of deification are profoundly religious. To the Japanese people, the dead are not really dead; and any amount of argument to the contrary will be of no avail when the race have lived throughout more than twenty-five centuries with such a conviction and consciousness as their ancestral heritage. . . . .

It is futile and irrelevant to ask how the spirits of the soldiers who died in the battlefields in China came back and how they are invited to assemble in the compound of the Yasukuni Shrine to be deified. Suffice it to say that the Japanese race have always believed that their dead friends and relatives who died in foreign countries return somehow to their fatherland. They feel their ancestral spirits dwell in the land and haunt their home sanctuaries and the holy precincts of temples and shrines. So they daily offer food to the spirits of their ancestors, speak with them, invite them to the annual family reunion and pray for their well-being. They died for their country and live in the spirit world to be the guardians of their families and the nation instead of going to heaven. No land, therefore, is more truly a fatherland than Japan is to the Japanese race. On Monday night [October 17, 1938, the night of the enshrinement] all Japanese present felt that every one of the 10,334 spirits of dead soldiers was there at the Yasukuni Shrine waiting to be deified.[6]

This passage is not simply an accurate statement of the religious faith of the Japanese people; it also sets forth clearly the underlying presuppositions of the official rites themselves. The spirits of the dead are assembled in a solemn service of prayer and priestly ritual and, after having been given temporary residence in a portable ark, are transferred with stately processional to the inner sanctuary of the grand shrine and deified there with further impressive prayer and ceremony. To say that this is merely symbolical and memorial in its primary significance may express the beliefs and wishes of individuals here and there and may be of more or less utility, political and otherwise, in making explanation to foreign audiences, but it is not easy to make a rational adjustment of such an interpretation to what we know about the true character of the rites and their supporting beliefs.

Common to official rite and popular faith is the belief that the spirits of the warrior dead, now exalted to the ranks of the *kami*, have become guardian deities of the state, especially of its military affairs, and that they protect soldiers on the field of battle and watch over the destiny of the nation with the same intensity of devotion that once inspired them to shed their life's blood in patriotic duty. Here again there is high and indubitable evidence in support of these statements. The business office of the

Yasukuni Shrine has published a booklet containing several poems written by Emperor Meiji with the war heroes of this shrine as the theme. To these, the shrine authorities have added explanation and commentary. In 1904, during the Russo-Japanese War, Emperor Meiji wrote:

> Tatakai no
> Niwa ni tafureshi
> Masura wo no
> Tama wa ikusa wo
> Nao mamoramu.[7]

This has been translated to mean:

> Souls of men fallen in action
> May be seen
> Protecting men on the field of battle.[8]

The commentary says that these words mean that the brave spirits of the men who have died in frustrating the enemies of Japan go on ahead of the imperial armies, when war breaks out, to the field of battle and fight, just as in life, for the protection of the imperial arms.

When in 1905 the victorious armies returned from the Russo-Japanese War, the emperor wrote:

> Totsukuni ni
> Kabane sarashishi
> Masura wo no
> Tama mo Miyako ni
> Ima kaeruramu.[9]

Which may be rendered:

> The souls of heroes whose bones lie bleaching
> On foreign strands
> Have even now returned home [lit. "to the capital"].

The commentary explains: "All unseen by mortal eye, the souls of the men who died on land and sea and left their bodies exposed in foreign lands, have now come back to the national capital with the returning armies."

In 1906 the consort of Emperor Meiji commemorated a visit to the Yasukuni Shrine with two short poems which have been translated:

May you safeguard as deities the fatherland
With truth and fidelity as intense
As the patriotism with which you fought for your noble cause.

And, again:

Parents and wives, who anxiously waited for the safe
    return home
Of their sons and husbands,
Are seen offering before the shrine their earnest prayers
    in tears of gratitude
And worshiping the departed souls now venerated as
    deities here.[10]

Much evidence in the same direction can be found in the ritualistic prayers or *norito* read by the officiating priests on the occasion of all important ceremonies at the Yasukuni Jinja. These constitute the very heart and soul of the services of State Shinto, here as elsewhere. I cite from a prayer offered to the spirits of the war dead in a ceremony held on the fourth day of the first month of the third year of Meiji (1870) to honor those who had recently lost their lives on behalf of the newly established imperial power.

The prayer is offered by the minister of war of the time, acting as the representative of the emperor. It begins:

I, Yoshi Akira, Minister of War, having received the august command of His Majesty the Emperor, in the presence of all the spirits [enshrined here] make utterance . . . .
[There then follows a statement of the occasion of the *norito* and an account of the offerings that are being presented to the spirits. In conclusion is the following prayer:]
Protect and prosper the august reign of the Emperor to ages as eternal as the everlasting rocks. Bring it to pass that all the officials of the government, even to the officers of the urban prefectures, feudatories, and provinces, defend the country—not with divided loyalty, each one for himself—but with uprightness of heart; and bring it to pass that they serve the Emperor with diligence.[11]

Important affairs of state are made known to the deities of the large shrines in a formal statement known as a *saibun* or ceremonial message. The *saibun* which announced the opening of the Russo-Japanese War before the spirits of the Yasukuni Shrine contains the following prayer:

Quickly smite and subdue the foe that is advancing on land and sea and cause the glorious power of the Food Country [poetic name for Japan] to shine throughout the world; give victory and restore long-enduring peace. Guard and prosper the country as long as the ever-lasting rocks shall stand. In reverent awe we ask that ye give heed to these august words from His Majesty the Emperor.[12]

The question has sometimes been raised as to what deities are recognized by the emperor when he participates in the great state ceremonies held before the altars of this shrine. Does he make prayer to the spirits of his subjects, however lowly may have been their stations in this world prior to death? The answer is evident from the citation just given. The emperor recognizes the spirits of the warrior dead, regardless of previous character or rank in human society.

As can be surmised from this fact, subtle ethical problems have arisen in connection with the worship of the dead at Yasukuni Jinja. In December, 1920, the late Dr. Sakuzo Yoshino, a professor in the Imperial University of Tokyo who eventually was ousted from his position for his liberal views, wrote in a magazine called the "Central Review" (*Chūō Kōron*) an article entitled "The Ethical Significance of Worship at the Shrines" ("Jinja Sūhai to Dōtoku teki Igi"). In the course of his discussion he raised an ethical issue connected with the deification of the war dead at the Kudan shrine.

The problem brought up by Dr. Yoshino arose from certain questions that had been asked by his children concerning the reasons for school vacations on the festival days of the state shrines. The writer confessed that he had had difficulty in explaining the matter to the entire satisfaction of either the children or himself. He said that he would welcome a statement from the government officials concerned giving good ethical reasons for vacations on shrine festival days and for worship at the shrines. In this matter he said that difficult questions had arisen even in connection with the enshrinement of the spirits of soldiers and sailors at the Yasukuni Jinja.

He then proceeded to cite a concrete example of the moral complications that were possible. The case had arisen in the family of a friend, not long after the close of the Russo-Japanese War. The father of the family had been asked by one of his children why the souls of dead warriors were enshrined in the Yasukuni Jinja. He had replied that it was because they had given their lives for their country. The child had then asked if a certain servant who had been employed in their home and who had lost his life in the Russo-Japanese War was enshrined there. The father said that this was the case; that this former servant had died in the military service of his country and that accordingly his spirit was enshrined in the hero sanctuary. The child knew that this particular person had been a notoriously bad character. He was dissipated, a liar, deceptive in money matters, and an outright thief. Shortly after having been called to the colors he had been killed in action and his spirit had been deified in the Yasukuni Jinja. The father found great difficulty in explaining all this so as to satisfy the conscience of the child, to whose artless way of thinking it appeared that no matter how much of a good-for-nothing a person might have been, if he died in battle for his country, his former sins were blotted out and he became a *kami* worthy of the worship of the best. The father was much perplexed by the influence of this incident on his child. He felt that the example of a bad person who had been elevated to the ranks of deity, even though on the merits of the sacrifice of life in battle, was of dubious utility as material for the moral education of the young. This is the summary of the account made by Dr. Yoshino in the *Chūō Kōron* twenty years ago. In its issue for September 18, 1938, the *Teikoku Shimpo*, an influential Tokyo newspaper, resurrected this article and made a vigorous attack on the liberal professor. He was accused of having insulted the national structure and of having heaped indignity on the sacred spirits of the warrior dead and the holy cause in which they had given their lives. A person once called to the colors in Japan is summoned to participate in what can never be other than fundamentally and forever righteous. The sacred quality of the divine emperor attaches to a Japanese war. All the wars of Japan are holy wars since they are under the supreme command of an emperor who can do nothing wrong. No matter how much the evil and crime with which an individual may have been defiled, it is all wiped away as soon as he has been placed under military command. We may translate directly at this point:

No matter how much of a wrongdoer, no matter how evil, a Japanese subject may have been, when once he has taken his stand on the field of battle, all his past sins are entirely atoned for and they become as nothing. The wars of Japan are carried on in the name of the Emperor and therefore they are holy wars. All the soldiers who participate in these holy wars are representatives of the Emperor; they are his loyal subjects. To put the matter from the side of subjects, we may say that every Japanese, regardless of what kind of person he may be, possesses the inherent capacity of becoming a loyal subject and of being empowered to put that loyalty into operation. The matchless superiority of the Japanese national life lies just here. . . . .

Those who, with the words, "Tennō Heika Banzai" ["May the Emperor live forever"], on their lips, have consummated tragic death in battle, whether they are good or whether they are bad, are thereby sanctified.[13]

The sanctification is thus twofold: it is by participation in a military cause that has been hallowed by the will of the sacred emperor and it is by a glorious death in his holy cause. From the person of the emperor emanates an influence that accomplishes atonement for sins. A national institution that presents to the members of the armed forces the prospect of joining the ranks of the sanctified *kami* through obedience to the sovereign and death in battle thus becomes the inspiration of the utmost devotion on the part of all those to whom genuine faith in these teachings is possible.

We must now journey from the sanctuary of the warrior dead on Kudan Hill in Tokyo to the ancient center of Yamato culture in the area that surrounds the old capital of Nara and turn our attention to the sanctuary of the sun-goddess at Ise. This takes us from the people to the imperial throne and into the very heart of State Shinto. The great deity honored at Ise, Amaterasu Omikami, is officially defined as the ancestress of the royal line. It is largely by means of the governmentally supervised worship of the sun-goddess that the virtue of devotion to the state is infused with the sentiment of religious faith and baptized with the sense of majesty and holiness that transcends the will of man. We have here excellent opportunity to observe how the god-world of Shinto is arranged on the pattern of the state structure and how the latter is supported and made inviolable by the sanctions of the former. The eternal Japanese state was founded through a sacred edict that is placed in the mouth of this supreme deity. We but follow the constantly repeated words of Japanese educators and statesmen when we say that in the beginning this deity saw far into the future and in her divine wisdom foreordained the structure of a state that was to last forever. Thus the unique national organization rests on a dogma that came out of heaven itself. In it is lodged a divine fiat that supplies Japanese institutions with a norm that is superhistorical in the sense of being a revelation out of the inner and everlasting over-world of spirit. Human thinking cannot touch it; man can only receive it with gratitude, interpret it, and apply it to his greater good. We can understand why it is that a dominant interest of the rulers of Japan is to magnify the sun-goddess at home and to carry her shrines into every territory to which Japanese soldiers have spread the glory of the national arms. Loyalty to the imperial dynasty and the worship of the sun-goddess are one and the same thing. The emperor, ruling in a line that reaches back unbroken to her historically manifested person, is the extension in time and space of her very body and soul. The god-emperor and the great deity mediate one and the same will. Reverence for the one is reverence for the other. To fail to honor the sun-goddess is to fail in the first duty of a subject of the state; it is treason against the sacred national structure itself. Every shrine to the sun-goddess is an altar to the imperial throne.

The edict promulgating the foundation of the state, just referred to, is found in the *Nihongi*, as previously cited. It will be recalled that the "divine edict" appears in the form of a commission laid on the grandson of the sun-goddess when she sent him down out of Takama-ga-Hara, the heaven of the old mythology, to take possession of the territory that was to become the new racial home on earth below. The text has already been noted. Its central importance, however, in all Japanese interpretations of their national structure justifies its reconsideration here.

This Reed-plain-1,500-autumns-fair-rice-ear Land [a rhetorical name for Japan] is the region which my descendants shall be lords of. Do thou, my August Grandson, proceed thither and govern it. Go! and may prosperity attend thy dynasty, and may it, like Heaven and Earth, endure forever.[14]

Dr. Shōzō Kōno, head of the Shinto College of Tokyo, the man who is chiefly responsible for the training of the Shinto priesthood, has said regarding these words:

This august message of the Imperial Ancestress has been looked upon by later generations as an expression of the Divine Will co-existent with heaven and earth. It is also considered as the fundamental faith of the nation and the motivating force of all activities. Furthermore, it is the source and foundation of Article I of the Japanese Constitution which reads, "The Empire of Japan shall be reigned over and governed by a line of Emperors unbroken for ages eternal."[15]

The same authority says regarding the sun-goddess:

Then what is the essence or nature of Amaterasu-Ōmikami? It signifies the sublime and mightiest power of the nation, namely the Throne, and the great-august-heart or the soul of the ruler, which is embodied in the Throne. In other words, it represents the divine soul of the ruler of the empire, the Emperor. The Emperor is the divine manifestation of Amaterasu-Ōmikami and rules the empire in accordance with her will. Thus the Emperor and the Imperial Throne, transmitted in an unbroken line, are sacred and inviolable.[16]

The real story of the Grand Imperial Shrine of Ise is closely connected with the guarding of the regalia emblems of the Japanese dynasty. These consist of a mirror, a sword, and a stone necklace, received by each sovereign at his accession. Their ceremonial commitment to the new ruler is the chief rite of the enthronement ceremonies of the Japanese state. Like primitive regalia emblems everywhere, they originally accomplished the magical transfer of imperial authority across the mysterious and dangerous break of death. Today, after the lapse of many centuries, they are still guarded as the god-given seals of imperial authority. The Grand Shrine of Ise is built about the mirror of this sacred triad.

The founding of the Dai Jingū—to use the Japanese title—carries us back to the year 5 B.C. of the Western calendar, according to the officially prescribed chronology. At this date a shrine to house the regalia mirror was built on the banks of the Isuzu River in the old province of Ise. Ever since then the mirror has remained in the holy of holies of this place safely protected from all defilement. On this reckoning the Ise shrine has an antiquity approximately the same as that of Christianity. Even this early date—if we may trust the chronology again—does not carry us back to the very beginnings. We read in the *Kogoshūi* and the *Nihongi* that, nearly one hundred years before this, the ruler of that time, Sŭjin Tennō, was in personal possession of the regalia mirror and the sacred sword. He kept them under the same roof with himself and on his own couch-throne. The mirror and the emperor were waited on with equal deference by courtiers and attendants. The mirror was a deity. The close proximity of the regalia emblems filled the sovereign with uneasiness, however; we read that he was "greatly overwhelmed by their awe-inspiring divine influence."[17] He accordingly had a new home prepared for them and a vestal virgin of royal blood placed in charge as guardian priestess. The exact location of this earlier shrine is unknown. Then after the passage of some nine decades, in the reign of the succeeding ruler, the mirror was housed in a new sanctuary at Ise, where it has remained to the present, and the sword was removed elsewhere. It is very important that we have these few "historical" details in mind in order to make clear to ourselves the original nature of the worship at the Grand Shrine of Ise. In a noteworthy passage of the *Kogoshūi* this regalia mirror itself is called Amaterasu Omikami.[18] Applying this bit of information to the officially inspired interpretation that we have considered previously, we get the interesting result that the supreme ancestress of the Japanese people and the founder of the state was a mystery-filled mirror. In numerous other places in the ancient Shinto classics the name "Amaterasu Omikami" is applied either to the sun or to the spirit that possesses and controls the sun. In other passages, under the obvious influence of political patterns, Amaterasu Omikami becomes an anthropomorphic deity that presides over the councils of the gods.

No student of early Japanese history and mythology who is really equipped to work in this field and who is free from the coercion of the state utilitarianism that controls body and soul in Japan today can deal firsthand with the evidence and fail to conclude that the Amaterasu Omikami concept rests on a primitive sun worship. Sun worship was the center of the religio-economic life of the rice-culture people of Kyushu whom we find on the scene when Japanese prehistory opens. In the course of time these southerners conquered central Japan and set up a succession of capitals in that district. Eventually this culture flowered into the magnificent Nara civilization of the eighth century A.D. Centuries before this, however, they had begun a program of military expansion into the main island territories to the northeast and had subjugated rival clansmen congregated on the shores of the Japan Sea to the westward. This protracted political and military struggle was reflected in the god-world. In fact, the principal means of centralizing conquest and unifying political control was through the concentration of religious sentiment in the worship of the sun-goddess as the ancestress of the conquering dynasty and the divine being to whom supreme allegiance was due. Historical criticism of the literary records shows us how, in the middle of the seventh century, the old nature mythology was revised in terms of this centralization. Ever since then a solar ancestralism has been the bedrock of political Shinto. In the same general period, however, a new and mighty force that was to make all things different entered the field.

In the middle of the sixth century Buddhism came into the land, and with its attendant riches of a superior continental culture, a more profound philosophy, and a higher ethical code, as compared with the old indigenous forms, it placed the native Shinto in a relatively inferior position against which it was to struggle for thirteen centuries. The subordination of Shinto reached its climax in the Tokugawa era, beginning with the seventeenth century and extending to the middle of the nineteenth. In this period Buddhism was to all intents and purposes the state religion. Then came the great change that was ushered in by the Restoration of 1867. Here begins the story of modern Japan. It was significant for the future that the major powers in the accomplishment of the overthrow of the Tokugawa shogunate were the descendants of the warriors from the south and west who had unified old Japan under the aegis of the sun-goddess. Their day had come again. The Satsuma and Chōshū clansmen who overthrew the Tokugawa government were inspired by the ancient Shinto faith, now revitalized with a Confucian ethic, and their first step after securing political dominion was to set up once more the worship of their sun-goddess. A state religion centering in Amaterasu Omikami was re-established.

From that time onward its influence has augmented with the passing years until it has become the strongest force in contemporary Japan and the chief inspiration of her purpose as she extends her cultural and political domination throughout the Far East.

Against the perspective of this brief historical outline we are in a position to estimate the validity of the various interpretations of the nature of Amaterasu Omikami that one finds in Japan today.

First of all is the ancestral and political view. Amaterasu Omikami is the genuine flesh-and-blood ancestress of the reigning emperor, the remote head of the imperial line and the national family, and the beneficent founder of the state. We have already noted some of the explanations of this position which the directors of thought in Japan today set forth. To dare to broach anything other than this nationalistic-ancestral theme is to invite arrest by the police and legal prosecution in the courts. The whole scope of education in the entire school system of Japan today, from kindergarten to university, is completely dominated by definite instruction in a politico-religious ancestralism centering in Amaterasu Omikami. Here we may present only enough of this material to get the matter more clearly before us.

One of the textbooks on ethics published by the Department of Education for use in all the primary schools of the nation, as part of the technique for deepening the sentiment of reverence for the first imperial ancestress (Amaterasu Omikami), calls the attention of the pupils to the manner in which the imperial family itself reveres the shrine of Ise and worships the great deity enshrined there. In this connection it cites a poem by Emperor Meiji which reads:

> Tokushie ni tami yasukare to inoru naru
> Waga yo wo mamore, Ise no Ōkami[19]

This may be translated:

> I pray that thou wilt keep the people in peace forever
> And guard my reign, O Thou Great Deity of Ise.

Then, in explanation and exhortation, the text continues:

Thus he [the Emperor] wrote, and prayed for the aid of the divine spirit of the Imperial Ancestress.

Children! Thus deeply does the Imperial Family revere and worship the Grand Imperial Shrine! Furthermore, the people of the nation, beginning with ancient times, have never once ceased in their adoration (*sūkei*) of the Grand Imperial Shrine. And even people living in remote places, having once made the pilgrimage to the Ise shrine, and having bowed deeply in the divine presence, and raised their eyes to the sacred majesty, have felt a life-long desire fulfilled. We who are born in the Empire of Great Japan must always revere the Imperial Ancestress and, regardful of the exalted foundations of our national structure, must make it our purpose to support the Imperial Destiny, which is as imperishable as heaven and earth.[20]

Another of the textbooks on ethics contains a lesson which says:

You children have learned that Tennō Heika [Emperor] is the great ruler of our Empire of Great Japan. The Ancestress of the Emperor is called Amaterasu-Ōmikami. The Kōdai Jingū [Imperial-Great Shrine] is the shrine where the Great Deity is enshrined. The Emperor holds this shrine in special reverence and each year, on the occasions of the most important festivals, sends thither Imperial messengers who present offerings.

Inasmuch as Amaterasu-Ōmikami is the Ancestress of the Emperor, she is the most venerated deity in our land of Japan. And since the Grand Imperial Shrine is the sanctuary where this Great Deity is worshiped, those who are Japanese, in addition to being obedient to the Emperor, must always revere and honor this shrine. You children should also await a suitable opportunity for making pilgrimage to the Grand Imperial Shrine, and, in addition to gaining an understanding of the majesty of the national structure, should pray for the prosperity of the Imperial Family. (*Kōshitsu no onsakae wo inori tatematsuru beki nari.*)[21]

A second form of interpretation of the sun-goddess is similar to the one just described but differs from it in being less definite. It recognizes, on the one hand, some of the historical impossibilities that attach to the out-and-out ancestral view of the government as supported by an obedient corps of officially chosen scholars; but, on the other hand, it finds it necessary, or at least expedient, to make concessions to the official position. Accordingly, Amaterasu Omikami becomes the symbol of the unknown historical ancestor who must antedate the known line of authentic sovereigns and who must stand somewhere in the dim and distant past as the racial head. The kind of reverence that here appears is suggestive of the commemoration of the unknown soldier in the Occident. It gives us on the Japanese side a symbolic veneration of the institutions of the past and still makes possible a participation in the stipulated worship of the state. This form of interpretation of Amaterasu Omikami is privately maintained by a certain number of educated people in Japan today. No one knows how many. The view is manifestly one that cannot be openly announced outside of limited circles, since it casts a fog of indefiniteness over the governmentally sponsored position. It is a compromise solution seized on by certain individuals whose range of information gives rise to conscientious scruples, and who, nevertheless, as good and loyal subjects, must make open and formal compliance with the state cult.

A third form of interpretation grows out of a combination of nature worship with ancestor worship, both of which elements are supposedly discovered in the makeup of primitive Shinto. This might be designated the solar-ancestral view. It has been advocated in the past by a small group of Shinto scholars who are too well informed to pass by the nature worship in the old religion entirely. For example, Dr. Genchi Katō, the well-known Shinto authority, has said:

I am of the opinion that the origin of Japanese religion partakes of both nature worship and ancestor worship; the two elements being mingled together. . . . .

It is possible that ancient Japan had a female sovereign, Amaterasu-Ōmikami by name, like the Empress Jingō or Himiko of Tsukushi, and whose political career was inseparably connected with solar myths in so remote a mythical age. So understood, it may be not unreasonable to consider Amaterasu-Ōmikami as partly mythological (the solar myths as ascribed to her in the *Kojiki* and the *Nihongi*) and partly historical. Not all the *Kojiki*, the *Nihongi* and the *Kogoshūi* narrations are purely mythological, or wholly lacking in historical significance; on the contrary, it is quite certain that they furnish historical materials of ancient Japan, though they were not compiled in book form until the eighth and ninth centuries.

There Amaterasu-Ōmikami has indeed an aspect of a solar deity and yet at the same time it is possible that she has an aspect of the great ancestral deity from whom the Japanese Imperial family are sprung.[22]

Here again is a compromise solution in which Japanese scholarship attempts to adjust itself to valid knowledge, on the one hand, and political necessity, on the other. Dr. Katō speaks for the historical significance of the mythological sections of the ancient classics. A full recognition of the historical value of this material would require a more rigorous historical approach than that which he reveals. We would have to recognize the influence of social and political patterns in providing the scheme in which the myths are cast and take account of the dominant interests of dynasty and government that selected, reconstructed, and emphasized certain elements of the mythology to the neglect of others. Otherwise we can never give a really satisfactory account of how a sun-goddess, born from the left eye of a sky-father, and sister of the moon and the storm, ever came to be an ancestor of the royal line and the founder of the state.

According to a fourth construction, Amaterasu Omikami has cosmic significance. In this form of thinking the Amaterasu Omikami concept is either equated with a spiritual monism or the Japanese divinity is made the historical manifestation of the Great Life of the Universe. Both Buddhist influences and those of occidental theology are discernible here. Buddhist thinkers early worked out an adjustment with Shinto in which the various divinities of the latter were interpreted either as the particular avatars of spiritually existent Buddha-forms or the appearances in the Japanese historical sequence of the primary world-soul. This planted seeds in Shinto from which a forest of speculation has germinated. At the same time the mono-theistic example of Christianity has inspired numerous Shinto thinkers to try to set up an ancient and independent monistic or trinitarian structure. In the latter kind of speculation Amaterasu Omikami is either equated with the "Father-god" of the trinity or made the space-and-time manifestation of this "Father." When once we have accepted premises of this kind, we can go anywhere and tie up with anything. We are dealing with theoretical adjustments that are as nebulous as a cloud. Amaterasu Omikami is thus, at one and the same time, the world-soul, the historical Japanese manifestation of the world-soul, the racial head of the nation, the founder of the state, and the ancestress of the imperial family. Contemporary Japan is pretty well flooded with speculation of this sort. It is especially rife among the Shinto sects and has been worked into systems by philosophically minded individuals outside the sects who are seeking to give a speculative texture to the state religion. We may pause here for only a single example of the infra-rational depths to which these thinkers sometimes descend. I quote from Dr. Katsuhiko Kakehi, a prolific writer on Shinto and a former professor in the law school of the Imperial University of Tokyo.

The primordial ancestor, offspring of the gods and herself a deity, was Amaterasu-Ōmikami, the Sun Goddess. The goddess everlastingly manifests Herself in the person of the Mikado, the August Ruler, the representative of the unbroken line of the Imperial Family, and in the firmament reigns supreme over the planetary system.[23]

The last form of approach to the unfolding of the mysteries of Amaterasu Omikami is strictly historical. It utilizes the methodology of scientific study and comes to the conclusion that a sun myth is the key to the understanding of the original nature of the great goddess. This kind of investigation was possible in Japan twenty years ago. Today it finds itself guilty of lèse majesté.

In its actual functional value to modern Japan, the primitive solar mythology has been modified and enlarged by the influence of social and political patterns and impressed by the ulterior motives of tribal, dynastic, and racial aggrandizement, until, reshaped into its modern politico-religious mold, it becomes the symbol of the eternal state. As such, it is the central element of the national spirit, the chief ground for the belief in the one-tribe origin of the nation as all descended from a common ancestor, the inspiration of a spiritual mobilization program that is carried in a thousand ways to the length and breadth of the empire, a basis of unity and authority in human affairs that broadens its dominions over men with every success of Japanese arms, and the embodiment of the highest political authority elevated to the position of deity—in a word, the deification of the political might of the military state.[24]

NOTES

1. *Kokugakuin Zasshi* ("Kokugakuin Magazine") (Tokyo), July, 1932, pp. 79–80.

2. Masaharu Anesaki, *The Religious Life of the Japanese People* (Tokyo, 1938), p. 15.

3. *Yomiuri Shimbun*, May 26, 1940.

4. "A Brief History of the Yasukuni Jinja," by Momoki Kamo in *Meiji Seitoku Kinen Gakkai Kiyō* ("Transactions of the Meiji Japan Society"), L (autumn, 1938), 2–3.

5. Anesaki, *op. cit.*, p. 18.

6. *Japan Advertiser*, October 21, 1938.

7. *Ōmi Kokoro* ("Selected Poems of Emperor Meiji") (Tokyo: Yasukuni Jinja, 1923), p. 7.

8. *Meiji Seitoku Kinen Gakkai Kiyō*, L (autumn, 1938), p. 6.

9. *Ōmi Kokoro*, p. 6.

10. *Meiji Seitoku Kinen Gakkai Kiyō*, p. 7.

11. *Yasukuni Jinja Shi* ("Documents of the Yasukuni Shrine") (Tokyo, 1911), p. 82.

12. *Ibid.*, p. 106.

13. *Teikoku Shimpō* ("The Imperial News"), September 18, 1938, p. 2.

14. W. G. Aston, *Nihongi* (London, 1924), I, 77.

15. *Monumenta Nipponica*, III, No. 2 (July, 1940), 11.

16. *Ibid.*, p. 10.

17. *The Kogoshūi or Gleanings from Ancient Stories* (A.D. 806), trans. Genchi Katō and Hikoshiro Hoshino (Tokyo, 1924), p. 35.

18. *Ibid.*, p. 44

19. *Jinjō Shōgaku Shūshinsho: Kyōshiyō* ("Textbook of Ethics for Ordinary Primary Schools: Teachers' Manual"), VI (Tokyo, 1931), 3.

20. *Ibid.*, pp. 3–4.

21. Vol. III of the *Jinjō Shōgaku Shūshinsho* series (Tokyo, 1931), p. 55.

22. Genchi Katō, *A Study of Shintō: The Religion of the Japanese Nation* (Tokyo, 1926), pp. 53–54.

23. Katsuhiko Kakehi, "An Outline of Shinto," *Contemporary Japan*, I, No. 4 (March, 1933), 586–87.

24. For the study of the shrines of State Shinto the reader equipped to do work in the Japanese language is referred to *Jinja Taikan* ("A Survey of the Shrines") (Tokyo, 1940), and to *Shintō Daijiten* ("Encyclopaedia of Shintō") (3 vols.; Tokyo, 1937–40). Among the thousands of shrines listed in these studies, those that invite special investigation, in addition to the two noted in the text, are the Meiji Jingū of Tokyo (Meiji Tennō and consort), the Kashiwara Jingū of Nara Prefecture (Jimmu Tennō), the Toyouke Daijingū of Uji-Yamada (the ancient Shintō food-goddess), the Kamo Wake Ikadzuchi Jinja of Kyoto (Waki Ikadzuchi no Kami), the Atsuta Daijingū of Aichi Prefecture (the regalia sword), the Ōmiwa Jinja of Nara Prefecture (the oldest shrine of Shinto) (Yamato Ōmononushi no Kami), the Kashima Jingū of Ibaraki Prefecture (Take Mikadzuchi no Kami), the Katori Jingū of Chiba Prefecture (Iwanushi no Kami), the Idzumo Taisha of Shimane Prefecture (Ōnamuchi no Kami), and many others. Among all these shrines, the last named is perhaps the best known to tourists.

CHAPTER III

NATIONALISM AND UNIVERSALISM

THROUGHOUT the whole of her history two sets of forces have stood over against each other in Japan and, by their interplay, their conflicts, their temporary compromise and reconciliation, and their maladjustment as well as their adjustment, have made the story what it is. On the one side have been arrayed the forces of insularity, fear, conservatism, antiforeignism, ethnocentrism, and nationalism; on the other, those of cordiality toward foreign culture, liberalism, incipient democracy, and universalism. At one time, one set of forces has been in the ascendant; at another time, the other; but more often history has been made by a mingling of the two in which liberalism has appeared in one direction and, simultaneously, conservatism and reaction in another.

Modern Japan has had to struggle for the unification and co-ordination of her national life in the face of strongly diversifying, not to say disintegrating, tendencies. There has been much internal heterogeneity to overcome. The particularism of a feudal regime that was split into rival clans and pocketed behind mountain barriers and secluded on separate islands has not even yet been fully transcended. Religious diversity has revealed itself in a tendency toward separatism that seems to reflect what amounts almost to a national genius for sect-making and for breaking up into small esoteric groups. This tendency has been accentuated and complicated by the incoming of nearly every form and feature of the organized religious life of the Occident on top of practically everything that India and China had to offer, including Buddhism, Confucianism, Brahmanism, Mohammedanism, Taoism, and Shamanism, in addition to a vast mass of Asiatic folklore and superstition. Under the circumstances Japan has come to present a spectacle that has well been called a constant exhibition of a world's fair of religions not to be duplicated elsewhere on earth.

Localism manifested in feudal survivals and religious separatism, complicated as they are, are only certain aspects of a much more intricate situation. Modern Japan has constantly been confronted with the dilemma of how to take over the experience and skill of the West without going down before it. If she takes in beyond her capacity to assimilate, she perishes of national indigestion; if she shuts herself off from the new, she perishes from lack of nutrition. In the one case she goes down because she has failed to master the materials and technique of creation and competition; in the other, because of sheer weakness. She has had to solve the difficult problem of gaining the new while somehow preserving the old. Contact with the wonderland of the West has meant improved technique in business and industry, modern sanitation and medicine, scientific education, a different kind of art and literature, and an entirely new culture. And as part of this mighty stream flowing out of the West have come in new conceptions of the nature of man and new and dangerous ideas of the nature of the state. Democracy, individualism, liberalism, even socialism and anarchism, have touched the soul of the people here and there with their flame. Sometimes this flame, fed with the materials of Japan's own internal tensions and maladjustments, has grown into a fire —a fire that has blazed up only to die down again.

Thus far the forces on the conservative side have always been more than sufficient. Protecting Japan against any threat of a conflagration of popular liberalism has been her heritage of insularity that has always made it easy for the ruling classes to stimulate in the masses a fear of foreignism as a threat to security. All the ills that plague the peasant are due to non-Japanese influences that have poisoned the pure and wholesome Yamato ways. This has made it possible to brand liberalizing movements of all sorts as a departure from the tried and safe national pathway and as an unpatriotic repudiation of the peerless Japanese nationalism. This technique of revolutionary control holds the citadel in Japan today. It dominates every approach to the national life. A growing military totalitarianism is thus successfully identified with what is called Nipponism—a name which is often little better than euphemistic camouflage for the most inexorable kind of reactionism.

The diversity of which we have spoken has generally been well under the control of a relatively small, highly trained ruling class, which, when need has arisen, has been able to act with aristocratic swiftness and efficiency without the democratic handicap of being unable to take any important political action prior to educating a supporting majority in the rank and file of the nation. It is this weakness of democracy—its operative lag—that partially accounts for the vehemence with which it has sometimes been attacked in modern Japan. Thanks to the heritage of the experience of Tokugawa feudalism, acquired under circumstances in which a small group of military aristocrats had devised ways and means of keeping millions in control, and thanks again to the unusually high quality of her leadership, Japan has been able to establish and maintain a form of government which in its flexible effectiveness is one of the strongest in the world. Every significant step in the progress of modern Japan has been from above downward—the work of small groups of exceptional men. Without this, the swift adjustment to the conditions of world intercourse and competition and the consequent preservation of the national existence would have been impossible.

Beneath this leadership has stood a patient people among whom the training of centuries has made unquestioning obedience the chief virtue—a people so accustomed to receiving all the authorizations of thought and action from external sources in police offices that they have come to identify truth itself with the asseverations of officialdom. Under such conditions of national psychology, every form of communal enterprise, Christianity included, is in danger of becoming a set of rules.

What has been said thus far has been only the statement of generalities, necessary as a background against which we may see the perspective of detail, but in need of vitalizing by the sketching-in of particular events. We must turn to this latter task. The historical reality which we now encounter is too complicated to make possible the depiction of more than a few outstanding features. These are selected in the line of our chief interest, that is, the tracing of trends in the religious life. They will deal mainly with the nationalistic attitude toward Christianity and the apprehensions, criticisms, and attempted adjustments of the former with respect to the universalism of the latter.

The story opens with the establishment of the newly revived imperial government in Tokyo in 1868. Christianity is under the ban. Signboards spread thickly throughout the country make it a criminal offense to embrace its tenets and offer liberal rewards for information regarding violators. Experience with the Catholic missions of the earlier part of the Tokugawa era has brought the internationalism of Christianity under suspicion; it is feared as the first stage of invasion by foreign powers, its universalism threatening to weaken national loyalty at a time when the new government is in the throes of the struggle to unite a disorganized land that is still feudal in all its ways; and, worst of all, Christianity's claim of obedience to a heavenly father and to a world savior in Jesus Christ runs counter to the veneration of a god-emperor around whom the state moves and has its being.

In 1873 the Japanese government ordered the edicts against Christianity removed. When we seek to discover the reasons for this action, we lay bare an illuminating example of the struggle between the inflowing liberalism and the indigenous conservatism that we have already remarked on. For a document bearing on the issue we can turn back to a letter written on November 10, 1873, by C. E. Delong, minister of the United States of America to Japan, to Rev. Jonathan Goble, in which the former answers certain inquiries raised by the latter concerning the matter before us. Mr. Delong says:

Relative to the repeal of the Edicts against Christianity or their supposed repeal the truth is this. The Edicts were taken down and removed from public observation by order of this government [i.e., the Japanese government] but were not repealed. On the contrary when they were removed officers of the government detailed for this express purpose called on all of the Japanese residents and warned them that although the Edicts had been taken down they still remained in force and must be obeyed as laws. When this action came to my knowledge, I taxed one of the Assistant Ministers for Foreign Affairs with bad faith. He in reply entreated me to not so consider it, at the same time saying: "The liberal party in Japan is yet in its infancy, but I assure you it is increasing rapidly. We have been able to secure two triumphs, one the return of the exiled Christian converts, the other, the removal of these Edicts." These matters, he assured me, had been attained mainly upon the strength of advices received from one of the Ambassadors, Governor Eto, who in a communication addressed to his government written from Europe had advised them that wherever he went he was met by the strongest appeals, in behalf of these exiles and for religious toleration; and he felt assured that unless his government acceded to the first request and evinced a disposition to be somewhat liberal as to the other matter that it might look in vain for friendly concessions on the part of foreign powers in treaty with Japan. He assured me of the disposition of his party and himself to go much farther at once but that it was deemed unsafe to do so as yet; as undue haste might ruin all.

Placing full faith in these representations I consented to let matters rest for a season and wait a more favorable opportunity. This statement proves that no particular man or government is entitled to the credit of having obtained these results. They are the fruit of the earnest labour of Foreign Representatives at this Court, Christian missionaries in this Empire and Christian statesmen and gentlemen abroad who had access to this Embassy, and improved the opportunity they enjoyed. . . . .

Less than four years ago the Japanese government met the Foreign

Representatives in Council on the question of sparing the converts at Urakami from the persecutions then being inflicted upon them. The Chief of that Council was Sanjo the present Prime Minister; the second officer in rank was Ewackura. That Council met all of our protestations with bold assurances of a determination to pursue the policy announced by the Government and Ewackura went so far as to state that the government was based upon the idea taught by the Sintoo and Buddhist priesthood, that the Mikado was of divine origin. This theory he said the teachings of Christianity dispelled, hence its propagation was calculated to undermine the throne; and therefore it was resolved to resist the propagation of that faith as they would resist the advance of an invading army. . . . .

I believe the opposition to religious toleration in this Empire to be confined mainly to two classes, viz. the highest and the lowest. The former actuated by a fear that a disabuse of the religious idea of the Mikado's divine origin would lead to a reorganization of their government, and the latter actuated by a hatred and fear of the doctrines of Christianity that has been instilled into them from infancy and which as yet they entertain.[1]

The above extracts are from a much longer document. The citations given justify a number of observations. In the first place, the removal of the anti-Christian edicts at the beginning of the Meiji era and the permission of freedom of propaganda to Christianity were not the unconditioned manifestation of religious toleration on the part of the Japanese government of the time. These things grew rather out of a political necessity created largely by pressure from Western powers and by Japan's willingness to compromise, in view of her relative weakness at the time and her desire to appear before the world as a reliable modern nation and thus place herself in position to conclude equal treaties with foreign governments. This interest continued to the end of the century, when the unequal treaties were finally abolished. It deeply affected Japan's treatment of the religious problem. It is plain that toleration was eventually extended to Christianity as a means of securing favorable concessions from foreign governments. We shall see that in recent years, with the vast development of economic and military power that has been achieved simultaneously with the entanglement of the

Western world in depression and war, Japan's attitude toward the religious issue has changed to a remarkable degree. A complication of events, foreign and domestic, has placed Japan in a position where she can deal with Christianity with such independence of action as she finds necessary. Undoubtedly Japan has been encouraged in this direction by the examples of Germany and Russia. In the second place, the necessity of protecting the institution of divine imperial sovereignty and of supporting it with the unification of government and religion existing in State Shinto has also profoundly affected the handling of the religious problem and in particular the treatment accorded Christianity.

When we place ourselves before the panorama of modern Japanese history, we can distinguish two general periods of cordiality toward foreign culture. Each period runs through a cycle of bias toward the West and its goods, amounting at times almost to an infatuation and worship that threaten to obliterate all marks of the old life. This is followed by reaction and a strong reassertion of self-sufficient nationalism. The first of these epochs began with the opening of the land to free international communications at the beginning of the Meiji era in 1868 and met its check in a powerful rise of nationalism in the latter part of the eighties of the last century. A second accentuation of pro-foreignism marks the years that followed the close of the Russo-Japanese War. England and the United States of America had been friends of Japan in this crisis, and its aftermath saw a natural turning toward these two countries. This fact was of signal importance for the expansion of liberalism in Japan, since these two countries were not only the strongholds of Protestant Christianity but also the chief seats of democracy in the West. In spite of the formidable growth of reactionary tendencies, especially among the younger officers of the armed forces, this second wave of liberalism continued well on into the third decade of the present century. It was not until the military coup d'état of July, 1937, had started Japan on her "holy war" for the control of East Asia that the final stand of freedom was routed.

We must go back to the beginning once more. Notwithstanding the apprehensions that prevailed in certain influential circles of the government at the opening of the Meiji era, we know that Christianity was admitted and that it eventually met with favor, at least in limited circles. Christianity came into Japan on a great tide of occidental culture that is comparable with the mighty stream of influence that flowed out of China in the wake of the admission of Buddhism in the middle of the sixth century A.D.

The Japan that faced the outside world in 1868 was not blind to the disparity that existed between her own material and technical deficiencies and foreign strength. Her greatest assets then, as since, lay in the quality of her leadership. She was rich in the possession of a number of extraordinary men, close to the throne, who knew that their land could not live by pride and conservatism alone. They had the sagacity to discern quickly the sources of foreign power, and they saw clearly the main steps that had to be taken in order to make their country strong. No less remarkable were they for their liberal aspirations and purposes. They knew that their country must go to school to the West. Simultaneously with the restoration of direct imperial rule Emperor Meiji promulgated in 1868 a charter oath in five articles which gave these purposes the status of imperial policy and which ever since that time has been the sacred scripture of the supporters of constitutionalism and liberalism.

This document stipulates that, when the country is ready for the step, a national representative assembly shall be established and thus government made to rest on public opinion. It exhorts all classes to unite in promoting the welfare of the whole nation, and it declares that all subjects of the realm shall have opportunity to satisfy their legitimate desires, that outmoded manners and customs and superstitions shall be abandoned and justice and righteousness made to regulate all actions, and, finally, that knowledge shall be sought for over the entire earth that thereby the foundations of imperial polity may be strengthened.[2]

This remarkable document, which has been called the Magna Charta of Japanese liberalism, gave the unqualified authorization of the new government to opening wide the doors of the nation to the culture of the West. Japan immediately set about putting into practice the provisions of the Charter Oath. We are especially interested in the last article. A host of foreign technical experts, advisers, and teachers were invited to come to Japan, many of them already men of eminence in their special fields. Some thirteen hundred distinguished Westerners were employed in high positions by the Japanese government at the time, and, if we add the long list of independent teachers and missionaries, the total multiplies several fold. At the height of their influence there were close to five thousand of these foreign representatives in the land. From them Japan learned Western science, educational method, industrial and agricultural technique, medicine, navigation, and shipbuilding, architecture, jurisprudence, military science, and Western religion—the whole gamut of the theory and practice of civilized life in its occidental forms.

In such an atmosphere Christianity flourished like a plant in the warmth of spring sunshine. By the middle of the eighties the Christian movement had established itself widely and firmly in the land, with the roots of numerous churches and schools well down into the soil, and with a Japanese leadership, that, relative to numerical strength, was second to none in the world. Then followed the characteristic and inevitable reaction. In proportion as Japan achieved her purposes in taking over the knowledge of the

West and placing herself in a position where she could match the strength of the foreigner with an equal strength of her own, her ancient self-assertiveness found opportunity for expression, and she began to seek means to check the dangerous infatuation with the West. The forces that stood for caution and conservatism, represented by the personalities of highly placed national leaders, now dictated that their nation had traveled outward far enough, that she must return to her tried and true self, stop copying the West, and take time to assimilate the newly acquired skill and knowledge in terms of form and spirit that expressed the age-long genius of the race.

The center of the problem of meeting the threat against nationalism was in the nature of the unrestricted religious propaganda that had been going on under the protection of cordiality toward things foreign, especially that under Christian auspices; and the center of the religious problem, from the point of view of the authorities, was the schools. Japan now turned herself against religious instruction in the schools. By the famous Order Number Twelve, issued August 3, 1899, religious instruction in all schools, whether governmentally or privately founded, was prohibited. Meanwhile, instructions in State Shinto—the meaning of its rites and ceremonies, the nature of its deities, the relation of all these to loyalty and patriotism and the subject's duty of participation—were all carefully established as foundation courses in the national instruction. A Shinto-motivated ethic was to displace that which had been set up in certain areas on a religious basis. Thus followed the impossibility of admitting that State Shinto was a religion. Since the date just given, representatives of the Japanese government have been particularly emphatic in insisting that State Shinto is not a religion. We shall see presently that this Shinto ethic has large Confucian importations and that it is not without its religious presuppositions.

The sacred text of this reassertion of nationalistic realism is the Imperial Rescript on Education—all things considered, the most famous and influential document yet produced in the history of modern Japan. It was issued on October 30, 1890, preceding by nine years the order withdrawing the right of general religious instruction in the schools. The two belong together. To the Western reader who takes up the rescript for the first time, its brevity and compactness will come as something of a surprise. He may feel that a document that is made to carry so much should be more generous in its proportions. It has all the brevity of a Japanese poem and is perhaps expressive, in one and the same way, of a national character that draws only in primary outlines and that leaves great areas to the response of the soul. The rescript has been supplemented, however, by a vast amount of commentary which supplies the extension not found in the original. In the official English translation the Imperial Rescript on Education reads:

Know Ye, Our Subjects:

Our Imperial Ancestors have founded Our Empire on a basis broad and everlasting, and have deeply and firmly implanted virtue; Our subjects ever united in loyalty and filial piety have from generation to generation illustrated the beauty thereof. This is the glory of the fundamental character of Our Empire, and herein also lies the source of Our education. Ye, Our subjects, be filial to your parents, affectionate to your brothers and sisters; as husbands and wives be harmonious, as friends true; bear yourselves in modesty and moderation; extend your benevolence to all; pursue learning and cultivate arts, and thereby develop intellectual faculties and perfect moral powers; furthermore, advance public good and promote common interests; always respect the Constitution and observe the laws; should emergency arise, offer yourselves courageously to the State; and thus guard and maintain the prosperity of Our Imperial Throne coeval with heaven and earth. So shall ye be not only Our good and faithful subjects but render illustrious the best traditions of your forefathers.

The Way here set forth is indeed the teaching bequeathed by Our Imperial Ancestors, to be observed alike by Their Descendants and the subjects, infallible in all ages and true in all places. It is Our wish to lay it to heart in all reverence, in common with you, Our subjects, that we may attain to the same virtue.

The 30th day of the 10th month of the 23rd year of Meiji.

(October 30, 1890)   (*Imperial Sign Manual, Imperial Seal*)

We have the word of no less a person than the man who, under the command of the emperor, drafted this document, Akimasa Yoshikawa, minister of education at the time, in affirmation of a fact that we should infer on other grounds—that this document was drawn up and promulgated as a definite means of checking the overprecipitate Westernization of Japan that was going on at the time. On this point Mr. Yoshikawa has written:

At the time of the Restoration the late Emperor declared it would be the guiding principle of his government to introduce western civilization into the country and to establish New Japan upon that civilization. Consequently every institution in Japan was westernized and the atmosphere of the "new civilization" was felt in almost every stratum of society. Indeed, the process of westernization was carried to extremes. Thus, those who advocated the virtues of righteousness, loyalty and filial duty brought down on themselves the cynical laughter of the men who professed as their first principle the westernization of Japan every way, and who declared that the champions of the old-fashioned virtues were ignorant of the changed social condition of the Empire.

But if any tendency is carried too far, inevitably there comes a reaction. The excessive westernization of Japan very naturally aroused strong opposition among conservative people, especially scholars of the Japanese and Chinese classics, who thought it dangerous for the moral standard of this Empire to see this process carried even to the moral teachings of the people.[3]

The reference to the attitude of scholars of the Chinese classics in the latter part of this citation means Japanese Confucianists, and the recognition of their powerful influence in now checking the inroads of Western thought points to the remarkable characteristic of the Japanese moral life that exists in the apparent inability to formulate a satisfactory social ethic apart from a Confucian model. In crisis Japan has always fallen back on her innate predilection for Confucianism. Her educational system today, as well as the texture of her public life, is of Confucian fiber. She has made one great modification of her own, however. Confucianism sanctions the overthrow of incompetent rulers and the setting-up of new ones by popular choice. Japan's structure of divine imperial sovereignty treats this as treason and blasphemy and stipulates as the central institution of the state an inviolable and inalienable sovereignty in a single unbroken line of blood succession.

The dependence of the Imperial Rescript on Education on Confucianism is practically admitted by Mr. Yoshikawa in the sequence to the statement just quoted. After reciting the story of the heated controversy that arose among scholars, publicists, and teachers, which was even shared in by officials inside of governmental offices, over the question as to what should be put into the proposed platform of national moral education, Mr. Yoshikawa says:

As people know, the Imperial Rescript on Education was based on four virtues: benevolence, righteousness, loyalty and filial piety (*jingi chūkō*). The making of these four virtues the foundation of the national education was, however, strongly criticized at the time, and some scholars even declared that these virtues were imported from China and ought never to be established as the standard of the nation's morality. Others again said that should such old-fashioned virtues be encouraged among the people it would mean the revival of the old form of virtue typified by private revenge, etc. But I strongly upheld the teaching of these four principal virtues, saying that the essence of man's morality is one and the same irrespective of place or time, although it might take different forms according to different circumstances, and that therefore the aforesaid four virtues could well be made the moral standard of the Japanese people.[4]

The statement then goes on to say that, in spite of criticism and opposition prior to promulgation and much apprehension regarding its future, the Imperial Rescript on Education was issued in its original form and soon became established as the moral standard for the nation. The account of the origin of this famous document from the pen of the minister of education of the time, which we have just reviewed, makes no mention of the religious issue, that is, there is no expressed juxtaposition of Christian universalism and Japanese nationalism; but the issue was present all the time, nevertheless, and protagonists of an exclusive

nationalism were soon on hand to declare that this antag-
onism was directly implied in the wording of the rescript
itself. As we shall soon see, these national leaders vigorously asserted the impossibility of reconciling reverence for
ancestors and the characteristic Japanese national structure with the demands of Christian worship. The grounds
of this difficulty are more apparent in the Japanese original
than in the English translation.

In its opening sentence the Imperial Rescript on Education says, "Our Imperial Ancestors have founded Our Empire on a basis broad and everlasting." The Japanese expression here rendered "Our Imperial Ancestors" is *Waga
Kōsokōsō*. While in its general reference this means exactly
what the English says, in its specific meaning it includes
two classes of imperial ancestors: those preceding the first
traditional emperor and those following him. There is
some difference of opinion as to whether Jimmu Tennō,
the first emperor, belongs in the former or the latter group.
According to the interpretation given in the commentary
that accompanies the Department of Education publication, "The Fundamental Meaning of the National Structure," the meaning of the *kōso* element is: "The deities
(*kamigami*), beginning with Amaterasu Omikami, who
laid the foundations of the imperial glory, and Jimmu
Tennō, who established his authority over the country,
spread abroad the imperial influence and was the first human emperor."[5] The second, or *kōsō* element, means the
line of historical sovereigns from the second emperor to
the father of the reigning emperor. We can see from this
that the rescript makes direct reference to the greatest of
the Shinto deities, Amaterasu Omikami. This fact gives it
the quality of a religious document. It becomes the chief
sacred text of State Shinto.

Not long after the promulgation of the edict a number
of Japanese writers, supported on the one side by their
nationalistic devotion and on the other by their new knowl-

edge of the agnostic literature of the West, and taking for their theme an alleged incongruity between the Imperial Rescript on Education and Christian universalism, launched an attack on Christianity. They declared that the purpose and precepts of the rescript were so definitely nationalistic in their character that it was futile to look for any reconciliation with Christianity. The latter introduces a divided loyalty, a religious absolute that stands forever over against the single devotion to the divine state that is demanded of every Japanese subject as his first duty. There is an unbridgeable chasm between the two.

Dr. Tetsujirō Inouye, at the time a professor in the Imperial University of Tokyo and the author of many books on Japanese national morality and religion, wrote:

Christianity advocates universalism and a love that knows no distinctions, and consequently it cannot be harmonized with the purport of the Imperial Rescript on Education which is nationalistic. Moreover, Christianity places its Heavenly Father and its Christ above the Emperor and therein it contradicts the principles of loyalty and filial piety of the Imperial Rescript on Education.[6]

In 1907 Dr. Hiroyuki Katō, also a professor of the Imperial University of Tokyo, wrote:

The doctrines of Christianity are quite irreconcilable with the Imperial Rescript on Education. In the Imperial Rescript on Education there is not a single word about the Heavenly Father who is the object of absolute love and reverence in Christianity. The rescript speaks only of the Imperial Ancestors. For this reason they [the Christians] cannot have it in their hearts at all to read the rescript acceptably. They must practice deception.[7]

Regarding the futility of attempting to incorporate Christianity into the national life, he says:

It is altogether impossible to assimilate Christianity to the national structure of Japan. If Christianity ere to be assimilated to the national structure of Japan, the fundamental teachings of Christianity would have to be completely destroyed. As long as Christianity possesses its characteristic nature, it can never be said that it is not injurious to our national structure. Sovereignty in Japan is vested in a single Race-father, a form of government without peer among all the nations of the world. It is, therefore, not to be tolerated that a sovereign should be accepted who receives reverence above and beyond the Emperor and the Imperial Ancestors. Our national structure makes it impossible to permit the acceptance of a "One True God" above the Emperor. For this reason it is entirely clear that the teachings of Christianity and our national structure can never stand together.[8]

At the height of his nationalistic apprehension he declares:

If in the future Christianity should gradually grow in power so that the Heavenly Father should be revered more than the Emperor, greater value given to the world than to the nation, and cosmopolitanism should be esteemed more than the Japanese race—if ideas such as these should in some measure arise, I fear that loyalty and devotion as they have existed up to now would be severely weakened or destroyed.[9]

The manner in which Japanese Christians met this attack can be studied in an extensive apologetic literature. Christian writers pointed to the defects of Confucianism "which recognized no spiritual emergency, no moral claims of a redemptive nature, no demand for extraordinary sacrifices overriding the claims of family and state."[10] They declared that Christianity strengthened ancestor worship by deepening faith in immortality and that it gave new breadth to loyalty and filial piety by the infusion of the teachings of forgiveness and redemptive love. They called attention to the fact that statements of the most ardent patriotism were sometimes accompanied by immoral living and unsocial actions, while sincere reverence for the national deities could only be revealed when heart and deed were pure—as Christianity taught. It was impossible to build a sound national ethic merely on the virtue of dying for one's country—supremely noble as that was—but that a loyal living was fundamental to real national greatness. They pointed to the Christian record of contribution to a wholesome nationalism written in terms of the widespread relief of suffering, the promotion of positive social well-being, and the deepening of devotion. The Christian was the best patriot. In the end, Christian apologists, by demonstrating in deed and word the manner in which their faith enriched and supplemented the interpretation of the Imperial Rescript on Education, carried the war into the camp of their enemies and eventually succeeded in vindicating and maintaining the Christian position before the nation.

The second general period of foreign influence in Japan begins with the close of the Russo-Japanese War in 1905. We have now an even better opportunity to observe the interaction of the forces of conservatism and liberalism, of nationalism and universalism, than we had in the earlier period. As already stated, the favorable position in which Japan was placed at the close of this war, especially with respect to the United States and Great Britain, opened the nation to a new phase of democratic and liberal influence. Christianity as the gospel of the release of human personality and of universal brotherhood met with deepened cordiality. In addition to these influences, however, came others that were to create profoundly disturbing situations for the directors of the national life and thought. A wave of fascination for Marxism swept over the land, especially in university and higher school circles, and leftist social theories became popular among students and professors as well as in labor groups. Even communism dared to raise its head. All sorts of isms had vogue in groups here and there, and the authorities looked on in growing alarm. Police measures were, of course, applied with characteristic thoroughness, but these did not touch the social and psychological roots of the malady. In searching about for means wherewith to check the infatuation with "dangerous thoughts," the directors of the national life now turned to the examination of the resources of religion as a thought-control agency. The record of Christian opposition to Soviet atheism and the Roman Catholic position on Marxism were plain before them. Christianity now basked in official favor, so much so that representatives of Buddhism and Shinto complained to the government that they were being discriminated against in favor of a foreign religion. Christianity was presented with an opportunity for an impressive apologetic that it immediately seized upon. The gospel of Christ was portrayed as the faithful mongoose that killed the communist viper; it was the devoted watchdog that kept away the burglar of radicalism; it was the guardian angel that protected the citadel of the national life against the demons of unsocial license. It inspired a true religious faith that brought the blessings of God upon the soldiers that faced ungodly forces across the Siberian border.

It would be a mistake, however, to give the impression that Christianity alone was the object of official encouragement. Buddhism and Sectarian Shinto shared in it. A brief and none too successful flirtation was carried on with Mohammedanism. A glance at the motives underlying Nipponese adventures in this last-named direction furnishes considerable illumination of the attitude toward religion prevailing in certain powerful circles. During the early 1939 session of the imperial diet, in the course of the debate on the bill that later became the "Law Governing Religious Organizations," the government was reminded that the treatment extended to Mohammedanism was intimately related to Japanese policy on the continent of Asia and that it was advisable to have Islam specifically named in the law along with Buddhism, Sectarian Shinto, and Christianity. The press pointed out that, although in Japan itself Islam was a negligible influence, on the continent it was espoused by vast millions of devoted adherents, who might be drawn into Japanese support by favorable treatment. The *Tōkyō Nichi Nichi* gave voice to a representative point of view when it declared:

For Japan to carry out her activity on the Asiatic continent, it is extremely necessary to keep up friendly and co-operative relations with them [Moslems]. Especially is it so when we consider the fact that Chinese Manchurian Moslems live scattered in the so-called Asiatic anti-communistic regions.[11]

The religious utilitarianism that here comes to expression as an instrument of foreign policy was even more authoritatively formulated in the domestic situation toward religion in general. The official purpose to encourage religion as a remedy for the unrest and disorder in the soul of the youth of the nation came to a noteworthy head in the autumn of 1935. At that time the Department of Education issued a statement which practically amounted to a reversal of Order Number Twelve of 1899, which, it will be recalled, had prohibited religious education in the schools.

The new statement encourages religious education in the homes and through various religious organizations and, while declaring that school education should take a neutral position in religion as far as sectarianism is concerned, takes pains to point out that care should be taken not to injure the religious sentiments cultivated in the home and in society. It goes on to say:

Although religious education is strictly prohibited in the schools, yet in order to develop character it is necessary to try to foster religious feeling through religious education.

School education has its basis in the Imperial Rescript on Education and, accordingly, religious education must avoid attempting to cultivate religious sentiment by the use of materials and methods that are inconsistent with the Imperial Rescript on Education.[12]

The statement then proceeds to specify methods by which religious sentiment may be cultivated in the schools. It enumerates more emphasis on the religious aspects of subject matter in teaching ethics, civics, philosophy, and national history; the building-up of a library of good reference books on religion in each school; occasional memorial services of a religious nature; lectures by well-known religious leaders; and the formation by students and teachers of extracurricular organizations for the study of religion and the deepening of the religious feelings.

As far as the official position of the educational authorities is concerned, this is where the matter now stands. The fact that religious educators have not entered more conspicuously into the possession of the opportunity here opened to them is due mainly to three causes: first, a general deficiency in leadership, both religious and educational, competent to meet the needs of youth and really inspire their respect; second, the mounting tensions of the political and social life of Japan today created by the urgency of subordinating everything else to the successful consummation of military purposes in Asia, producing a situation in which extraordinary regimentation makes every person and agency in the nation cautious; and, in the third place, the fact that, after all, the authorities, in their new generosity toward religion, are motivated not so much by an interest in religion for its own sake as they are by the utility of religion in promoting state interests. This third matter deserves special attention.

Behind the invitation from the Department of Education to the religious forces of the nation that they contribute more positively to the attempt to strengthen the foundations of character in youth, it is possible to discern a recognition on the part of the directors of Japanese state affairs of the fact that their formalized, stereotyped education in national morality has in no small measure failed— at least, that it lacks inner dynamic and inspiration. The attempt to identify the reasons for this failure must be limited to a partial statement of only the most important. In the first place, we must recognize an overemphasis on the duty of sacrificial dying for the state without a corresponding inculcation of the responsibility of upright living for the state and, in the second place, a failure to relate the ends and methods of moral education to real emotional interests in the young, that is, a fundamental misconception of the nature of character education on the part of governmental authorities and educators alike. The standardized moral training of the schools, and of the entire nation for that matter, is ceremonial, external, and coercive. It has emphasized unquestioning obedience and thereby has helped to dry up the inner wellsprings of responsible conduct. In the past few years this kind of regimentation has vastly increased. In the third place, we have to admit the devastating effects on character produced by the official demand for outward conformity to unhistorical, and even irrational, elements in the national stereotype. For the undiscerning, docile rank and file this may not be a problem, but for all thoughtful people it introduces an unfortunate dualism and hypocrisy into the moral life. Important areas in the study of history, ethics, government, economics, and even anthropology and ethnology cannot be uncovered and brought out into the light where they may be examined on their own merits. Multitudes of teachers and students, as well as informed people in other walks of life, know this very well. They are obliged to make statements and give tacit assent to propositions that they know represent not historical fact but an extraordinary tissue of truth and fiction, mythology and history, that has been put together under the necessities of bureaucratic utilitarianism. It frequently comes to pass that, although the members of intelligent groups are fully aware that a given situation has more than one side, they are obliged to say that only one exists and that any others are the creation of a mistaken, if not vicious, imagination. Thus scholarship and self-respect are degraded, and the moral life that the state would like to see healthy and vigorous is damaged by the state itself. A make-believe attitude that cherishes form more than substance, a proneness to take refuge behind an emotional fog bank and merely say, "You do not understand us," when issues arise that cannot be openly approached with candor and clarity, a tendency to substitute convenient verbiage for bedrock realism—these are some of the less favorable psychological results of overregimented, formalized moral education of contemporary Japan.

This is, of course, all of one piece with the story of subordination of individualism to the demands of collective security that is being repeated all over the world. If Japan's nationalistic education, conscious of some of its shortcomings, reaches out to religion with one hand, it reaches back into its own conservative past with the other. If the events of recent years have convinced the leaders of the national life that moral education must be deepened and enriched, they have at the same time convinced them that these same ideals must be attained through the use of Japanese instruments. The governmental generosity toward religion that we have just noted is possible only because religious organizations have pretty well accepted this position; and, as we shall see later, even this has not protected Christianity from the suspicion and attack of certain aggressively nationalistic forces in the public life. One of the most prominent characteristics of Japanese nationalism just now is the unanimity with which its advocates heap up the total ills of the body politic on the doorstep of foreign individualism. Significant also is the fact that Japanese intellectual circles, especially the economics department and the law department of the Imperial University of Tokyo, have been singled out for criticism on grounds of an advocacy of dangerous pro-foreign individualism, that surpasses anything directed against Christianity, in spite of the foreign affiliations of the latter.

A statement in the *Teikoku Shimpō* for September 18, 1938, reveals the quality of this kind of criticism on its more rabid and chauvinistic levels. The article makes an attack on the Imperial University as a center of antimilitaristic teaching and a hotbed of communism. It says in summary:

After the Russo-Japanese War there was a great expansion of national self-esteem in Japan. But in spite of American exclusionism and her attempts to frustrate Japan's plans on the continent of Asia and in spite of unfortunate experiences with other countries, especially with England and France, a wave of pro-foreign feeling swept over the country and a blind worship of the West appeared in intellectual circles.

Naturalism and hedonism, along with a fascination with the idea that everything existed merely for the pleasure of the moment, and free thinking and acting that had in them the ruin of the land, ran rampant. The center of this degenerate infatuation with foreign error was the law department of the Imperial University of Tokyo.[13]

The list of names which this newspaper then gives of the men who had been poisoned with foreign democracy, liberalism, and socialism includes practically the entire law department of this school.

For an example of nationalistic repudiation of Western individualism as the source of all the maladjustments of the public life, coming from more dignified and responsible sources, we have an unusually significant document to draw on. It is the publication, *Kokutai no Hongi* ("The Fundamental Principles of the National Structure"), issued in 1937 by the Department of Education. This book has been introduced at an earlier point in the discussion. We should add that it was compiled while an army officer, General Senjurō Hayashi, was minister of education, and, as might be expected under the circumstances, is a manifesto of the principles of military totalitarianism in a Japanese setting. The Introduction states the general attitude of the whole toward Western culture and philosophy. After giving an account of the complexity of the influences that have converged to the creation of modern Japan, the text says:

All of the evils of thought and society in our country today are the result of the excessive and extreme introduction of the manifold and complicated European and American culture, institutions, and technique subsequent to the beginning of the Meiji Era, taken in connection with the fact that we were prone to forget our (national) origins and rush for results, and being deficient in rigorous and sound judgment, we failed to accomplish a fundamental purification (of this foreign culture).

As a matter of fact the Western thought that came into our country was for the most part the thought characteristic of the *Aufklärung* of the eighteenth century and later, or else an extension of this thought. The fundamental world-view of this kind of thinking, as well as its philosophy of man, is a rationalism and a positivism that are defective in historical orientation. (This philosophy) finds the highest value in the individual man and proclaims individual freedom and equality, at the same time revering an abstract universalism that transcends nation and race. As a result, this form of thinking attaches primary importance to an abstracted individual and his groups in isolation from the historical whole. Whereas political theory, social theory, moral theory, educational theory, etc., founded on this kind of world-view and philosophy of man, have, in one direction, contributed to various kinds of reformation in our country, in another direction, they have exerted deep and wide (negative) influences on our indigenous thought and culture.[14]

Following this, the text presents a brief outline of the historical stages of the introduction of Western thought into Japan, the various forms it assumed, and the manner in which it was adjusted to the traditional culture and the state philosophy. We then come to what is probably the most significant statement in the book:

As a matter of fact, in the last analysis, radical systems of thought like socialism, anarchism, and communism are all founded on the individualism that lies at the basis of recent foreign thought and are nothing other than the various manifestations of that individualism.[15]

If it seems puzzling to one familiar with the true history of Western social theory to find such thoroughly collectivistic systems as socialism and communism attached to the root of individualism, he should remember that the key to the understanding of the philosophy of man that controls Japan today is the all-sufficiency of the virtue of unquestioning obedience on the part of subjects. Social and personal evil arises as soon as the individual asserts himself over against the fixed forms of the past or the commands of the rulers of the present wherein absolute values are mediated. In such a psychology it is inevitable that everything that threatens the status quo should be attributed to an arch-evil of individualism that has come into being through unpatriotic infatuation with foreign error. Thus, much domestic discontent arising entirely out of internal maladjustments is shrewdly loaded onto a foreign scapegoat and the glory of the tried and true Yamato ways preserved intact. All this indicates that we should look to the army as one of the main sources of antiforeign teaching, and, if we search in this direction, we shall not be disappointed. Lieutenant General Seishiro Itagaki, former minister of war and later one of the high commanders of the Japanese forces in China, early in 1940 issued a pamphlet in which he says:

The fundamental cause of the outbreak of the present China incident, which has resulted in the unfriendly position of the two Oriental nations, is a lack of realization by them of their true culture and their running after the individualistic conception which forms the basis of the culture of Europe and America. The rulers of China have depended too much on European and American countries. The Japanese people, boasting of their country's superior position, have been insulting China and worshiping things Occidental. These factors have combined to bring about the present predicament. Therefore, it is up to both the Japanese and Chinese people to correct fundamentally the present Sino-Japanese relations on the basis of awakening consciousness of their position as Orientals.[16]

This statement does not make specific mention of Christianity, yet there is plenty of evidence that no small amount of uneasiness exists in military circles regarding the harm that may come to traditional institutions and thought from the Christian world-view. Although this has not reached the stage of the responsible official expression that is manifested in the repudiation of foreign individualism as such, seen in the pamphlet just cited, it nevertheless crops out now and then in surface stones of apprehension that suggest interconnection with a massive bedrock beneath.

A case in point is found in the famous questionnaire sent out under the date of March 4, 1938, by the chief of the thought-control office of the gendarmerie of the Osaka area to representatives of the Christian movement in that district. Although distributed originally only to a small group of Christian leaders in this city, the questions quickly found their way throughout the entire nation, and Christians in widely separated places attempted to answer them. They have been taken by some as indicative of the nature of the apprehensions toward Christianity entertained by wider military groups. The questionnaire asks that Christians submit their views on the following subjects: the Christian idea of God, the nature of the eight hundred myriads of deities of Japan, the relation of the emperor of Japan and the God of Christianity, the relation of the rulers of other countries (for example, the king of England) and the God of Christianity, the relation of the Imperial Rescript on Education and the Christian Bible, the difference between the educational policy of the Imperial Rescript on Education and education according to the principles of Christianity, views regarding Japanese ancestor worship, that is, ideas relating to participation in the ceremonies of the shrines of State Shinto, ideas regarding the divine spirits of the imperial ancestors, the nature of the supreme condition of faith, ideas regarding freedom of religious faith, the reasons why Christianity calls Japanese Shinto and Buddhism idolatrous superstitions, and the relation of Christianity to the Japanese spirit.

As a means of appraising the nature of Christian adjustment to Japanese nationalism it would be of considerable value to us to be able to study some of the replies to these questions in detail. We cannot, however, enter into such a task here. Christian accommodation to Japanese nationalism is dealt with as a special problem in the following chapter. We are interested just now in the other side of the situation, that is, the light that the questionnaire sheds on the attitude of military authorities toward Christianity.

The Osaka questionnaire is only one out of several cases in which military officers have assumed the roles of investigators of Christian activities. In a book published in the summer of 1938 one of the most distinguished and honored members of the Christian constituency of Japan took up the problem of the threatened superintendence of Christian operations by army men and reviewed the outstanding issues. He cites the evidence in the cases of the forced installation of a Shinto god-shelf in the *jujutsu* hall of one of the Christian universities (Dōshisha) by night and without the previous approval of the school authorities, the investigation of Christian thought in the Osaka area, efforts that have been made to extend to all the homes of the nation the use of god-shelves and the protective talismans from the shrine of the sun-goddess at Ise, along with the part that representatives of the army have taken in all this. He declares that if it is a question of wishing to know the nature of Christianity, it is possible to refer to the information on file in the bureau of religions in the Department of Education, where abundant reports on Christianity are available. He asks if it is not inconsistent that interrogations regarding Christianity should come from the gendarmerie rather than from the bureau of religions, to which Christian organizations are supposedly responsible, and continues:

Is the gendarmerie the office that superintends the affairs of Shinto and religion? . . . . The direction and management of the affairs of Shinto and religion by the gendarmerie is from the point of view of various relationships, a cause of anxiety and danger. In regard to the facts given above, I feel that there is a measure of encroachment, anxiety and coercion respecting the freedom of belief in Christianity.[17]

The tensions between nationalism and universalism in Japan today are thus concentrated in the area of the adjustment of Christianity to the claims of the military state. Japanese writers have sometimes declared that the problem of state and religion in their country hardly exists apart from this particular opposition. The manner in which Japanese Christians have recently attempted to meet this situation now calls for consideration.

NOTES

1. Michio Takaya, *Matai Fukuinsho* ("The Gospel by Matthew," a study of early translations into Japanese) (Tokyo, 1940); see pp. 65 ff. for Delong's letter.

2. See translation of the Charter Oath in Inazo Nitobe, *The Japanese Nation* (New York and London, 1912), pp. 76–77.

3. *Japan Advertiser*, August 6, 1912; translated from the *Kokumin Shimbun* for August 5, 1912.

4. *Ibid.*

5. Fujisaku Miura, *Kokutai no Hongi Seikai* ("Commentary on the Fundamental Principles of the National Structure") (Tokyo, 1937), pp. 63–64.

6. Tetsujirō Inouye, *Shūkyō to Kyōiku no Shōtotsu* ("The Conflict of Religion and Education"), cited in Toraji Tsukamoto, *Gendai Nihon to Kirisuto Kyō* ("Present-Day Japan and Christianity") (Tokyo, 1932), p. 124.

7. Hiroyuki Katō, *Waga Kokutai to Kirisuto Kyō* ("Our National Structure and Christianity") (Tokyo, 1907), p. 63.

8. *Ibid.*, p. 56.

9. *Ibid.*, pp. 86–87.

10. Cited as the criticism of Bishop Honda in the article by S. H. Wainright, "The Course of Japanese Thought as Reflected in Christian Literature," *The Christian Movement in Japan, Korea and Formosa* (Tokyo, 1923), p. 121.

11. *Tōkyō Nichi Nichi Shimbun* ("Tokyo Daily News"); translated in the *Japan Times and Mail*, March 7, 1939.

12. From a document privately distributed to the schools by the Department of Education in the fall of 1935.

13. *Teikoku Shimpō* ("Imperial News"), September 18, 1938.

14. *Kokutai no Hongi*, p. 3.

15. *Ibid.*, p. 5.

16. Translated in *Japan Advertiser*, April 29, 1940.

17. Daikichirō Tagawa, *Kokka to Shūkyō* ("Religion and the State") (Tokyo, 1938), p. 141.

CHAPTER IV

JAPANESE CHRISTIANITY AND
SHINTO NATIONALISM

VIEWED in the perspective of the vast and complicated national life of Japan today, the Christian movement of that country appears as a small and relatively weak—sometimes impotent—minority enterprise. The annual statistical summary of Christian believers of all affiliations stands out with conspicuous disparity against the total population—some 340,000 members of the Christian churches in a total of 70,000,000 souls for Japan proper. Even if we admit, as some have claimed, that there are as many as a million private followers of Jesus who hesitate to attach themselves formally to the churches, and after full recognition of the magnificent contribution of Christianity to social melioration, the humanizing of education, and the emancipation of personality—with all due credit given this achievement, we must nevertheless admit, if we are to be realistic in our appraisal, that the Christian movement in Japan today is still too weak, in numbers as well as influence, to take more than a subordinate position when powerful forces in the state set about turning all the resources of the national life into directions that cut across those along which the Christian church has traveled. Under the circumstances the church has only two roads open to it: persecution and martyrdom or compromise and accommodation. The Japanese Christian church has chosen the latter. This has meant the surrender of much initiative that at one time was exercised with relative freedom.

The fundamental requirement of conciliatory readjustment laid on Christianity by Japanese nationalism has been well stated by Dr. Genchi Katō when he says:

Since a national religion which is closely united with the Japanese Empire in the form of State Shinto still reigns all over the country, it is in vain that an imported religion exerts itself with the object of extirpating and supplanting this national religion of Japan. Because such a religion could succeed in its mission only after having exterminated the Japanese nation and destroyed the national polity or the fundamental form and character of our nation. If anyone wishes to propagate a new religion in Japan, I believe that he has no other means than to admit, in the spirit of conciliation, the friendly relation of the two religions, both the indigenous and the foreign. . . . . There is no other means than this for the diffusion of an imported religion among the Japanese people, believers as they are in the nationalistic Shintō, ready to defend the indigenous religion at the cost of their lives, under the rule of the divine Emperor.[1]

Although this statement does not name Christianity in so many words, it may be taken as having special reference to the extension of the Christian movement in Japan today. We turn to the examination of some of the adjustments that are taking place in the consummation of "the friendly relation of the two religions," Christianity and Shinto.

The far-reaching nature of the accommodation of Japanese Christianity to the claims of national Shinto is nowhere more definitely revealed than in the almost complete compliance with the official requirements of participation in shrine ceremonies that now prevails in Christian circles. This is in marked contrast with reservations that were openly stated in earlier years.

In 1917 the council of the Federated Churches of Japan, representing nearly all the Christian forces of the land outside of Roman Catholic and Russian Orthodox constituencies, declared: "To lead the people into a vague religious exercise under the pretext of reverence towards ancestors, and thus to mix the two things, is not only irrational, but results in harm to education and hinders in many ways the progress of the people."[2]

The Federated Churches of Japan eventually gave place to the National Christian Council. For years this latter body gave careful study to the Shinto problem through the agency of a special committee on the shrines. In 1930 this committee made an important statement from which the extracts given below are taken. The report was ratified by fifty-five Christian organizations, including Japanese national bodies, local ministerial and lay associations, and the various foreign missionary groups. It may be taken as thoroughly representative of the position of the Christian forces of Japan at the time. In its most significant sections the statement says:

> For many years we have deplored the fact that there has been no solution of the traditional difference of opinion and the confusion which has existed as regards the relation between Shrine Shinto and religion.
>
> While it is true that since the middle of the Meiji Era the traditional policy of the Government in its administrative treatment of Shrine Shinto has been to put it outside of the religious sphere, still, to treat the Shinto shrines, which from of old have been religious, as nonreligious has been unreasonable. The shrines of Shrine Shinto are actually engaged in religious functions. This has given rise to much confusion.
>
> Furthermore, recently the Government in its effort to foster religious faith has promoted worship at the shrines of Shrine Shinto and even made it compulsory. This is clearly contrary to the policy that Shrine Shinto is nonreligious. Moreover, the question has often been raised as to whether at times it has not interfered with the freedom of religious belief granted by the Constitution of the Empire.
>
> In the interests of the people's thought-life, this is a problem of such gravity that it can no longer be overlooked. . . . .[3]

Since the issuance of this statement the National Christian Council of Japan has been obliged to adjust its position on the shrine problem to the growing demands of governmental standardization. The nature and success of pressures that have been applied in this region may be gauged from the fact that in November, 1936, the National Christian Council went on record with the declaration: "We accept the definition of the government that the Shinto shrine is nonreligious." This may be taken as reflecting the opinion of the Christian community as a whole. In the place of the earlier reservations there now exists general and practically unanimous approval of the position of the government that the shrines of national Shinto are legally and inherently outside the religious classification, that the deities are the spirits of deceased emperors and others who have contributed meritorious service to the state, and that the purpose of the ceremonies is to commemorate the past, deepen patriotism, and sanctify the sentiment of devotion to the imperial throne.

The earlier position of the Roman Catholic church of Japan on the shrine problem was not manifested in any binding official statement of fundamental scope. But the history of this church in its struggle with State Shinto and the occasional pronouncements of individual bishops reveal beyond a doubt the reservations that Catholicism in Japan entertained toward Shinto as a state religion. We may take as an example a proclamation of the Bishop of Nagasaki, made in 1918:

> The members of the Catholic Church, without hesitation, will join in paying due reverence toward the nation's distinguished men as a part of patriotic duty. Nevertheless, however generous our frame of mind may be with regard to this view of the shrines [government view], we cannot give our support to it. . . . . Shrine worship is indeed poor in religious ideas judged from the inner worth of religion, but is amply furnished with a wealth of ceremonies fixed by law. It is an organized form of reverence paid to supernatural beings and must be regarded as a religion. Moreover, it is a religion forced upon the people, and if it be different from Shinto, it may not inappropriately be called shrine religion. . . . . We regret exceedingly that as Catholics we cannot accept the interpretation of shrine worship given by the government nor can we visit the shrines and engage in the services for the dead nor can we ever pay respect to the so-called gods.[4]

As late as 1931, the bishop of the same diocese, himself a Japanese, declared that State Shinto was "only a primitive religion" and continued a New Year's message to his people by saying:

> The Shinto shrines, so the high authorities of the government tell us, do not maintain a religion, but as a matter of fact the ceremonies that are performed therein have a full religious character. Thus the sacred right of religious freedom, given to the people in article 28 of the constitution, is forgotten and violated by the ministry of education itself, and students are forced to go to the shrines and punished if they refuse.[5]

It was not long after this, however, that the pressure of national standardization, exerted through police and military offices as well as through the ordinary channels of civil government, led the Church of Rome to hand down a decision that completely reversed the position of the Nagasaki bishops. On May 25, 1936, the Office of the Sacred Congregation of Propaganda Fide at Rome, after a review of the entire problem by the College of Cardinals, directed Catholic believers in Japan to accept the official definition of the nonreligious nature of State Shinto and comply with the governmental requirements in the matter of participation in the shrine ceremonies. The document justifies this action mainly on the ground of the alleged reliability of the Japanese official declaration of the purely civil character of the rites. In its most pertinent section the proclamation says:

The Ordinaries in the territories of the Japanese Empire shall instruct the faithful that, to the ceremonies which are held at the Jinja (National Shrines) administered civilly by the Government, there is attributed by the civil authorities (as is evident from the various declarations) and by the common estimation of cultured persons a mere significance of patriotism, namely, a meaning of filial reverence toward the Imperial Family and to the heroes of the country; therefore, since ceremonies of this kind are endowed with a purely civil value, it is lawful for Catholics to join in them and act in accordance with the other citizens after having made known their intentions, if this be necessary for the removal of any false interpretations of their acts.[6]

When we attempt to account for this reversal of the position of the Christian forces of Japan from rejection to acceptance, we are confronted with the fact that whatever changes have taken place have not been in the national religion itself. State Shinto in its inner nature remains today what it was at the beginning of the present century and essentially what it was at the opening of the modern era in 1868. The changes must be sought mainly in the attitudes of the Japanese Christians. If we should list briefly the main factors that have influenced this accommodation, we would have to take note of the success of the national educational program that has raised up a generation of loyal subjects who have been fully indoctrinated in the officially inspired utilitarian interpretation of the nature and history of the national structure; an overflow of patriotic sentiment, stimulated by the fears, as well as by the intensification, of a war psychology that engulfs all alike regardless of religious affiliation; and, most potent of all, an official compulsion that has made discretion the better part of valor and conformity the way of real wisdom.

During the last three or four years individual Japanese Christians have found conspicuous opportunity to impress the nation with the fact that, in loyalty to the ceremonies and beliefs of national Shinto, they do not compare unfavorably with the members of any other group in the nation, however devoted. Christians in high official positions have performed obeisance before the altars of the spirits of the Meiji emperor and his consort at the Meiji Jingū of Tokyo and before the spirits of the war dead at the Yasukuni Shrine on Kudan Hill; outstanding Christian leaders have announced Christian programs before the spirit of the sun-goddess at the Grand Imperial Shrine of Ise; and Christian schools within Japan proper have participated almost without exception in attendance at shrine ceremonies.

Occasionally this accommodation has taken the form of the presentation of *norito*, or prayers, to the deities enshrined in Shinto sanctuaries. On August 13, 1937, a group of prominent Christians appeared at the shrine of the sun-goddess in Ise and offered to this deity the following petition:

Prosper and favor the reign of the Emperor who rules over the Great Eight Islands [an archaic name for Japan] as Manifest *Kami* and make it a majestic reign and a prosperous reign. Grant that the august person of the Emperor be kept in ever increasing health and grace. Prosper the glory of the Imperial Throne with a glory that grows from more to more, unto an eternity as enduring as heaven and earth. . . . . Bring it to pass that the subjects of the empire may quicken and elevate the Japanese spirit as in the Age of the Gods; that they may exalt the glory of the national life; that they may make the sacred power of the Emperor to shine ever higher, ever wider, and for eternity; and grant that Japan may become the model for all nations.

Again, we pray that thou wouldst bring to fulfillment our spiritual, educational and social activities, whereby the early peace of the world is being promoted, and the seven hundred thousand inhabitants of [name of district omitted] are being awakened to the Japanese spirit and the glory of this spirit unfolded. Bring it to pass that all things may be done according to the Way of the Gods. . . . . This we say in solemn awe.[7]

This prayer is published in a study called "The Shrine Problem" (*Jinja Mondai*), written by Mr. Iwasaburō Okino, a pastor of the Japan Presbyterian church. After printing the text of the *norito*, the author says: "The fact that a group of Christians presented this prayer is truly a remarkable event in the history of religions in Japan."[8]

Further efforts of Japanese Christians to adjust their faith as followers of Jesus to the claims of nationalism appear in an ethical apologetic which makes the chief moral requirements of Christianity identical with those demanded by the state. Christianity is avowed to be primarily a religion of absolute obedience, while any emphasis on Christian teaching as fundamentally concerned with the development of creative personality and moral freedom on which can be built the intelligent co-operation of responsible men and women is suppressed if not openly repudiated. This is not to say that the conviction that Christianity should devote itself essentially to the enrichment of free personality has been entirely abandoned, but it has gone backstage and is discreetly inarticulate. In so far as the activities and utterances of the leaders of the Christian movement in Japan are open for objective examination, they show a purpose to fit Christianity fully into the scheme of comprehensive regimentation demanded by the state.

It is not by chance, then, that this ethical alliance between Christianity and nationalism has often sought to demonstrate to military and civil authorities the full reliability of the Christian subject in the totalitarian state by citing an appropriate scriptural basis. Christianity has protected itself by the frequent repetition of the Pauline injunctions that every soul should be in subjection to the higher powers and that the powers that be are ordained of God. The first seven verses of the thirteenth chapter of Romans have been a favorite passage for reading at public gatherings, especially those connected with the schools when representatives of the army have been present.

This laudation of the priority of absolute obedience in the ethical platform of Christianity is supplemented by a reassertion of its contribution to social progress and the establishment of higher standards of conduct. Supporting this is a review of the Christian record in the relief of poverty and suffering, the purification of the home and the dignifying of the status of woman, the elevation of private and public honesty, the strengthening of domestic morale, and the ministration to soldiers in the field. This kind of review sometimes extends to the publication of the value of Christianity to the nurture of military virtues and the enrichment of the code of *Bushido,* or the "Way of the Warrior." A study of this subject by Mr. Arimichi Ebisawa, published late in 1939, bears the title, "The Relation between the Ethics of *Bushido* and Christianity." It includes sections dealing with the persecutions of the early Catholic period and analyzes the spiritual and moral attainments manifested in the characters of the Christian martyrs. The greatest of these are renunciation of all desire for worldly wealth and fame, unyielding purpose to be worthy of life everlasting, vehement faith, extraordinary courage, and tenacious power of will. After setting forth this summary of the virtues of the martyrs, the author remarks: "We may herein observe that the Christian people further strengthened and enhanced the sense of honour and will-power peculiar to Bushidō, which had developed strikingly, notwithstanding all contradictory and adverse conditions which stood in the way of its development."⁹

It is not many pages after this remark, however, that the author reverses the relation of indebtedness by observing that the calm resignation with which the Christian martyrs often met unspeakably cruel death, "evincing no resentment against anyone, but on the contrary, offering prayers for the sake of their persecutors," that this sublime and inspiring attitude of the Japanese Christian converts "is mainly due to the unique idea and sentiment of Bushidō which had been cultivated for ages." Also, he says, "because of the traditional influence and inspiration of Bushido such glorious and blood-stained pages as are rarely seen in the chronicles of other nations have been added to the history of Japan."[10]

It is difficult for a Western chronicler to read this idealization of *Bushido* without protest. The Way of the Warrior truly leads through centuries of bloodstained pages, but where in all that story do we find a single example of that Jesus-like love that requites evil with good and offers prayers on behalf of the enemy and persecutor? The lurking revenge of the Forty-seven *Rōnin* is typical of *Bushido*, not the spirit that evinces resentment against no one.

The most authoritative recent statement of the identity of Japanese military ethics and the teachings of Christianity comes from the "Committee on Emergency" of the National Christian Council of Japan. Early in 1940 this body issued four propaganda pamphlets designed to show the position of the Japanese Christian church on urgent national issues and programs. Their publication was accompanied by an explanation of purpose written by the man who was the executive secretary of the council at the time of compilation. Some of his observations are very much worth noting. He says:

Unprecedented crisis having befallen the Far Eastern countries, everything must be re-examined in the light of the new situation arising out of this tragic experience. The whole life of our nation is deeply affected and the mental attitude of the people is naturally undergoing a fundamental change. It is in line with the general psychological trend

of the day that our nation has been disillusioned by western civilization
and has lost confidence in the western powers for which they previously
had high respect as "Christian" nations.

Along with this awakening of national consciousness the Oriental
peoples began to turn their eyes toward the Christian institutions within our land which in the minds of the general public are yet closely
associated with these foreign nations. The foreignness of these institutions has been much criticized by unbelievers, and we must admit with
some justice; because to an extent Christianity in Japan is not yet
really rooted in the indigenous soil. Some have even gone so far as to
question the patriotism of the Christians in Japan. . . . .

New Christian apologetics to meet the newly arising national sentiment had to be introduced to the churches in Japan confronted by
crisis. As a consequence, the whole tone of writings and lectures of our
Japanese leaders of late has been along this line of producing new
apologetics for our new age and surroundings.[11]

One of these propaganda pamphlets includes a discussion of the matter immediately before us, the comparison
of Christian ethics and the code of the warrior. The title of
the booklet is *Seishin Hōkoku to Kirisuto Kyō* ("Patriotism
of the Spirit and Christianity"). The author is Mr. Saburō
Imai, a pastor of the Methodist church of Japan and formerly the chaplain of the Aoyama Gakuin middle school.
The sponsors and publishers are, of course, the National
Christian Council of Japan. The main points of the argument are summarized below.

Criticism on the ground that Christianity possesses an
indelible foreignness that cannot be assimilated to Japanese character and institutions is countered with the position that the rigorous Christian ethic deeply satisfies the
well-disciplined Japanese spirit and conforms in a special
way to the essential demands of its finest manifestations.
This is seen in the unique correspondence between Christianity and *Bushido*. Protestantism and Catholicism alike
have attracted to themselves an unusually large number of
the members of the military families. The leadership of the
Christian movement has come in no small measure from
the samurai class. This noteworthy fact is no accident of
history. It rests on a fundamental affinity between Chris-

tian ethics and *Bushido*. This leads to a comparison of the special characteristics of Christianity with the code of the warrior.

In its general aspects, the traditional spirit of *Bushido* is founded on the conception of righteousness. It is a way of life which above all things else magnifies the duty of sacrifice of self for ruler and nation. It teaches the obligations of succoring the weak, of putting down the strong, of the avoidance of evil, and of the fostering of sincerity, uprightness, and goodness. Five characteristics are listed:

In the first place, *Bushido* is founded on a strong sense of moral obligation. It fulfils to the utmost the claims of duty. That to which the warrior aspires is truth; that which he guards is uprightness. In all the world there is nothing greater than truth; there is nothing weightier than uprightness.

In the second place, *Bushido* holds strongly to the doctrine of sacrificial death. In the discharge of duty everything personal must be surrendered. In devotion to ruler and love of country, in loyal and courageous public service, there must be no regard for the advantage or comfort of the individual.

In the third place, it is a resolute and intrepid spirit that always goes forward in the strength of firm conviction. In the discharge of duty it raises no questions of disparity of numbers. It resolutely trains the mind to perform whatever duty is entrusted to it.

In the fourth place, it nourishes the spirit of compassion for the weak. Within its strength it bears a heart of love. Concealed within *Bushido* is a magnanimity that crushes evil and wrong on behalf of the oppressed.

Finally, it does not have its center in the military arts. In its fundamental aspects it is the spirit of loyalty to ruler, love of country, and devoted public service.[12]

For a statement of the primary principles of Christianity, the pamphlet goes back to the Meiji era and summarizes from the words of certain of the Christian leaders of the time the main points of the defense which they made against the nationalistic criticism that arose at about the turn of the century. The discussion recalls that, beginning about 1892, Christianity was attacked because it taught "Thou shalt have no other gods before me," and thus subverted absolute loyalty to the imperial throne; because it declared that in the love of the one true heavenly father all men were equal and without distinction, because from the point of view of such teachings it did not recognize the superior majesty of the emperor, being destitute of the concepts of loyalty and patriotism and lacking the ethical teachings of reverence for ancestors and filial devotion to parents; and, finally, because such a religion could not be harmonized with the unique Japanese national structure and spirit.

The Christian reply, taken from various publications of the time, extends to nine points. Summarized they are:

1. Although when considered from the point of view of religion the One True God of Christianity is regarded as a personality, when considered from the point of view of philosophy, He should be regarded as ultimate reality and the essence of the universe. [The unspoken inference is that no real conflict with personal loyalty to the emperor is involved, since the Christian doctrine of God moves in an area where the state sets up no claims.]

2. Christianity is a teaching that relates to the unseen world of God, and it is from this doctrine that its teaching regarding mankind arises.

3. When a person is saved according to Christian teaching, he is spontaneously enabled to meet the moral requirements of human ethical relations. [I.e., he becomes a good and reliable subject of the state. The Christian is the finest patriot.]

4. The essence of *Bushido*, in which the Japanese people take such pride, is to offer one's self as a sacrifice and to take the part of the weak. These teachings are also essential in Christianity, as seen in the words: "Thou shalt love thy neighbor as thyself," and, again, "Greater love hath no man than this that a man lay down his life for his friends." In this Christianity and *Bushido* are the same. It follows from this that Christianity is one with *Bushido* in promoting the welfare of the nation and love of country, and that the fundamental spirit of Christianity is the same as that of *Bushido* in rendering loyalty to the Supreme One who looks on his people with compassion.

5. The Japanese spirit esteems righteousness and hates iniquity. This again is highly honored in Christianity, as set forth in the teaching, "Righteousness exalteth a nation; but sin is a reproach to any people."

6. Christianity does not worship idols and makes absolutely no recognition of them. Japanese Christians, however, regard the Grand Mausoleum of Ise as the historical memorial of imperial ancestors and revere and honor it as the object of national devotion; and, again, it is hardly necessary to say that they revere and honor all the Shinto shrines

where those who have contributed distinguished service to the nation are enshrined.

7. The equality which Christianity advocates is not absolute equality. It is an equality that makes distinctions.

8. Loyalty and patriotism and honor for parents are fundamental teachings of Christianity. When the existence of the fatherland is threatened and when those appear who destroy the peace of the world, who flaunt their iniquity and strive against righteousness, then Christianity fights them with determination.

9. Opponents of Christianity assert that the authority of the state and the authority of a world religion cannot be reconciled, but this argument is mistaken at the root. It leads to inevitable error when we compare the state and religion on identical grounds, since the purposes of the two are quite different.[13]

The author applies this summary of an earlier Christian apologetic to the existing situation by the brief remark: "The above gives the main points of the argument from the side of Christianity. It is self-evident whether this statement is in conflict with *Bushido* and, more widely considered, with the Japanese spirit, or whether it harmonizes with them."[14]

The booklet does not attempt to define the purposes of a world religion in relation to those of the state beyond the outline which we have just reviewed. The explanation of the reasons for issuing these propaganda pamphlets by the National Christian Council, to which we have earlier called attention, does, however, make a statement which may be applied in the direction of the clarification of this relationship. In a word, it is the humanizing of the programs of the state. Describing the motives that led to the preparation of the pamphlets, the statement says:

We also took advantage of the opportunity to make clear that the final goal of the so-called "establishment of a New Order in East Asia" would be achieved only when the Christian principle of love and justice was observed, and that the problems of man-power and material resources which the whole nation is seriously considering would be solved only when individuals came to behave according to inner Christian motives.[15]

The actual nature of the adjustment that takes place under these conditions may be seen when we examine the discussion regarding Christianity and war. "Patriotism of the Spirit and Christianity" says:

Even well-informed people who feel that they possess a relatively sound understanding of Christianity fail to reveal a comprehension of the subject of Christianity and war comparable to their knowledge of Christianity in other respects. There are many who believe that some sort of contradiction exists between the two. This is something that we have experienced repeatedly in connection with the Emergency [war with China]. It has often come to our attention that even modern men with good education, men who if asked would declare themselves friendly to Christianity, men who ordinarily have permitted the members of their families to attend church and have sent their children to the neighborhood Sunday school, when once the Emergency arose have used indirect means to interfere with church attendance on the part of the members of their families. The reason seems to lie in the fear that connection with a Christian church is somehow an unpatriotic act.

What in brief are the grounds for this kind of thinking? It is true that Christianity proclaims a gospel of peace. Christianity loves peace among mankind. But to love peace does not mean in and of itself an opposition to war. The opposite of the love of peace is the love of discord. Are the Japanese a nation of people who love discord? Could anything be more absurd? Yet exactly this absurd argument is cast against Christianity when wars and emergencies arise.

We love our nation; we love our fatherland; and if ever our fatherland is in danger, we immediately arise and place ourselves on guard. We are not among those that love war. When, however, the fight is against an unrighteousness that is trampling righteousness under foot, when the fight is for the establishment of true peace, we count it glory to enter the field of battle and stand as a shield against iniquity. "Think not that I came to send peace on the earth: I came not to send peace, but a sword."[16]

In relation to the practical aspects of military operations in East Asia, this conception of the relation of Christianity and war becomes little more than a republication of the idealizations already made by the Japanese government. Regarding this, the pamphlet goes on to say:

When those who should mutually love each other do not practice this love, when far eastern peoples of the same racial stock and written language, who should act in co-operation do not co-operate, nay rather, when they resort to arms and recompense blood with blood, how regrettable it all is. One can have only the most profound sympathy for the people of China when their government, which should have guided them in ways that were good and planned for the peace of the Far East, rather, because of its mistaken policy of opposition to and contempt for Japan, incited this unfortunate affair.

There is nothing so pitiable as a people who are treated as puppets, deceived by their government, and instigated by flattering, lying demagogues. The people of China in their everyday lives, even in their national readers, were entangled in a movement of contempt for Japan and of opposition to the Japan of their own racial stock and written language. This they believed was the New Life Movement which was to bring them happiness.

When the Emergency began, Premier Konoye repeatedly issued warnings that they should take knowledge of their sins. He tried to persuade them that nothing was so important to the happiness of the people of both countries as co-operation between them for the establishment of the peace of the Far East; but evil is indeed like a blind man who fears not the serpent in his path. Finally our country proclaimed a Holy War.

It is our mission to protect the Chinese people from having their whole body cast into Gehenna, even though their right eye must be plucked out. With love in our hearts we have resolved on the completion of the Holy War. With tears in our hearts we have raised aloft the whips of love, and the time may yet come when these will bring the people of China to perceive their error. We hope and believe and pray that on that day when the peace of the Far East opens before their eyes, their time of thanksgiving will come.[17]

An equally noteworthy example of this same kind of apologetic was published in the early summer of 1939 in commemoration of the second anniversary of the outbreak of the war with China. It is from the pen of Mr. Akira Ebisawa, who was at the time the executive secretary of the National Christian Council of Japan. Central to his argument is the identification of the Christian conception of the Kingdom of God on earth with the extension of Japanese political sway in eastern Asia. On this point the author's words are worthy of special attention. He says:

What is then the plan for the long-term reconstruction of East Asia? Its purpose is that of realizing the vision emblazoned on the banner, "The world one family"; and that purpose, we must recognize afresh, coincides spontaneously with the fundamental faith of Christianity. The policy of extending even to the continent our family principle which finds its center in an Imperial House so that all may bathe in its holy benevolence—this policy, can we not see?—is none other than the concrete realization on earth of the spiritual family principle of Christianity which looks up to God as the Father of mankind and regards all men as brethren. This is the Christian conception of the Kingdom of God. The basis of the Japanese spirit also consists in this; and thus, wonderful to relate, it is one with Christianity. Nay, this must indeed be the Great Way of Heaven and Earth.[18]

It is the duty and opportunity of the Christian to work to keep this great extension of Japanism true to its inner spiritual nature and forever devoted to high moral purposes. Mr. Ebisawa says regarding this:

Herein is the reason why we, in this emergency, must make it our supreme and immediate duty to serve the country by preaching the gospel of Christ. To store up spiritual strength to regulate the various dislocations that the "affair" (jihen) produces within the nation itself; to help the people to make that progress in both physique and character which will fit them for the fulfilment of their mission; to enable them to burn with the ideal of the establishment of a new East-Asia; and to stand firm in the assurance that it will be accomplished; thus to make us as a nation, face to face as we are with unprecedented difficulties, ready to sacrifice gladly for the development of the life of the ancestral country; with penetrating discernment of the international situation, at the same time to take long views of the history of mankind; and embracing a wide vision, and in firm and steadfast understanding holding on to the faith that the final victory is with truth, to urge a brave and straight-forward advance that knows no limit—all this, we believe, can be the work only of those who share the faith and life of Christianity.

We have thus to demonstate the true value of these ideals by the way we make our contribution both at home and abroad; and we believe that it is our Japanese spirit manifested through Christianity that can prove to be the spirit of leadership needed to establish a genuine cooperating "Bloc," thereby inducing all people who are neighbors in East-Asia to submit to our lead, to follow gladly and to trust implicitly.[19]

A further and definitely theological form of Shinto-Christian accommodation that has been taking shape in modern Japan over a period of years should come up for attention at this time. Stated in a word, this is an attempt to find a primitive monotheism at the basis of Old Shinto and hence central to the true and indigenous Japanese worship. Although the sponsors of this kind of doctrinal syncretism are relatively few in numbers, they are sufficiently influential with their pens and voices to have brought their position prominently before the Christian church, particularly during the past few years. The situation which they reveal to us may be taken as symptomatic of Christian psychology in Japan today and is well worthy of the attention of Western students of the history of Christianity in the Far East—this in spite of the fact that the syncretism in question is repudiated by many of the Christian leaders of contemporary Japan on the ground that it is in essence little better than a pious wishful thinking whose valid historical roots are almost entirely imaginary.

It is undoubtedly true that those who support this doctrinal *rapprochement* between Christianity and Shinto are consciously or unconsciously led by the urgencies of stress and strain in political and social situations to seek an accommodation with Shinto which, while ostensibly bringing to fulfilment the latent truth of the national religion, will at the same time furnish Christianity with a protective apologetic much needed in a time when it is under suspicion in certain influential quarters as subversive of traditional institutions and beliefs. Beginnings are thus made at setting up a distinctively Japanese Christian system—a desideratum ardently longed for by some of the Christian patriots but little realized up to the present; the alleged original universalism of Shinto is brought to light; and, most significant of all for the security of the Christian movement in contemporary Japan, it is supposedly demonstrated that the worship of the far-off ancestors of the royal line—and therefore the correct worship of the nation as a whole in the present—was originally directed toward a great deity who is nothing other than the one true God of the Christian faith.

In brief outline the argument runs as follows. The oldest extant Japanese literary document, known as the *Kojiki*, or "Record of Ancient Matters," and dating from A.D. 711, at the very beginning of its account of the creation of the world, names first, in a long list of gods and goddesses, a deity called the "Lord of the Center of Heaven," in Japanese, Ame-no-Minakanushi-no-Kami. We should note the opening words of the *Kojiki*, since much is made to depend on them. The text says:

The names of the deities that came into being in the Plain of High Heaven when Heaven and Earth began were: the Deity Lord of the August Center of Heaven, next, the High August Producing Deity, and, next, the Divine Producing Deity. These three deities were all deities that were born alone, and hid their persons.[20]

This passage from the *Kojiki*, brief as it is, has been made to bear a tremendous load of doctrinal superstructure. The name by which the first-mentioned deity is called has invited elaborate speculation. Correctly understood, so we are told by the Christian syncretists and others in the ranks of Shinto as well, it stands before us as evidence of the existence of traces of primitive monotheism in Old Shinto. As "Lord of the Center of Heaven" this deity is described to us as the center and ruler of all things, that is, as the supreme inner life of the spiritual universe and the creator of the manifest world. As partial evidence for this conclusion the name by which he is called in the *Kojiki* is placed alongside the title of "The Lord of the Universe and the Maker of the World and All Things Therein," which appears in Paul's sermon delivered in the midst of the Areopagus to the men of Athens. These two names "agree like a seal and its counterpart," enthusiastically remarks one of the best known of the contemporary advocates of this view.[21] It must be admitted that the ideographic representation of the title of the deity met with in the beginning of the *Kojiki* is suggestive of the text of the Japanese translation of the attributes of the unknown God expounded in the twenty-fourth verse of the seventeenth chapter of Acts, providing that the former is properly interpreted in terms of the well-known meaning of the latter.

Not only is the name itself taken to be highly significant, but also the fact of priority in the *Kojiki* pantheon is regarded as an attempt on the part of the early writers to attribute to this deity both temporal and functional superiority. He is first in time—or even prior to time—and first in worship. Furthermore, he appears in immediate conjunction with two other divine personages who are offered as evidence of the existence of trinitarianism in ancient Shinto. These two deities, as introduced above, are the "High August Producing Deity" (Taka-Mimusubi-no-Kami) and the "Divine Producing Deity" (Kami-Musubi-no-Kami). Ancient Shinto, we now learn, begins with a triune creation deity who is the source of the other deities and the visible universe of man and things.

This trinitarianism is supported by the citation of the rather remarkable passage that says, "These three deities were all deities that were born alone, and hid their persons." This is Chamberlain's translation. It follows some of the most authoritative of Japanese scholarship. From this point of view the passage is taken to mean that the three deities under consideration came into existence spontaneously or without being procreated in the manner usual to gods and men and that afterward they disappeared; in other words, died. The syncretists, however, say that this is wrong. They take it as an explicit statement of an early belief that this deity, though existing in a threefold operation or mode, was nevertheless one. From their point of view the correct meaning of the passage is: "These deities together came into existence as one deity and they were unseen." In the very beginning they were regarded as a triune and transcendent spiritual being. Thus, as the oldest element of Shinto belief that can be identified, we find a primitive monotheism expressed in trinitarian form.

Judicious selections are then made from other parts of the early classical literature to support the thesis. For example, it is stated in the *Nihongi*, or "Chronicles of Japan," dating from A.D. 720 and covering approximately the same ground as the *Kojiki*, that the sun-goddess, Amaterasu Omikami, cultivated sacred rice fields for the purpose of producing offerings to be used in religious rites and that she celebrated the feast of first fruits. It is impossible to think that she did all this in order to worship herself, although there have been Shinto apologists, bent on making their national faith begin and end with the sun-goddess, who have said this very thing. It must mean that Amaterasu Omikami worshiped deities that existed prior to herself. As a matter of fact, the original sources leave us to guess as to what particular deity or deities were intended. Not so the modern Christian syncretists, however. They hasten to declare that it is plain that Amaterasu Omikami —the august head of the royal line and the founder of the state—must have worshiped in particular the triune creation god of the *Kojiki*, the one God of heaven. Thus Shinto classical literature when properly interpreted shows us a god above the gods, a deity worshiped by Amaterasu Omikami herself. Shinto brought back to its true beginnings lays bare a bedrock that coincides with that of Christianity.

It may be worth our while to let a modern Christian writer speak on this point. Pastor Ojima, a Christian authority widely known for his studies in Shinto, says:

As an original deity, Amaterasu-Ōmikami must be taken in a political sense rather than a religious one. Accordingly, the Great Creative Parent is not Amaterasu-Ōmikami but rather the original deity who begot Amaterasu-Ōmikami. This original deity is the Triune Creation Deity who is named at the very beginning of the *Kojiki*. The ancient teaching regarding this triune deity resembles a heretical form of trinitarianism. The *Kojiki*, after naming the persons of the threefold Deity of Creation, says, "These three deities were all born as one god (or born alone) and hid themselves." If we eliminate the single word "all," this becomes straightforward trinitarianism. We can interpret this as a doctrine of trinitarianism in which the triune god is regarded as embracing a threefold consciousness of fatherhood, sonship, and holy spirit. This "Celestial Deity" (*Amatsu Kami*) is indeed the central object of worship of true religion. . . . . We must remember that Amaterasu-Ōmikami herself worshiped the One True God of Heaven. This is a matter of central importance in determining the place of religion in the cultivation of the Japanese spirit.[22]

This position, if it could be historically and soundly validated, would equip Christianity with perhaps its strongest apologetic in the face of criticism and apprehension from the side of Japanese nationalism. It would completely undercut the charge of foreignism leveled against the Christian faith and make the highest loyalism of the Japanese subject one and the same thing with devotion to the God of Christianity. Unfortunately, there are factors in the situation that raise difficulties for a clean victory of this sort. For one thing, the first and greatest member of this Japanese trinity, after a bare mention in the opening lines of the *Kojiki*, disappears completely from the pages of this document. He appears once in the *Nihongi*, but in a subordinate position. Again, the worship of Ame-no-Minakanushi-no-Kami at the shrines of Shinto, past and present, while not entirely nonexistent, is so rare as to be almost negligible. Christian apologists, however, meet these facts by declaring that the Japanese race has not been faithful to its original and true traditions, which were monotheistic. There is a further difficulty arising from the fact that the worship of this deity has been identified in Japanese history with star worship, and arguments can be developed to show that Ame-no-Minakanushi-no-Kami ("The Lord of the August Center of Heaven") is either the pole star or the Milky Way.

It must be admitted, however, that the position of the Christian apologists whose thought we have just examined is very much strengthened by the existence of similar arguments from the side of Shinto. In fact, the reputed discovery of traces of monotheistic (or trinitarian) universalism in the ancient foundations of the Japanese national faith was originally made from the Shinto and not the Christian side. Prior to his death in 1843, Hirata Atsutane, the outstanding scholar of his day, had drawn up an account of Ame-no-Minakanushi-no-Kami into which he had written a spiritual monism that suggested the influence of the Christian idea of God. Some of the later interpreters of Hirata have insisted that this is just what happened; that he studied and used discussions of Christian theology written by Jesuit missionaries in China and that for him to take over whatever he needed from this source and graft it onto a Shinto stem was entirely consistent with his conviction that by judicious selection from foreign writers Shinto should be made to include all the knowledge necessary to man. Shinto scholars who followed in the early part of the Meiji era and later have repeated and elaborated Hirata's contribution. It has been accepted by one of the chief of the contemporary Japanese authorities on Shinto, Dr. Genchi Katō. Today the belief that Shinto rests on a doctrinal basis of spiritual monism expressed in a primary trinitarianism is ordinary orthodoxy in many of the popular sects. For example, one of the most influential of the leaders of this phase of Shinto has recently said:

Ame-no-Minakanushi-no-Kami ("The Lord of the August Center of Heaven"), the first god named in the *Kojiki,* is correctly understood as the central existence of the universe, the primary source of all things, both animate and inert. All the phenomena presented to the human senses are the manifestations in time of this Absolute God. The Absolute functions in time in the form of the two creation deities, Taka-Mimusubi-no-Kami and Kami-Musubi-no-Kami. These two beings represent activities of opposite kinds (positive-negative or "male-female") from which the phenomenal world has its origin.[23]

It will be clear from this that the discovery of the idea of an absolute and supreme God at the very beginning of the oldest extant Japanese documents and at the center of Shinto faith cannot be accredited to the modern Christian syncretists. Shinto scholars themselves first formulated it, perhaps under Christian influence. From this point of view, modern Christianity, in finding something of its own god-idea in original Shinto, is simply taking out at one end of the pipe line what it put in at the other.

Similar to the identification of Ame-no-Minakanushi-no-Kami and the God of Christianity which finds an ancient

and indigenous monotheism in the *Kojiki* is the attempt
to show that Amaterasu Omikami and Jehovah are one and
the same. Other Christian apologists have tried to make a
connection between Christianity and Japanese tradition
by utilizing the Japanese classics such as the *Kojiki*, the
Nihongi, and the *Kogoshūi* in place of the Old Testament.
Another group adjusts the problem of conflicting absolutes by accepting outright the dogma that the emperor is
God in a full religious sense. They teach that the Godhead
has four persons: the Father, the Son, the Holy Spirit, and
the Japanese emperor; that the God of Christianity has a
twofold incarnation: in Jesus Christ, who is the savior of
the soul, and in the Japanese emperor, who is the nationalistic or the political savior of the world.

A special phase of the theological accommodation of
Christianity to Shinto is concerned with the meaning of
kami. To many Christian apologists in Japan today this is
regarded as the center of the problem of adjustment. If
Christian devotion and Japanese loyalty focus on one and
the same conception of the divine or sacred, and if the rites
of the state cult connote an homage which is close to, if not
identical with, the act of worship of genuine religion, then
the followers of Jesus in Japan are confronted with the in-
soluble dilemma of subordinating either the supreme
being of the Christian faith or the man-god manifested in
the person of the emperor.

Christian evangelism of all sorts, Protestant and Roman
Catholic, Japanese and foreign alike, has been criticized
for heightening this problem by a failure to distinguish
properly between the meaning of *kami* on the Japanese
side and that of *theos* on the side of New Testament teaching. Christian propaganda literature commonly writes
Kami for the God of Christianity. The Japanese transla-
lation of the Bible does the same thing. For example, the
first part of John 4:24 in the revised Japanese translation
of the Protestant churches is rendered, *Kami wa rei narebe*

—"God being spirit." "The Son of God" is rendered *Kami no Ko*. The usage of the Roman Catholic church has been criticized for similar ambiguity. In the early period of the missionary activities of this church in Japan, "God" was rendered either by the Latin *Deus* or the Portuguese *Dios*. Later, after the settlement of the Rites Controversy in China, the expression *Ten Shu*, "The Lord of Heaven," was favored. Until very recently, however, the usage of the Roman Catholic church in Japan has not been officially unified, and *kami* has been employed both by individuals and by responsible literary agencies of the church. A Catholic translation of the New Testament by E. Rage, issued in Tokyo, renders *theos* by *kami*. It can also be found in certain places in the Catechism and the prayer-books, where *Kami* is used for "My Lord" and "My God."[24]

A Protestant writer, Mr. Kiyoshi Maejima of the Japan Episcopal church, has recently drawn attention at some length to the problem of the translation of the New Testament *theos* into Japanese. He advances the opinion that the main problem of adjustment between Christianity and Shinto is to be found in the difficulty of setting forth the Christian idea of God by means of the word *kami*. He believes that the translation of "God" by *Kami* is unfortunate and misleading. He says that the confusion began when the Protestant missionaries first entered Japan in the early part of the Meiji era. Some of these missionaries had labored in China prior to their entering Japan and during their service in the former country had had their attention drawn to some of the difficulties inherent in the problem of the proper translation of *theos*. For certain reasons they had come to favor the Chinese term *shen* and upon arrival in Japan had discovered that the ideogram employed by the Japanese to express their word, *kami*, was none other than the *shen* that they had employed for translating the New Testament term *theos*. They naturally concluded

that "God" and *Kami* had the same meaning and forth-
with initiated the usage which has persisted to the present
day of using the latter as a translation of the former. Regarding the inadequacy of this equation, we can permit
Mr. Maejima to speak for himself:

But although the ideograms for the Chinese *shen* and the Japanese
kami are the same, their contents differ. Also, their backgrounds are
entirely different. The Chinese term *shen* is entirely religious and represents nothing more than a crude conception of an age of spiritism. The
Japanese *kami*, however, as used in national Shinto, although it possesses a spiritual content, does not have a religious meaning. Furthermore, in China the *shen* are worshiped by the vulgar common populace,
while in Japan the *Kami* are revered and commemorated by the State.
Thus the force of the backgrounds are entirely different. There are
those who believe that, since in China *shen* is used by Christianity to
designate its object of faith, there will come a time when *shen* is changed
completely into a Christian term, just as the word "god" of various
Teutonic peoples was adopted and absorbed by Christianity until it was
entirely a Christian term. In Japan, however, this can never take place.
Kami is not a religious word. Inasmuch as this word, as used in Shinto
shrine terminology, is an important agency for fostering the national
spirit, no change in content is permissible. The declaration of the Christian world that "God is the one and only creator of the universe, that
He is uniquely omnipotent with no other gods besides him" is not realized in any term in the Japanese language. The Japanese *kami* is not a
word that indicates such a Christian meaning, and since the significance
of this word cannot be changed, Christianity on its part must select
another word in place of *kami* for the expression of its religious terminology.[25]

Another Protestant writer, Mr. Antei Hiyane of the
Methodist theological school of Tokyo, has likewise recently said:

The *kami* (gods) connected with shrine worship are the spirits of
Amaterasu-Ōmikami, of our emperors and of persons in history who
have rendered meritorious service to our country. The God of our [i.e.,
Christian] worship, however, is the almighty Creator of heaven and
earth. It is unfortunate that misunderstanding has come about through
the use of *kami* to connote both meanings.[26]

Other Christian writers could be quoted in the same general vein. The evidence goes to show that the solution
which they offer to the problem of Shinto-Christian accom-

modation is a favorite one among Christian apologists of today. According to these men, the choice between rival objects of supreme homage does not have to be made, for the reason that the Christian idea of God and the Japanese idea of *kami* are two entirely different things. The Japanese conception of *kami* as found in national Shinto is a secular-state term and is not genuinely religious, at least in the Christian sense. To point the difference between the two, the Roman Catholic church has recently decreed that the designation *Ten Shu*, "The Lord of Heaven," shall be used exclusively as the name of the supreme object of Christian worship.

The presentation which Japanese Christian writers have made of this subject opens a large issue in the religious world of Japan—one that reaches out beyond the Christian church into wider circles of the national life. *Kami* is probably the most meaningful concept in the entire range of the Japanese vocabulary. At the same time it is probably the most difficult to render adequately in any foreign language. Volumes have been written on its meaning. It has had a long history and has varied in significance from period to period in the course of that history. Japanese writers who possess sufficient insight and information to enable them to speak with respectable authority on the matter have pointed out that the roots of the *kami* concept go back to a preanimistic level of emotional experience in which, as the great eighteenth-century scholar, Motoori Norinaga, said: "Anything whatsoever which was outside of the ordinary, which possessed superior power, or which was awe-inspiring, was called *kami*." The thunder was *kami*; a fearful animal was *kami*; a mountain, the sea, even the stump of a tree could be *kami*. In its original and characteristic historical connotation the word *kami* was exactly what the Christian writers cited above say it was not. The ancient psychology still survives in the folkways of the present and is not entirely absent as an unseen but subtle influence in the official cult of the state itself. Beyond this preanimistic stage we have a complicated development. Very quickly in the story we meet an animistic polytheism of extraordinary proportions, probably the most extensive in the whole history of religions. Practically every object of nature and every significant force either in the natural world or in the affairs of men is equipped with a resident and controlling spirit or a personified *kami*. We are here introduced to the eighty myriads of gods and goddesses of Shinto. This stage of evolution has also survived in force to the present and influences the state cult as a powerful underground stream. Then grafted on to the old Shinto god-world we find the transcendent pantheism of Buddhism and the ethics of Confucianism, with the result that the *kami* concept has been purified and equipped with moral and religious content of a high order. The *kami* world is further enriched by the addition of the spirits of outstanding human beings, those who have served the state gloriously, especially those who have given their lives fighting for the protection of the empire.

The fact of the matter is that in the presence of the actual historical and contemporary meaning of *kami* among the Japanese people, their state cult included, we are quite unable to agree with the position that *kami* in the national usage is not a religious term. *Kami*, today as in the past, and in the state usage as in the popular usage, is fundamentally a religious word. To the non-Christian Japanese it connotes dependence on the invisible powers of the spirit world and a profound responsibility to these spiritual existences. Christian apologists have attempted to find a needed refuge in the position that Shinto is not a religion at all because its *kami*, properly understood, are nothing but human personalities endowed with higher rank than their fellow-men. If we are going to be true to the actual facts, however, we shall have to accept Dr. Genchi Katō's unqualified rejection of this compromise view. He says:

We have a view that Shinto expresses a relation not between God and man, which is truly a religion, but rather a relation between man and man, from which morality indeed may spring, but never religion. There is, in my opinion, no view more erroneous than this. In Shinto a man of an ethically noble character may be worshiped, not because of his human nature, but because of superior divine nature which in reality is above and transcends that of humanity.[27]

We can conclude, then, by pointing out that, although it is perhaps an advantage to Japanese Christianity to be able to designate the supreme object of religious devotion by its own special term, yet it would be a great mistake to conclude that the fundamental issues of co-ordination with Shinto and nationalism have been very much affected by this process. The real problem of the adjustment of the universalism of Christianity, with all that that implies, with the purposes of the Japanese state is not solved by a shift in the names of the supreme being. Private conscience over against the suppression of individuality; the duty of prophetic challenge over against a static uniformity that tolerates neither discussion nor criticism; creative and co-operative personality as an educational ideal over against a regimentation of the soul that inculcates absolute obedience as the supreme virtue—these are some of the real issues. Not until the content of the service of the Christian to the loving Father-God revealed in Jesus Christ has been fully differentiated as over against the loyalty demanded by the state and the two found mutually complementary and without conflict—not until then is it possible to adjust a homage that renders unto Caesar the things that are Caesar's, on the one hand, with a devotion that renders unto God the things that are God's, on the other. There is plenty of evidence that the directors of the Japanese state life know this well enough and that the real grounds of their apprehension regarding Christianity are just here. From their standpoint it is fairly certain that the full nationalization of Christianity simply means the unquestioning acceptance on the part of Christians of the duty of absolute obedience to the imperial will as mediated and interpreted by the high officials of the state, both military and civil.

NOTES

1. Genchi Katō, "A Trait of the Religious Character of the Japanese People in Close Connection with Their Institutional Life, as Illustrated by Shinto: A Study of the National Faith of the Japanese," *Young East*, VII, No. 4 (1938), 15.

2. *Japan Evangelist*, November, 1917, p. 413.

3. *Japan Christian Quarterly*, V, No. 3 (July, 1930), 276.

4. *Japan Evangelist*, May, 1918, pp. 180–81; *Kirisuto Kyōhō* ("Christian News"), March 28, 1918.

5. *Die katholischen Missionen*, LVIII (1930), 247; cited in J. B. Aufhauser, "Die Jinsha-Frage im Heutigen Japan," *Umweltsbeeinflussung der Christlichen Mission* (München, 1932), pp. 167–68.

6. "Instructions" (official English trans.), Sacred Congregation Propaganda Fide, given at Rome on May 25, 1936.

7. Iwasaburo Okino, *Jinja Mondai* ("The Shrine Problem") (Tokyo, 1939), p. 149.

8. *Ibid.*, p. 150.

9. Arimichi Ebisawa, "The Relation between the Ethics of *Bushido* and Christianity," *Cultural Nippon*, VII, No. 4 (December, 1939), 27.

10. *Ibid.*, p. 31.

11. Akira Ebisawa, "New Apologetics for the New Age," in the *Japan Christian Quarterly*, April, 1940, pp. 161–62.

12. Saburō Imai, *Seishin Hōkoku to Kirisuto Kyō* ("Patriotism of the Spirit and Christianity") (Tokyo, 1940), pp. 22–23.

13. *Ibid.*, pp. 25–26.

14. *Ibid.*, p. 26.

15. Ebisawa, "New Apologetics for the New Age," *op. cit.*, p. 162.

16. Imai, *op. cit.*, pp. 36–37.

17. *Ibid.*, pp. 41–42.

18. Akira Ebisawa, *Tōa Shinchitsujo no Kensetsu to Kirisuto Kyō* ("Christianity and the Establishment of the New Order in East Asia"), *Bulletin of the National Christian Council of Japan*, No. 183. June, 1939, p. 1 (translation by Bishop J. C. Mann).

19. *Ibid.*

20. B. H. Chamberlain, *Kojiki* (Kobe, 1932), p. 17.

21. Daikichirō Tagawa, *Nippon to Kirisuto Kyō* ("Japan and Christianity"), (Tokyo, 1939), p. 56.

22. Saneharu Ojima, *Kokutai Seigi* ("The True Meaning of the National Structure") (Tokyo, 1938), pp. 3–8.

23. Kazusaku Kanzaki, *Shintō Honkyoku no Kyōri* ("The Doctrine of Shintō Honkyoku"), in *Uchū* ("The Universe"), January, 1930, p. 13.

24. An outline of Roman Catholic usage of *kami* is given in J. B. Aufhauser, *Umweltsbeeinflussung der Christlichen Mission*, pp. 173–74.

25. *Meiji Seitoku Kinen Gakkai Kiyō* ("Transactions of the Meiji Japan Society"), art. "Kirisuto Kyō ga Tōyō Dendō Shijō ni Sōgu seru Nammondai" ("Some Difficulties Encountered by Christianity in the History of Oriental Missions"), No. 52, autumn, 1939, p. 72.

26. Translated by W. T. Thomas in the *Japan Christian Quarterly*, January, 1940, p. 47. The original is in *Kirisuto Kyō no Nippon-teki Tenkai* ("The Development of a Japanese Christianity") (Tokyo, 1938).

27. Genchi Katō, *What Is Shintō?* (Tokyo, 1935), p. 13.

CHAPTER V

BUDDHISM AND JAPANESE NATIONALISM

THE story of the nationalization of Buddhism is one that Japanese writers like to tell. Not infrequently it is presented as the most conspicuous example in Japanese history of the remarkable union of assimilative power and unchanging racial spirit that are exhibited in the national character. A world religion has been molded and transformed until some of her chief interpreters today can say that Japanese Buddhism is merely another name for Japanism. The success and even the survival of Buddhism within the national environment are attributed to an extraordinary adaptability to the prior interests of the state. Deliberate and far-reaching accommodation was practiced from the beginning, and today, when the greatest crisis of all Japanese history confronts the nation, the resources of Buddhism are already marshaled to the single service of the new order in the Far East. These are the claims. They are symptomatic of a great concern on the part of present-day Buddhist writers to justify their faith before the nation. Why this concern, what the nature of Buddhist accommodation to Japanese nationalism, and what the form of apologetic used by Buddhist writers in setting forth the essential agreement of their belief and practice as good Buddhists with national institutions and ideals? The approach to finding the answers to these questions can best be made through a brief examination of the history of Shinto-Buddhist adjustments in modern times. In this connection relations with Confucianism must be touched upon.

The traditional date of the introduction of Buddhism into Japan is A.D. 552. Ever since that time Buddhism, in spite of periods of disorganization and degeneration, has had to her credit a brilliant record of contribution to the national life, and her supporters point with justifiable pride to her devotion to the highest interests of the country. The situation becomes difficult, however, when loyalty to the national welfare calls for almost complete surrender to a Shinto-dominated state initiative. This is where Buddhism stands in Japan today, and she does not seem to be altogether comfortable in her position, certainly not entirely confident. In the face of the deep penetration of state regimentation into the affairs of religion, Buddhism, although still relatively powerful and assured of the support of millions of the Japanese people, is hardly in better position to assert herself positively than the numerically weaker and even less confident Christianity. The vast authority of the state, manifested in the last analysis by the physical force of police and soldiers, makes independent action futile even when existing as a latent possibility, while powerful conditioning influences working through the all-inclusive nationalistic educational system have produced a psychological receptivity to official guidance that effectively sterilizes both individual and group initiative at birth.

The control to which Buddhism must adjust herself is not merely that of political authority asserting itself through the ordinary channels of civil administration. It is permeated through and through with Shinto religious devotion and Confucian class ethics. This is not the first time in modern history that Buddhism has had to head her ship into a heavy Shinto-Confucian sea. When the modern period of Japanese history began in 1868, Buddhism had long been facing bitter attack from this same double source. If the Christianity of the time was under suspicion as a danger to national unification and a subtle force that was calculated to break down morale behind the lines preparatory to foreign dominion over the country, Buddhism, in spite of her long history in the land, was even more feared and suspected. This apprehension did not grow solely out of the fact that Buddhism had been favored by the defeated Tokugawa shogunate and was therefore politically dangerous. It was all this and something more. Modern Japan came into existence on a flood tide of intense Shinto-Confucian enthusiasm. The hands of the clansmen from Satsuma, Chōshū, Tosa, and Hizen who overthrew the Tokugawa shogunate were held aloft by a powerful group of Shinto and Confucian scholars whose theory of state was dyed deeply in the doctrine of *Haibutsu-ron*, "Down with Buddhism." Shinto, resuscitated from medieval lethargy by a brilliant school of nationalistic writers, had reached the conclusion that her contribution to a strong nation had been weakened by too much fraternizing with Buddhism. For a thousand years previously Shinto had moved in a Buddhist shadow, more or less absorbed in a superior Buddhist philosophy and molded to the will of extraordinary Buddhist priests. That Shinto had benefited much in both doctrinal and practical affairs by this long tutelage under Buddhism did not lessen her determination to set herself free.

On the part of Confucianism, antagonisms with Buddhism were no less real. Confucianism, with its practical concern for the effective organization of human society, has always turned a suspicious eye on the transcendental, otherworldly ethics of Buddhism. Buddhism has been accused of being primarily concerned with funerals, ceremonies for the dead, and the upkeep of graveyards. Confucianism boasts that it brings the full impact of its teachings to bear on the problems of the improvement of government and the establishment of proper relations among living men. Confucianism is aristocratic, absorbed in the nice definitions of political and social propriety, devoted to standardization, and concerned with the adjustment of classes and interests in such manner as to preserve essen-

tial distinctions and at the same time to make their inter-
actions harmonious and frictionless. Buddhism, when true
to her inner genius, is democratic, devoted to universals,
international, and the friend of common man. In these directions lie deep cleavages which sometimes have widened
into open breaks.

The immediate result of the mid-nineteenth-century attack on Buddhism was disastrous. The opening years of
the Meiji era are marked by an organized persecution of
this great faith on the part of the government of the time.
The union of Shinto and Buddhism was strictly prohibited.
Members of the royal family were debarred from continu-
ing in Buddhist orders; Buddhist ceremonies in the imperial palace were prohibited; Buddhist temples all over the
land were attacked and destroyed. A blind fury of mis-
placed patriotic zeal committed precious Buddhist writings, fine sculptures, bronzes, wood-carvings, and paintings
to the flames, broke them in pieces, cast them away, or
sold them for a pittance to whosoever would buy. Buddhist priests were prohibited from participating in Shinto
ceremonies. They were subjected to beatings and threatened with military force. Monks and nuns in large numbers were obliged to take up secular callings. Although this
persecution lasted for only a few years (1867–72), it left
deep wounds and threw Buddhism into a disorder that
was overcome only after decades of struggle.

The main factor in easing the anti-Buddhist policy of
the state was the recognition of the strength of Buddhism
in the common life. Shinto-Buddhist bonds might be severed in official areas and in the public institutions of the
two religions, but not so in the homes. The faith of the
masses was too deeply immersed in an inseparable merging
of Shinto and Buddhism to make an open attack on the
latter a safe administrative policy. This did not mean a
danger of popular Buddhist uprising. It meant, rather,
that in a land in which millions of households worshiped

jointly before the Buddhist home altars and the Shinto god-
shelves, faith in the one could not be uprooted without
deep injury to the other. A government that attacked
Buddhism only undermined its own foundations of popular
confidence. The result of the recognition of this important
fact in official circles was a brief attempt to work with a
new union of Shinto and Buddhism as a state religion.
When this also proved impracticable, the two were again
separated, but not now on the basis of a governmentally
inspired opposition to Buddhism. Shinto was preserved as
the cultus of the state. Buddhism was set free to work out
its own destiny as a recognized religion along with a number of unofficial Shinto sects that were springing into existence and eventually also with Christianity.

This in brief summary is the outline of Shinto Buddhist
relations in the early part of the Meiji era. From the Buddhist point of view it was not an experience calculated to
strengthen confidence in the impartiality of a Shinto-dominated state. Following this came the period of cordiality
toward foreign science and thought, and then at the very
close of the last century the inevitable reaction that showed
itself in the reaffirmation of traditional Japanese culture
and the repudiation of Westernism. In matters of faith
this came to a head in the antireligious movement of the
schools, inspired by the Department of Education. Religious education was to be displaced in favor of a more directly state-centered nationalistic ethical training founded
on the recently issued Imperial Rescript on Education.
Here, again, Buddhism was affected more than Christianity, for her interests in religious education were considerable, and once again she was obliged to make the best
terms she could with a Shinto-Confucian state policy.

The twentieth century brought the Russo-Japanese War
and a turning toward the democratic institutions of the
West, then World War I and a widespread, though often
masked, radicalism in social and political thought in the

universities, accompanied by an ever mounting unrest in industrial and agricultural circles. Marxism made inroads in proportion as economic disorder deepened and as traditional religious sanctions weakened. This situation multiplied difficulties for the authorities right up to the time when the opening of campaigns on the Asiatic continent, beginning with the Manchurian affair in 1931, gave occasion for placing the entire nation under a totalitarian discipline that has grown increasingly inclusive with the passing years. At the center of this regimentation lies Shinto with its yet more inner nucleus of Confucianism, a Shinto more powerfully asserted and more all-pervasive than ever before in modern times.

The above remarks may suffice to prepare us for the observation that it is possible to find in the literature of the last three decades sharp criticisms of Shinto from the pens of Buddhist writers. Until very recent times a noncompromising attitude toward State Shinto was especially conspicuous in the powerful Shin sect. This body consistently refused to have anything to do with the practice of *hōben*, or accommodation, as applied to Shinto. Certain outstanding Zen scholars have also shared this position.

Buddhist writers have repeatedly emphasized the debt of the national faith to Buddhism. They have declared that the umbrage afforded Shinto by Buddhism during the long period of the amalgamation of the two prior to the beginning of the modern period in 1868 protected the former from natural decay, saved many of its documents from probable oblivion, and actually made possible the survival of Shinto as an organized system into the present. Buddhism imparted a depth and meaning to the old Shinto mythology and made it philosophically respectable and acceptable to educated men. In other words, Buddhism equipped Shinto—a primitive religion—with a worthy doctrinal and ethical content. At the same time Buddhism could find satisfaction in the recollection that it once was

able to subordinate Shinto to itself by its practice of reading the sutras before the altars of the Shinto deities—for
their edification—as well as by the doctrine that all Shinto
kami were merely the temporal manifestations of pre-existing Buddhist divinities.

Buddhist writers have declared that Shinto, important
as it is to state unification, is only one form of the manifestation of the versatile national soul. The fundamental
Japanese spirit is a disposition of sincerity, integrity, loyalty, and love of purity. It finds its highest institutional
expression in the imperial line "unbroken for ages eternal"
and in the peerless and everlasting national structure. The
unchanging strength of the Japanese national character
appears in a unique assimilative power which is able to
take in diverse cultural elements from foreign sources and
make them truly Japanese. Thus Buddhism has been
woven into the texture of Japanese history and institution
until it has become as much the racial religion of Japan as
is Shinto. The Japanese spirit is reduced to poverty if it is
interpreted merely in terms of the mythological tradition
of a preliterate age.

In more aggressive mood Buddhist writers have pronounced Shinto an artificial construction, abounding in
superficialities and contradictions and built on a mythology that is the common possession of many peoples. Shinto
has been criticized for lacking adequate philosophical support for its ethical ideals, as defective in logical thoroughness, as suppressive of the inner life of the spirit, as buried
in conventionalities, emphasizing system, devoted to hierarchy and mechanical formalism, and depending on bureaucratic manipulation for propagation. Most serious of
all, Buddhism has charged Shinto with attempting to make
all the agents of the governmental bureaucracy participants in the sacred nature of the imperial ancestors, thereby extending a divine character and authority to political,
military, and educational practices.

Furthermore, an official fostering of superstition is alleged to exist in the sale and distribution of charms. Buddhism has repeatedly accused the government of inconsistency in its religious policy. Evidence for an actual religious character for State Shinto has been declared to exist in the *norito* or prayers read at every important Shinto service, in which supplication is made to the deities of the shrines for good crops, prosperous business, happy homes, and a strong state; in the *shinsen* or offerings presented to spirits which are believed to be actually present and participating in the ceremonies, though unseen; and in the *harai* or purification rituals whereby demonic and ceremonial defilement is expelled from the nation.

Shintoists on their part have not been meekly silent in the presence of this criticism. They have denounced Buddhism as lost in ceremonial formality, devoid of practical utility, immersed in superstition, dominated by a priestly class that has paid only lip service to ethical ideals, and concerned with the dead rather than with the living—in a word, as totally unimportant to the vital concerns of society and state. Current Japanese patriotic zeal exhibits a marked tendency to glorify the distant days of pre-Buddhist culture into a golden age of happy people who preserved in Shinto a simple rational ceremonial for the commemoration of ancestors and heroes. This was corrupted by the incoming of Buddhism with its accompanying deluge of superstition and magic inherited from Hinduism or picked up in the course of Buddhism's long journey across Asia. Thus primitive Shinto was transformed into a religion.

Conditions of disharmony between these two great faiths have supposedly been greatly modified by the accommodation of Buddhism to Shinto-military requirements. The high priests of the different Buddhist sects have certified their patriotism by public worship at the Meiji Shrine, the Yasukuni Shrine, the Grand Imperial Shrine of Ise, and

elsewhere and thus have set good examples to their followers. Buddhism has accepted the doctrine that the emperor
is the direct descendant of the sun-goddess and is thereby
divinely authorized to rule as god manifested in human
form—the dogma of *Arahitogami*. The temples are cov-
ered with propaganda placards advertising the new order
in East Asia and the support of the domestic front. The
various sects have carried out extensive educational programs for strengthening the movement for the cultural unification of Asia and the economic and military protection
of the nation. They have recruited from their youth vol-
unteers for pioneering in Manchuria and Mongolia. They
have given enthusiastic support to the movement for the
"general mobilization of the national spirit." Temples
have been used extensively for funeral services for the soldier dead. Priests have taken prominent parts in the dedication of war memorials and have ministered widely to the
needs of soldiers in the field.

The purely patriotic services suggested in this summary
are only such as would devolve on any people in time of
war. In the hour of great national crisis Buddhism has
steadfastly accepted her responsibilities and is attempting
to discharge them faithfully. It is possible to discern in
this nationalistic accommodation, however, evidence of an
awareness on the part of Buddhism of the need of present-
ing her case favorably to the scrutiny of a Shinto-military
control in the state. An apologetic trend is manifest in the
veritable flood of patriotic literature that has poured from
the Buddhist press since the beginning of the Manchurian
affair in 1931. The issues discussed exhaust the public and
private duties of good subjects: loyalty and filial piety in
relation to Buddhism, the new mission of Japanese Buddhism, the political development of Mahayana Buddhism,
the Japanese national structure and Buddhism, expanding
Japan and the new Buddhism, Buddhism and Japanese
culture, patriotism and Buddhism, Japanese education and

Buddhism, the new Japan and the Buddhist view of nationality, Buddhism and Shinto, Buddhism and the Japanese spirit, Buddhism and Asiatic development, Buddhism and the new mission of the Japanese race, Buddhism and the Japanese imperial family. Areas of discussion such as these suggest the completeness with which Buddhism is attempting to present her case to the nation.

It is true that the appearance of this literature may be accounted for partially as the manifestation of Buddhist desire to seize a good opportunity for evangelism, but this is far from being the whole story. Internal evidence shows Buddhism's awareness of the need of an apologetic in the presence of misunderstandings arising out of nationalistic prejudice. In a recently published work entitled *Nippon Seishin to Nippon Bukkyō* ("The Japanese Spirit and Japanese Buddhism")[1] the late professor Yoshitaru Yabuki of the Imperial University of Tokyo, a man recognized as one of the leading contemporary authorities on Buddhism, presents a significant discussion of the question of whether or not Buddhism contravenes the Japanese spirit. Some of the details of his account should be noted for the illuminating picture they give of Buddhism's sense of uncertainty. The book includes an outline of the nationalistic criticisms of Buddhism that have come under the author's notice in recent years, and while Professor Yabuki rightly declares that they represent the point of view of only a section of the Japanese people, it may not be too much to say that his entire book is an attempt to overcome them with a correct statement of the Buddhist cause. According to Dr. Yabuki, the present-day indictment of Buddhism includes the following charges.

In spite of the length of time that has passed since the introduction of Buddhism into Japan, it is from first to last a foreign doctrine that mixes with the traditional Japanese spirit no better than oil with water. Even though it is recognized that many threads of foreign culture, including

Buddhism, have been woven into the pattern of Japanese national life, yet the true strength of that fabric lies in the fact that the warp is always uniquely Japanese. Or, granting that Buddhism has contributed in a measure to the development of the Japanese national structure, it is far from being the support to the state that Shinto is. The treason of the priest Umako (Soga no Mumako), who assassinated Emperor Sushun (A.D. 588–92), and the crime of the priest Dōkyō, the adviser of Empress Shōtoku (A.D. 765–69), who plotted to place himself on the imperial throne (A.D. 769), are sins of Buddhism which would have been impossible to the uncontaminated Japanese spirit. The humanitarianism that calls all men equal is steeped in the world imperialism of the great powers and is ill suited to the fostering of a strong national spirit. The main effort of Buddhism goes into the promotion of her own organization; her purpose to work for the real interests of the nation is weak. The first need of the nation in the time of crisis is unity; Buddhism fosters sectarian divisions and thus indirectly promotes the disorganization of the national mind. Buddhism does not develop a vigorous and progressive spirit on the part of her followers; on the contrary, she fosters the idea of the degeneracy of the present age and is thereby a detriment to wholesome national progress. Mingled with Buddhism is a great deal of superstition, some of it corrupt and unethical. In addition, the teaching of a philosophy of escape and withdrawal from the world is not in harmony with the lively spirit of the Japanese people with their love of life in the present. Regarded superficially, Japan may appear to be a Buddhist country, but this is in reality nothing more than an outworn clinging to the past. Buddhism talks much about her contribution to society, but as a matter of fact she is without either practical program or competency to promote real progress. The support of more than one hundred and ten thousand temples and places of propaganda throughout the land is a serious drain on the economic resources of the common people, and, especially in a time of national crisis, the maintenance of the vast Buddhist organization is a great economic liability to the country. Even toward the modernized activities of the various sects Buddhist followers take merely the parts of onlookers. Buddhism has shown no strong force of opposition to socialism. Even within Buddhist ranks there are people who are promoting antireligious movements. All this is a walking in the path of ruin. Buddhism talks about the co-operation of the many sects, but in matters of faith there is no unity.[2]

Most of these charges, says Dr. Yabuki, are founded on misunderstanding. They have their correction in an enlightened view of history and an intelligent insight into Buddhism's contribution to stability and unity in the present. Organizations in need of institutional reformation are not confined to Buddhism. Corruption in modern Japan has had its center in politics and business, and this has extended a pernicious influence in all directions. It is true that the various sects are engaged in doctrinal propaganda each according to its own view of truth, but in the large affairs of the national life and destiny they are united.[3]

When we look merely at the outward strength of Buddhism, with her 71,300 temples, her 40,000,000 believers, and her six universities, we see that she is a powerful reality that cannot be set aside with indifference.[4] We will not consider here appraisals advanced on the ground of a discrepancy between the actual Buddhism and the Buddhism that ought to be. We may say, however, that a man's wife is not a stranger, and to turn her out because her mother and grandmother came from an outside family is to indulge in a kind of conduct which in and of itself is a viola-•tion of the Japanese spirit.[5]

It is a remarkable fact that one of the most outstanding Buddhist scholars of modern Japan should find it necessary to write in this manner. Only a real sense of uncertainty in the presence of threatening and unsympathetic forces in the national life could lead a loyal subject of the state to go to such pains to justify the existence of a religion that was introduced from foreign shores fourteen hundred years ago.

The book from which the above summary has been taken was published under the auspices of the Buddhist Federation of Japan (Bukkyō Rengōkai), the official incorporation of all Buddhist sects and schools. It was written at the request of this organization, and, although the author assumes the responsibility for the language used, he says that he has tried to make the account representative of Buddhism as a whole. With this in mind it is of considerable importance to note the following statement which the book makes regarding the ten main characteristics of Japanese Buddhism in relation to nationalism.

1. The separation of Shinto and Buddhism effected by the governmental authorities in the early part of the Meiji era, the movement for the preservation of national traits in the eighties of the last century carried out by those devoted to the ancient ways, and following this the Japanism of the nineties, and after this the antireligious movement that began in the Taishō era (1912–26) were all forms of pressure and attack against Buddhism, but they did not result in such a blow to Buddhist organization and especially to the faith of the people in Buddhism as was expected.

2. Practically all the cultural programs that have been undertaken since the beginning of the Meiji era have owed their development to governmental protection and policy, with the single exception that toward Buddhist institutions alone there has been no constructive protection whatsoever [on the part of the government]. Buddhism has been maintained entirely by the strength of the people themselves.

3. In the religious statistics of Japan the believers of Buddhism maintain by far the largest numbers. Even though legal administration does not accord Buddhism the leading position in religious thought, yet in the faith of the people of the nation, in their customary usages, in their emotional life, and above all in the quantitative aspects of the situation, Buddhism fills a very significant role.

4. It is a great mistake to think that a Buddhism that possesses this vast body of believers has been entirely unrelated to the progress of the national destiny of new Japan during the sixty-odd years of modern history.

5. It is true that Buddhism is divided into thirteen sects and some fifty subsects; but, if it attains unification and leadership under suitable

policy and direction, it can become a most effective instrument for the state.

6. While conscious of a humanitarian and world mission, it is yet a religion that is one with the national structure and national usages. It is a religion that has been assimilated to the fundamentals of national morality. Unlike the Buddhism of India and China, it is not dominated by the priesthood. It is a religion that the Japanese people themselves have fully absorbed. In contrast, the new thought that has recently come in from abroad shows very little that actually harmonizes with the national structure and with national usages.

7. The doctrine of Japanese Buddhism, on the side of its philosophical foundations, holds a position of superiority over all other religions. Since the beginning of the Meiji era it has accomplished the amalgamation of new religion and new philosophy and has manifested the profundity of its teachings.

8. Japanese Buddhism, as Buddhism, has affinities with the Buddhism of other lands, but in addition it differs from that of India and China in being the Buddhism of the Japanese people, sharing the fate of the Japanese race. Japanese Buddhism is like iron sulphide formed from the chemical combination of iron and powdered sulphur. Japanese Buddhism is not a visiting housekeeper; she is a wife. This national spirit and usage is something that cannot easily be destroyed.

9. Out from the Japanese race have come many sect founders in Buddhism. The worship of these sect founders has been tempered in the national practice of ancestor worship, and an influence has thus been imparted which cannot be blotted out. In spite of the fact that from the point of view of Buddhist doctrine temples are not inevitably merged with tombs, nevertheless Japanese Buddhism in response to ancestor worship has created certain unique usages. It can hardly be said that all this is unrelated to the family system and in wider realms to the conception of the national structure.

10. The vast number of temples, scriptures, books, scholars, and educational institutions connected with Buddhism surely gives Japan the crown among all the nations of the world. These are matters that cannot be passed over in relation to the progress of the national destiny. For statesmen and officials to turn to good use an institution already in existence, and one that can easily be utilized, would be an exceedingly enlightened policy, while to cast away voluntarily a strength which in the nature of things ought to be possessed is a course that involves much labor and little gain.

Accordingly, the feud between Shinto and Confucianism on the one side and Buddhism on the other which existed from the close of the Tokugawa shogunate onward into the Meiji era should be liquidated as a matter of course by contemporary Japan. At the same time it should be pointed out that the nationalism of Japan must inevitably pursue a course different from that of Italy and in particular from that of present-day Germany.[6]

This statement is presented as evidence of the degree to which the growth of a Shinto-centered nationalism has thrown Buddhism on the defensive. This impression continues when we examine more of the elaborate apologetic with which Buddhism is calling attention to her contribution to the progress of the national destiny. In the examples of her greatest priests, in her ministration to general social welfare, in education, art, literature, and scholarship, in public morality, and philosophical resourcefulness alike Buddhism promotes the national interest and protects the state. We should note enough of the details of this situation to make the account specific.

The phrase *Hōkoku Bukkyō*, "Buddhism guarding the land," is met with constantly in contemporary propaganda literature. "Buddhism," says Dr. Junjirō Takakusu, professor emeritus of the Imperial University of Tokyo, member of the Imperial Academy, and dean of modern Buddhist scholars, "responds to nationality. Especially in Japan, Buddhism from the very beginning has devoted her entire self to the safeguarding of the nation." The great heroes of Japanese Buddhism, her founders, saints, and eminent priests, labored to make the state strong and great. Shōtoku Taishi (A.D. 584–622), "the Constantine of Japanese Buddhism," promulgated a national constitution on a Buddhist foundation and made Buddhism a support for government by exploiting its function as the chief agency for the integration of the disorganized cultural life of his time. He early recognized the superior qualities of the new religion and made it a primary means for the realization of the ideal of national unity in the presence of widespread division and unrest among rival clans. Kōbō Daishi (A.D. 774–835), the founder of the Shingon sect and the famous Mount Koya temples, exhorted the people to mercy, loyalty, and filial piety. The priest Eisai (A.D. 1141–1215), who propagated in Japan the teachings of Zen which he had studied in China, taught the doctrine of

Kōzen Gokoku, "Zen for the protection of the country."
Nichiren (A.D. 1222–82), the founder of the strongly nationalistic sect which bears his name, labored to make the
doctrine which he sponsored the chief bulwark of the state.
He was loyal to the imperial family in an age of feudal dis-
sension and declared, "How true it is that our land of
Japan is above all nations, excelling India and China and
superior to all other countries." The priest Dōgen (A.D.
1200–1253), the founder of the Sōdō sect, was a contemporary of Nichiren and, like him, labored in Kamakura for
the restoration of direct imperial rule. The priest Shinran
(A.D. 1174–1268), the founder of the Shin sect, defied the
traditional practice of priestly celibacy, married a daugh-
ter of Fujiwara Kanenori, and thus founded genuine lay
Buddhism by identifying the family system with approved
social practice. The priest Rennyo (A.D. 1415–99), the re-
former of the Shin sect, taught that loyalty to the sovereign
was the basis of all Buddhist conduct.[7]

Great temples and monasteries have been built for the
purpose of protecting the nation. Such activity was especially prominent during the golden age of Buddhism in the
seventh and eighth centuries, but the distinction remains
even in the present. These widely scattered Buddhist
strongholds have served as colonization centers from which
have radiated influences that have tended to overcome
localism in favor of interests that comprehended the nation
as a whole.

Buddhist apologetics are able to tell a story of vast and
brilliant contribution to the general social well-being.
Early Buddhism was the main highway along which the
rich resources and skills of a superior continental culture
flowed into Japan. Great Buddhist priests were the chief
agents of the establishment of this culture in its new home.
They founded magnificent temples, taught agriculture, and
introduced sculpture, wood-carving, and the casting of
bronze; they taught ceramics, painting, weaving, and

brewing and the manufacture of sugar, ink, and paper. They brought in new and useful fruit trees, promoted sericulture and forestry, built roads and bridges, made new harbors, drained swamps, and constructed canals, ditches, and dikes. They improved communications and opened extensive new tracts of land to a more enlightened industry and agriculture than primitive Japan had ever known. They introduced a better medical practice, established health resorts, and taught the healing properties of mineral baths. They founded hospitals, dispensaries, almshouses, cemeteries, and free funerals for the poor and brought widespread relief to famine and pestilence. They founded the scientific study of astronomy and geology, taught calendar-making and the keeping of records, established schools, introduced literature, taught the people how to read and write, and were the first to compile Japanese histories. They fostered the love of nature and deepened toleration and human brotherhood. They broadened the religious feelings of the people and introduced resplendent rituals. They universalized the primitive and insular Japanese mind and instilled a compassionate idealism both in philosophy and in conduct. They made possible the golden age of old Nara culture.

The modern period continues the later chapters of this wonderful story. Buddhism, when once she had recovered her balance after the Shinto-Confucian attack of the early Meiji era, set before herself the task of attempting the alleviation of some of the social damages of a capitalistic economy in a manner worthy of her best traditions. Today she maintains an imposing array of social welfare activities, expressed in public dispensaries, hospitals, infirmaries, maternity homes, foundling homes, orphan asylums, nurseries, kindergartens, schools and homes for the blind, the deaf and dumb, and the feeble-minded, libraries, information bureaus, social education institutions, settlement houses, continuation schools, reform schools, employment

offices, asylums for the aged, offices for the legal protection
of the poor and needy, cheap lodging-houses, restaurants,
loan offices, pawnbroker shops, co-operatives, prison chap-
laincies, and guidance for former convicts. Even this list,
extensive as it is, is not exhaustive.[8]

A recent report of social welfare activities on religious
foundations published by the bureau of religious affairs of
the Department of Education credits Sectarian Shinto
with 136 institutions of this character, Christianity with
1,493, and Buddhism with 4,848. These figures suggest the
magnitude of Buddhist operations in this field. They do
not include educational institutions.[9]

It is impossible here to do more than mention in briefest
terms Buddhist contributions in this last-named area. Numerous Buddhist educational establishments, ranging from
kindergarten to university, cover the land. They provide
even more extensively for secular education than for the
training of priests. For the most part they follow the state
pattern, as do those of all other religious foundations.

In calling the attention of the Japanese people to their
contributions to art, literature, and scholarship, Buddhists
are also able to draw upon a rich history: Japanese art is
largely a Buddhist art; her literature is largely a Buddhist
literature; the first studies of Shinto itself were made by
Buddhist priests; Buddhism has preserved the heritage of
the past, secular as well as religious, by protecting in her
temples and archives the rare documents of other days;
Buddhist scholars have brought renown to their country
by their proclamation to the world of the greatness of
Buddhist philosophy and their critical study of the classical texts.

In the fields of private and national morality Buddhism
leads the way toward everlasting peace, promotes happy
homes, and fosters gratitude, compassion, humility, perse-
verance, courage, resignation, and obedience. Buddhism
exhorts its followers to give first place to their duties as

loyal subjects of the emperor, to pay their taxes willingly, and to perform their military services gladly. Buddhism has enjoyed great favor with the royal family and has been sponsored by successive generations of sovereigns.

Finally, Buddhism is intimately related to progress in the world of thought. Dr. Takakusu asserts that Buddhism "is the greatest promoter of the culture of the intellect." It inculcates deep thinking, correct observation, and efficient teaching. In Buddhism this culture of the intellect passes beyond mere knowledge to the stage of a wisdom that enriches the human spirit with compassion and perspective. When this wisdom of Buddhism is arrived at, the motive of sheer economic profit is transcended by genuine co-operation based on universally valid principles. The new order will come in the Far East when economics are managed with an enriched Japanese spirit, which means a spirit that is "nourished with the depth of Mahayana Buddhism."

Buddhism further promotes the progress of thought through the affinity of its underlying philosophy with the most recent and reputable scientific synthesis. In this matter Dr. Takakusu says:

As to the rise of modern scientific thought, Buddhism wants almost no adjustments. While they [the scientists] were sticking to the three fundamental principles of nondestructibility of substance, preservation of energy, and the theory of causality, Buddhism had some objections to raise. As long as the modern physicist keeps the indeterminate principle (uncertainty principle) or complementary principle, relativity principle, quantum theory or wave theory, or wavicle theory, or curvature of space (with its relativity of time) and polarity principle, they have almost the same arguments as Buddhism. They are now said to go jointly with philosophy. We can further say that they go hand in hand with Buddhism. Buddhism started with the ever changing state of mind, and physicists have now reached the ever changing state of matter. A bridge seems to have been thrown over between them. One seems unable to proceed without the other.[10]

We have noted some of the main phases of contemporary Japanese Buddhist apologetics in relation to general cultural activities. Relations with the state must next be examined.

The Buddhist ideal of the state has been expressed in the affirmation: wealth, peace, and no resort to arms. These are the ideals. The fact that, when measured against the unadorned realities of actual human affairs, they embody an irreconcilable contradiction has subjected Buddhism to the same conditions of inner strain and compromise that we discover in the case of similar idealism elsewhere. Fundamental Buddhism incorporates a universalism that transcends the divisions of race and nation and clan. Buddhism has opposed the caste system of Brahmanism with the ideal of universal brotherhood; it has regarded the whole human family as one without distinction of class, color, or creed. This fact has been advanced as one of the main reasons why Buddhism has made so little progress in the land of its birth. Today in Japan, the land of its greatest strength, it is confronted with the difficult problem of implementing its loyalty to this original and characteristic universalism and at the same time of making room for its followers to discharge their duties as subjects of a state that claims the inclusion within its ethical scheme of all the idealism necessary to man.

With the aftermath of disillusionment that followed World War I, stimulating a determination to seek deeper means for the promotion of a better co-operation among men, a powerful section of Japanese Buddhism spoke in no uncertain terms on behalf of the rights of universal humanity that pass beyond the limitations of a narrowly conceived materialistic nationalism. The utterances of the best Buddhist leadership of the time gave articulation to the idealistic sentiments that stirred like-minded people everywhere. The doctrine of the state for the state and nothing above the state was repudiated. A state, to have a significance worthy of the devotion of intelligent men, must be founded on an adequate philosophy of man and must be infused with the spirit of a universally valid religion. In 1921 one of these Japanese Buddhists declared: "A state devoid of any spiritual belief in the destiny of human life on this earth has no meaning for its continued existence."[11] He continued:

There was a time when the phrase "for the sake of the state" wielded such a power as to suppress all other considerations, making the people subservient to the despotic will of statesmen, and even the spiritual leaders had meekly to submit to their sometimes arrogant and inflexible orders. This was all right if the state was representative of things that are good, just, and humane; but as history tells us, no state has ever proved in the past to be such a symbol. In fact, every one of the states that prospered and disappeared, or that are now prospering, has been anything but symbolic of justice and love and liberty. Hence the history of the world has been the record of constant struggles and untold sufferings. But fortunately, since the termination of the recent war, the world seems to be realizing the enormity of the loss and the foolishness of the greed for power. We are now growing more conscious than ever of the imperative necessity of emphasizing the spiritual side of human life and the fact that our lives are so closely interrelated that whatever things good or bad happen to one nation are sure to affect another. The time is come when we have to abandon the narrow conception of the state which puts one nation's welfare, especially material welfare, above that of the friendly neighbors. . . . .

Statesmen have been wont to urge us to sacrifice our personal interest for the state, to abandon our individual claims and even affections for upholding the state as the highest expression of human life. This is all right if the state is also the perfect and most rational symbol of all that we, as individuals, can conceive as good and just and lovable. If the state, on the contrary, betrays our thought of justice and freedom and countermands the dictates of love and humanity, it has no right to continue its existence. If it does not fall by itself, other states will not suffer its ever menacing existence. To obey blindly whatever is claimed by the state, good or bad, just or unjust, is to enslave oneself and to lose one's moral and spiritual individuality. . . . .

I believe in the existence of the state, for I think it necessary to the enhancement of real human welfare. But I cannot subscribe to the ideas stoutly upheld by some who, taking the state for an absolute form of human life, believe in its power of doing anything for its own maintenance, regardless of the consequences either to its own members or to the neighboring states. Inasmuch as no one absolute state can exist by itself and in itself, it requires other states to be its friendly neighbors, for no state can ignore the claims of other states, just as in the case of individuals. If it does this and goes on its own way ignoring its fellow-organizations, it is sure to meet a sad fate and lose its own existence before long.[12]

The theoretical basis of the Buddhist view of the state is found in the doctrine of mutuality or social and cosmic interrelatedness. The same author says:

Even a state is unable to maintain itself against the universal law of mutuality which is so strongly taught by Buddhism. Things can only exist as long as they keep up their harmonious relations with the surrounding objects; if one thing grows too domineering over others, the latter rebels against it; if the latter is too weak to resist, the predominant one will die of its own predominance, for an internal disruption is sure to break up within itself. This is the law inviolable. The balance ought under no circumstances to tip one way or another. Egotism that feeds itself too fat is bound to burst from within. All the evils, whether individual, social, or international, grow out of abusing the law of mutuality or interdependence. When the hard shell of the ego, cut away and isolated from others, is crushed, and merges itself in the oneness of things, that is, in the idea of universal brotherhood, the earth will really become a peaceful, comfortable place of abode.[13]

Practical adjustments to operations safely within areas marked out by the state are easily made, however, when such necessity arises. For illustrative evidence in this direction we can turn to the discussion of *The New Japanism and the Buddhist View on Nationality* by Dr. Junjiro Takakusu, an authority whom we have earlier introduced as one of the chief luminaries of the contemporary Buddhist world.

The Buddhist doctrine of selflessness, or *Muga*, is the antidote of the doctrine of individualism. Thus *Muga* is the true basis of a sound collectivism. Buddhism teaches a perfect principle of totalitarianism (the author calls it "totalism"). All events of time and space are indeterminate and mutually complementary; therefore, the possibility arises of the realization of a form of existence in which all things—mutually related and mutually dependent—are co-ordinated and accommodated to one another until complete harmony is attained. In Buddhism this state of full mutual adjustment is described in the *Isshin-Hōkai* doctrine, the teaching of a "Unified and True Universe." Again, it is called the *Kegon* doctrine, from *ke*, "lotus" and *gon*, "glory," meaning "the world as glorious as a lotus flower." This sounds like a philosophical formulation of the Christian doctrine of the Kingdom of God, but, like the Christian writers whom we have earlier examined, our author hastens to point out that it calls for nothing that carries either thought or action beyond the formulations legitimatized by the sacred state. He concludes: "The totalism of the *Kegon*-Doctrine should stand only as a principle, and it should not stand against or above the totalism of Japan. This is the real Buddhistic attitude toward the state."[14] Although Dr. Takakusu does not discuss the point, his conclusion calls to mind another well-known doctrine of Buddhism, that of *Hōben*, or accommodation: it is better to bend than to break.

All the highest ethical ideals necessary to practical life are already incorporated in the doctrine of the state. The state is not only all-powerful; it is also all-wise and all-good. Along with this, it is recognized that statesmen and soldiers are fallible like other human beings, that ideals and practice do not always go together even in the service of nationalism, that the resources of religion are in conscience and intelligence, and that religion can provide a training in character such as makes the realization of the high moral ideals of the state possible.

The completeness of Buddhist accommodation to the ethics of the state appears most clearly in connection with the problem of war. Here again the theory is lofty; the practice, whatever the state in its needs requires. "Buddhism," Dr. Takakusu says, "holds absolutely to the anti-war principle."[15] Eight fundamental concepts are advanced on which the Mahayana teaching is founded: (1) atheism, or the denial of the existence of God in the sense of a God of Creation, or a God of Superintendency, or a God of Judgment, but not necessarily the denial of the existence of spiritual life above the human; (2) "intellectualism," leading to self-enlightenment; (3) idealism; (4)

the elevation of personality; (5) noninjury; (6) compassion or "all-love"; (7) pacificism; and (8) equality.

All these principles, except possibly the first, bear directly on the problem of war. The truly enlightened man makes an art of living and includes in his wisdom the recognition of the world-wide reaches of mercy and love. True idealism creates genuine civilization which is the art of cooperative living, and to be complete this must be contributed to by the human race as a whole. The elevation of personality can never be attained apart from respect for the personalities of others. The compassion of the Buddha is an undivided all-mercifulness like the infinite love of a mother. Hence Buddhism needs no commandment, "Love your enemies," for the reason that it knows no enemies. All are friends. Equality means unreserved mutuality and a life of universal co-operation.

In the principles of noninjury and pacificism Buddhism proclaims even more direct teachings regarding war. The Buddha established the commandment of *Ahimsá*, or "non-waste of life," as prior to all others. For this reason the strict Buddhist cannot sanction the killing of any living thing or even the eating of meat. Dr. Takakusu says: "In the light of this principle it is irrational that man ill treat the animal, and it is more so when a man oppresses other men, and how much more so when a race hurts another race. And it is a most strange thing that a religion tolerates, even encourages, war on other religions. The ideals of noninjury are the foundation of universal love."[16]

The principle of pacificism is likewise based on rationality. Wars arise between nations because men pass erroneous judgments on other peoples and apply to them codes and conditions of action that they are unwilling to have applied to themselves and because of the incapacity of the human mind to include in the field of comprehension and sympathy more than a very limited area of life and interest. The radius of the ego is very small; the shell of

the ego is very hard and thick. Hence arise all sorts of
unenlightened discriminations—economic, religious, national, and racial. As an illustration of the Buddha-way of
overcoming the spirit of war, the example of the last king
of Burma is cited. Here we witness the sublime spectacle
of a devoted Buddhist ruler who gave away his country to
England, preferring personal humiliation and the loss of a
throne to a course which would have involved giving sanction to the slaughter of multitudes of his fellow-creatures.
In summary Dr. Takakusu says: "Buddhism has never
organized a crusade, declared a holy war, or slaughtered
the Jews or Negroes, or practiced lynching. If the world
would really demand a religion of pacificism, there is no
other religion but Buddhism recommendable."[17]

This is the theory. In actual practice the accommodation to the demands of the state is complete. While Japanese Buddhism, out of its devotion to compassion and
mercy, noninjury, pacificism, and rationality, upholds the
ideal of universal peace as the ultimate goal of human society, it nevertheless gives unrestricted precedence to the
state in matters of war. If, as Dr. Takakusu claims, Buddhism has never declared a holy war, it has nonetheless
proclaimed all Japanese wars holy. Japanese Buddhism today accepts practically without qualification the principle
that if the nation goes to war, by that very fact the war is
sanctified; it becomes a crusade for peace and good will on
earth.

Contemporary Buddhist propaganda dwells with satisfaction on the war records of the soldiers of the faith. Buddhists have served with conspicuous valor in the armies of
modern Japan. The three "dynamite soldiers" who with
their own hands carried a bomb against the wire entangle-
ments of the Chinese in the first Shanghai affair of 1932
and perished in the explosion were all adherents of the
Shin sect. The divisions selected by General Nogi for the
attack on Port Arthur in the Russo-Japanese War came

from Kanazawa and Kumamoto, districts where Buddhism is strong. The candidate for the Buddhist priesthood as part of his ordination examination is asked if he has paid his taxes and performed his military service.[18]

Zen Buddhism especially has always appealed to the warrior class. It has done so because at the height of the period of feudal wars in the twelfth and thirteenth centuries Zen found the center of its activities in Kamakura, the military capital of the time; also, because, out of all the Buddhist sects, Zen has manifested the greatest attraction to Confucian ethics, and Confucianism, with its severe definition of the mutual obligations of lord and vassal, has always been "a sort of religious philosophy for the military classes"; and, finally, because Zen stresses arduous physical and mental discipline, unyielding moral force, indomitable spirit, and courage that faces death with resignation. In all these ways Buddhism fosters the qualities of spirit that make for strong soldiers.[19]

Dr. Takakusu's statement that Buddhism holds absolutely to the anti-war principle must be read, then, with a strong emphasis on "principle" as over against practice. Pacifism is not rejected as a remote ideal. The "absolute" quality of adherence which the claim sets forth may perhaps best be understood as persistence in the pursuit of this ever receding goal. Actually, however, war is accepted as a necessity if not as a good. Exactly as in the case of the position which the Japanese Christians have had to accept, every Japanese war is by definition just. The identity of Christian and Buddhist adjustments at this point is undoubtedly due to the fact that both simply restate the rationalizations of the state education. The unqualified measure of Buddhist accommodation here is well set forth in an interpretation made in 1925 by Sekizen Arai, who at the time of speaking was administrative head of the Sōdō sect. The statement says:

Buddhism does not absolutely oppose having war..... Peace is man's natural ideal. It is the highest ideal of man. Japan is a lover of peace, so even if she goes into war, it is always a war for peace. . . . .

In advocating peace and racial equality, we must not forget the state we belong to. Real peace cannot be expected if we forget our state in our love of mankind. . . . .

If we forget our duty to our country, no matter how we advocate the love of mankind, there will be no real peace. . . . .[20]

A more recent example of the facility with which theoretical idealism is adjusted on demand to practical necessity comes from a statement made in 1934 by Ryūzan Shimizu, a professor of the Nichiren University of Tokyo, dealing with the teaching of this sect on war. The principle of universalism on which the Nichiren church is founded is supposedly saved from compromise by identifying the extension of Japanese political and military control with the spread of human brotherhood. In summary the author states:

It is not in harmony with the teachings of Nichiren, the founder, nor with the principles accepted by the church, to stir up the war spirit within the nation and adopt a militant and threatening attitude toward other nations, and thereby foster abroad the mistaken idea that Japan is militaristic and aggressive. The Hokke Sutra [the sacred text of Nichiren] is entirely devoid of a militaristic, punitive, warlike spirit. In the great wisdom of the Buddha, enemies had no existence. The spirit of Nichiren is the equality of all men. Though color and race may differ, all men are the children of the fundamental Buddha, and the fundamental Buddha is the parent of all. Human beings everywhere are brothers and sisters. It is the ideal of Nichiren to make the entire world one great Buddha-land.

The underlying principle of Nipponism is the enlightenmentl of the world with truth. Just as our brother Manchurians have come to follow us with affection, so also must we lead all the nations of the word into righteousness and establish heaven on earth, where brotherly love and world-wide peace shall prevail and where all men shall be Buddhist saints. This is the true ideal of Nipponism.[21]

The subordination of this righteous universalism to practical military requirements follows in the form of a note, attached by the author to his essay, which appeared first as a public lecture. We learn from this that, following the original discourse, a certain patriot in the audience arose and attacked the position of the speaker. The objector stated that in view of the actual status of international relations it was absolutely essential to the safety of Japan that armament be increased and hastened. He called attention to the fact that Nichiren himself had taught the duty of drawing the sword on behalf of truth and country. In reply the author adds:

I am by no means one of those who denies war. I was simply saying in this connection that it would be unfortunate to be in error in regard to the degree of preparation required and the relative urgency. Then again my objector was speaking from the point of view of realism. I was speaking from the point of view of pure theory.[22]

This illuminating paragraph may be taken as the key and conclusion to the accommodation of contemporary Japanese Buddhism to the demands of nationalism.

NOTES

1. Yoshiteru Yabuki, *Nippon Seishin to Nippon Bukkyō* ("The Japanese Spirit and Japanese Buddhism") (Tokyo, 1934). The book went through fifteen editions in two years.

2. *Ibid.*, pp. 43–46.

3. *Ibid.*, p. 46.

4. The statistics for Japanese Buddhism published in 1940 are:

Temples	71,326
Churches	7,753
Temple heads	55,930
Other priests	178,127
Adherents	42,249,229

5. Yabuki, *op. cit.*, p. 28.

6. *Ibid.*, pp. 3–6.

7. Junjirō Takakusu, *The New Japanism and the Buddhist View on Nationality* (Tokyo, 1938), p. 39.

8. *Outline of Japanese Buddhism* (Tokyo: Buddhist Federation of Japan [Nippon Bukkyō Rengōkai], 1937).

9. *Ibid.*, p. 93.

10. Junjirō Takakusu, *Life Questions and Buddhism* (Tokyo, 1939), p. 7.

11. Sonyu Otani, "The Washington Conference from the Buddhist Point of View," *Eastern Buddhist*, I, No. 4 (December–November, 1921), 259.

12. *Ibid.*, pp. 259–62.

13. *Ibid.*, p. 261.

14. Junjirō Takakusu, *The New Japanism and the Buddhist View on Nationality*, p. 22.

15. Junjirō Takakusu, *Buddhism the Fountain-head of Intellect* (Tokyo, 1938), p. 55. For the discussion that is summarized here see pp. 55–73 of this book.

16. *Ibid.*, p. 68.

17. *Ibid.*

18. Junjirō Takakusu, *The New Japanism and the Buddhist View on Nationality*, pp. 23–24.

19. Minoru Hashimoto, "Zen Doctrine and Its Influence upon the Samurai Classes," *Cultural Nippon*, VI, No. 1 (March, 1938), 51–64.

20. Sekizen Arai, "A Buddhist View of World Peace," *Japan Evangelist*, December, 1925, pp. 395–400.

21. Ryūzan Shimizu, *Risshō Ankoku no Taigi to Nippon Seishin* ("The Teachings of *Risshō Ankoku* ['On a Righteous and Peaceful Country'—by Nichiren] and the Japanese Spirit") (Tokyo, 1934), pp. 46–48.

22. *Ibid.*, pp. 47–48.

CHAPTER VI

THE OVERSEAS EXPANSION OF
STATE SHINTO

THE rise of modern Japan to ascendancy in Far
Eastern affairs has been accompanied by an impressive geographical expansion. This territorial
growth—achieved mainly by the force of arms—has been
safeguarded by the extension of elaborate political and
military administration, and this in turn has been accompanied by economic and cultural penetrations that are only
beginning to reveal their vast possibilities for the reorder-
ing of the new areas of control. We are witnessing in the
Far East today a bursting of old barriers of national life
and an outflowing of energies across new frontiers that
may prove as eventful for the fate of mankind as was the
great *Völkerwanderung* that marked the transition from
the ancient classical world to the Dark Ages of European
history. Japan is "moving in" onto the continent of Asia
with the totality of her cultural possessions. This movement is not merely military and political. In manufactur-
ing, agriculture, mining, engineering, business, education,
and religion, Japan is projecting something like a migration
onto the mainland, which, if carried through even to partial conclusion, will leave very little as it was either for
continental eastern Asia or for Japan. And even though the
actual movements of population may not be relatively
large, the completeness of the controls which the Japanese
genius for paternalistic organization is in process of establishing over conquered peoples threatens a momentous
change to the story of mankind.

The part which the national religion has played in this
great movement is not inconsiderable. The tenacity with

which the Japanese government has pressed the Shinto issue in Korea and elsewhere points to its significance as the
guaranty of the establishment of inner authority over subjected peoples. The scope of this issue can be partially
grasped if set against the brief outline of Japan's modern
geographical expression.

The original archipelago, sometimes called Japan proper
or the *Naichi*, the "Inner Land" of the Japanese language,
which made up the territories with which the nation began
its modern career, consisted of a swarm of some six hundred islands, not including small uninhabited islets,
stretching from Hokkaido on the north to the Oshima
group on the south. The total area of this original territory
was about 148,000 square miles, some ten thousand square
miles less than the state of California. At the close of the
Tokugawa era these islands supported about thirty million
souls. The population in the late pre-modern period remained practically static at this figure, owing to the operation of factors introduced by periodic famine, unscientific
disease control, transportation and agricultural deficiencies, and abortion. Saghalien, which had formerly been a
part of the Chinese empire, was annexed by Japan early in
the nineteenth century and then ceded to Russia in 1875
in return for the Kurile Islands. The possession of these
last-named territories, while adding only about 3,900
square miles—an area about the size of Puerto Rico—to
the empire, brought important fishing advantages and carried the Japanese line to within seven hundred miles of the
western outposts of the Aleutian Islands. The Bonin Islands were formally annexed in 1877 and the Loochoo Islands in 1879. Formosa was annexed in 1895 at the close of
the Sino-Japanese War, adding an area of 13,800 square
miles, a tract about the size of the Netherlands. By the
terms of the Treaty of Portsmouth at the close of the
Russo-Japanese War in 1905 southern Saghalien with an
area almost exactly the same as that of Formosa was taken

over. The annexation of Korea in 1910 brought an additional 85,000 square miles, a territory somewhat larger than the state of Kansas.

The close of World War I saw the Marshall, Mariana (excluding Guam), and Caroline Islands, formerly belonging to Germany, transferred to Japan under mandate of the League of Nations. Although this meant an increase of less than a thousand square miles, it carried the national holdings almost to the Equator and gave to Japan possessions of great strategic importance in the impending struggle for the control of Asia.

The successive steps here outlined created the existing territorial basis of the modern Japanese state. They constitute the legally incorporated areas of the Japanese empire. Altogether they make up an area of about 265,000 square miles. Pieced together they would give a continuous land mass somewhat larger than France and England combined. The islands stretch for 3,000 miles along the east coast of Asia, and, defended by a powerful navy, watched over by a skilful diplomacy, and protected by a strong national determination, they give to Japan a formidable position in the Far East. Since the beginning of the last quarter of the nineteenth century, Japan has expanded her national territories by 79 per cent over what she held at the close of the Tokugawa period.

When we take under observation the vast reaches of Manchukuo, where Japan has assumed exclusive authority and acquired corresponding privileges and opportunities, the expansion takes on truly heroic proportions. Here are some 503,000 square miles of land infolding rich agricultural plains that stretch away interminably like the horizons of Kansas and Nebraska, great coal fields, newly discovered oil resources, and mountains where recent surveys have found important minerals. This region has opened to Japan's expansion territories as large as the combined areas of old Germany and France. We can understand how

Japanese enthusiasm, warmed by the contemplation of this wonderland and seeking relief from the closed opportunities of the homeland, has sometimes declared that here it would set up a "paradise on earth."

The wide sweep of these various lands becomes more vivid to our comprehension when they are laid out to scale over a map of the United States of America. If we should place the most northeasterly of the Kuriles on the northeast corner of the state of Maine, the southern boundary of Kyushu would fall approximately at Austin, Texas; Formosa would lie on the west central coast of Mexico; the westernmost point of Korea would fall somewhat to the west of Oklahoma City; the Marianas would be near Panama; the Caroline Islands along a line formed by the borders of Columbia and Venezuela with Brazil; the Marshall Islands over British, Dutch, and French Guiana; the western boundary of Manchukuo would be near Pikes Peak.[1]

The population statistics are also impressive. In Japan proper, according to the latest available statistics, live 70,000,000 people; in Korea, 24,000,000; in Formosa, 5,000,000; in Saghalien, 330,000; in the South Pacific possessions, over 100,000. The total population for the empire is approximately 100,000,000. Manchukuo, including the Kwantung peninsula, boasts a population of 38,000,000, about 600,000 of this number being Japanese civilians.

The extension of control into realms beyond the island territories and the penetration of Japanese populations into overseas areas have had as their proper accompaniment the setting-up of Shinto shrines in new places and the worship of the deities of the homeland as the guardians of new ventures. Even more significant for the international aspects of Japan's rise to hegemony in the Far East is the fact that the conception of the unity of government and religion has necessitated the establishment of shrines to home gods as agencies of political administration. Given the nature of the Japanese state and its inseparable association with Shinto belief and ritual, it is impossible to think of a political control apart from a vigorous determination to secure the subordination of conquered populations to the central religious interests of the state. Where go the Japanese armies there go the Japanese gods.

That this overseas extension of State Shinto includes much more than a program of ministering to the needs of the members of the Japanese race in new homes is clear from various sources. Stimulated by the ever growing strength of the national consciousness, Shinto has become aware of a world mission as never before. This has given occasion for the formulation of what may be called a Shinto theory of foreign missions. A Japanese authority on Shinto has expounded this matter in a recent discussion. In the *Shūkyō Nenkan* ("Yearbook of Religion"), published in the early part of 1939, Mr. Hideo Horie writes on the subject, "The Shinto Shrine Problem Overseas" ("Kaigai ni okeru Jinja Mondai"). The major problem, argues Mr. Horie, is that of the adjustment of the exclusively nationalistic aspects of State Shinto to the universalism that ought to inhere in constructive international intercourse. The existence of the former elements is first recognized and strongly emphasized. The author calls attention to the consciousness of unique racial integrity that underlies the thinking of the Japanese people. He begins with the doctrine of the one-tribe origin of the nation. The true members of the Japanese race regard themselves as the offspring of the gods. They believe that their state was brought into being by the *kami* and that the people are the descendants of these ancestral deities. They hold that, in spite of the infusion of the blood of other peoples in times past, the genuine Yamato stock predominates and that for the most part the breed is pure. Communal solidarity is guaranteed and preserved by this fact of direct divine descent and by the bonds of spiritual communion with the gods. These bonds are kept strong by the ceremonies and beliefs of the national shrines. The sanctuaries of State Shinto are, then, the chief means for the integration of past and present about the sentiments of reverence, gratitude, loyalty, and obligation. To recognize them, support them, and participate in their ceremonies is the first duty of the subject. Wherever the national life finds it possible to express itself on its own terms and by means of its characteristic institutions there the shrines of State Shinto must be set up. The two cannot be separated. Shinto must go overseas, therefore, as the unique institution of Japanese political expansion.

The shrines of Shinto bring unity to the faith of our nation. They strengthen the corporate fusion of the race. They furnish the supreme and central power for refining the feelings, the manners, and customs of the people. . . . . Reverence for the shrines is rich with the significance of a solemn oath of loyalty to the great duty of improving and consolidating the state. The connection of the shrines and the state is so intimate that the two cannot be severed.[2]

All this, however, does not necessarily involve an exclusive attitude toward non-Japanese peoples. On the contrary, it affords opportunity for sharing the blessings of the matchless Japanese community life with other races and nations and furnishes grounds for the hope that thereby these gentile peoples may be deepened in feelings, united in loyalty, and broadened in human benevolence. Nationalism clothes itself with the righteousness of the missionizer. At the height of his argument the author says:

The nationalistic character found in the shrines does not inevitably veto a universal character. In cases where members of our Japanese race—so rich in the sentiment of reverence—are living together in a land with foreigners of like tendencies the practice of worshiping together at the shrines is not merely a matter to which there is no objection, rather it should be welcomed. Shinto, the Great Way of the Gods, is not a thing which the state or the people of the nation should regard selfishly. Shinto is broad. It includes humanitarianism and righteousness. The spirit of Shinto, which is the fundamental directive principle of our national life, must be utilized for the purpose of elevating the races of neighboring territories where the national relationships are complicated. Indeed, by means of this spirit of Shinto foreign peoples must also be evangelized. The self-interested internationalism, which has come into existence apart from the give and take of ordinary intercourse and which up to now has fought with the weapons of craft and deception, must be brought to its senses by the saving presence of the pure and holy spirit of Shinto.[3]

This statement invites us to attempt an exploration of the possibilities that State Shinto holds out to the universalizing of the human spirit. The virtues that are stressed in the national education of modern Japan have already been noted and need not be repeated. Fundamentally they are concerned with attitudes toward particular institutions of state and would seem to carry the corollary that Shinto cannot be propagated outside the realms of the Japanese emperor. Various Shinto writers have said this very thing. Only an authentic member of the Japanese race can accept and worship the traditional "ancestors." What generally valid principles does Shinto offer, then, that are applicable to all mankind and not restricted to a particular nation? When this question is put to Shinto authorities, they commonly answer in terms of a moral excellence called *makoto*, *magokoro*, or *shinjitsu*. All these words are probably best translated "sincerity." "Perfect sincerity," says Nobuyoshi Watarai, a seventeenth-century scholar, "is the supreme principle of Shinto."[4] From this moral straightforwardness or uprightness of heart stem all the virtues prized by *Bushido* and extolled in the idealistic literature. Side by side with the love of Christianity and the compassion of Buddhism is placed the sincerity of Shinto, and, just as Christian love and Buddhist compassion know no national barriers, so also Shinto sincerity is universal in its reaches. "Herein," says Genchi Katō, "we see an ethical spark of universalism in Shinto."[5] From this, says the same author, "springs the idea of universal fraternity and of love for all without distinction among friends and foes."[6]

The religious literature of the nation contains many noble passages in praise of sincerity.

Katō has rendered a fragment from the teaching of

Munetada Kurozumi, the founder of a Shinto sect that bears his name, by the lines:

> Blest be sincerity of virtues chief!
> Alone in it the world shall seek relief
> From doubt and fear—till men of every land
> In universal brotherhood do stand.[7]

Even more profoundly eloquent of depth of universal religious insight is a famous passage from the writings of the remarkable woman who founded the Tenri sect of Shinto:

> Sincerity is the attitude of an awakened spirit that has been swept clean of the eight dusts [moral contamination] and made free from evil fate. Your true self is spirit and this is sincerity itself. Sincerity when it works naturally is truth. Truth, therefore, is the principle of your spirit. And since your spirit is part of the spirit of God, the principle of your spirit is the principle of Heaven. Thus, the truth of the heart of sincerity is the truth of God, Himself, and sincerity which is revealed in truth is communion with God. "If in all the thoughts and acts which come before me," says God, "there be only a little sincerity, if only a bit of the truth of Heaven, then quickly will I accept it and quickly make reward." For sincerity and God are one and inseparable. . . . .
>
> Thus does God desire sincerity. And not until one prays with sincerity does prayer have power to prevail with God. Spiritual salvation is a blessing that comes only to sincerity.[8]

This is Shinto at its highest. It is more than "an ethical spark of universalism," as Dr. Katō calls it; it is part of the all-pervading fire of the world-wide human soul and inspires the conviction that, in spite of the blighting effects of nationalism, there is still such a thing as universal human nature. It is significant that the lofty interpretations of sincerity that we have examined come from the popular sects of Shinto. They reveal to us the soul and aspirations of the real Japanese people—something of what they would like to be— but not that soul as claimed by the state. In this latter area the fate of Shinto groping toward universalism is effectively determined by three factors that must be examined: (1) the governmentally inspired doctrine that the essence of sincerity consists in conformity to rule; (2) the conception of the national expansion process as involving the full assimilation of conquered peoples; and (3) the inseparable connection between Shinto and political administration.

It is one of the significant elements of strength in the domestic operations of the Japanese government that it possesses the shrewdness and power to turn the instinctive idealism of the people into directions that fit in with the expediency of administrative policy. This is a primary means of authoritarian restraint, perhaps its most effective agency of revolutionary control, on the one hand, and of emotional unification, on the other. All the idealism necessary to a full human life, all the avenues leading to the complete realization of self and community, are already established and included in the idealism of the state itself. The individual attains the maximum of security and satisfaction by obedience. The bearing of these observations becomes especially evident when we see what happens to sincerity in the hands of the official guides. We have already had occasion to note the important volume called "The Fundamental Principles of the National Structure" (*Kokutai no Hongi*), issued in 1937 by the Department of Education in Tokyo. At the center of its discussion of national ethics this book says:

> The heart of sincerity is the purest manifestation of the spirit of man. In sincerity man possesses the foundations of his life. By sincerity he becomes one with the universe. By this he gives life to the universe and attains harmony therewith.
> Both Kamo-no-Mabuchi[9] and Fujitani Mitsue[10] have written with special attention to sincerity. Sincerity means that true words become true deeds. By sincerity words and deeds are unified. That which is spoken by the mouth must surely be manifested in actions. At the bottom of words and deeds must be sincerity.
> Mitsue divided spirit (lit. "heart") into three forms: the onefold spirit, the one-direction spirit, and the true spirit. The onefold spirit is the spirit of egoism. The one-direction spirit is the spirit of obstinacy and ignorance. Neither of these can be called a complete spirit. The true spirit follows the desires of the heart and yet does not go beyond the rules. When such a spirit appears in deeds and words and practice, it knows neither let nor hindrance. It is the pure heart and the pure deed

that are separated from selfishness. Verily, sincerity harmonizes and unifies the universe and brings it freedom and consummation. Revealed in art, sincerity becomes beauty; in the moral world it becomes goodness; in the affairs of knowledge it becomes truth. The source from which beauty, goodness, and truth are born is sincerity. Sincerity means the clean and upright heart; it is the heart of purity. This is the very foundation of our national spirit.[11]

This passage is a remarkable mixture of noble moral idealism and statecraft, the former harnessed to the purposes of the latter. Commenting on the statement that sincerity is a spirit that does not go beyond the rules, the standard commentary on the book that we have before us says, "It is a spirit that does not break the fixed regulations, one that carefully obeys the rules, one that does not jump the track."[12] This is itself a violation of the human spirit. The history of goodness, beauty, and truth is witness to the indispensability to human progress of people who do "jump the track."

In a system of moral and political control under which truth is identified with official standardization it is easy to see how the essence of sincerity becomes conformity. The great liberalizing principle of Shinto, its contribution to the universalizing of the spirit of man comparable with the love of Christianity and the compassion of Buddhism, now, in its practical manifestations, finds its scope of expression only within the specifications of military and political utilitarianism. It is simply the old body of nationalism again, clothing itself in outer garments of beauty. The early summer of 1940 found Manchukuo placarded with a slogan which in translation read, "One heart, one virtue" (*Isshin-ichidoku*). When questioned as to what this might mean to the Manchurian subject under the domination of the armies of Japan, a non-Japanese resident who had spent his life in the country replied, "It means a heart of fear and a virtue of absolute obedience."

The best that can be said of a situation like this is that, in so far as the governmental laudation of sincerity is itself sincere, it may be taken as a chief example of the remarkable capacity of the official mind to hold on to positions that are violently opposite, without sense of either logical or moral incongruity. This same thing is to no small extent a characteristic of Japanese psychology as a whole. Truth is the establishment of official asseveration, not the logical relation of inner parts.

A second influence limiting the reciprocal operation of any universalism that may be latent in State Shinto appears in the apparent determination of the Japanese authorities to effect the full assimilation of subordinated peoples wherever possible. This aspect of Japanese expansion can be studied to best advantage in the two older cultural areas that have been incorporated into the empire in modern times, namely, Formosa and Korea, and applies to all phases of the lives of the people, administrative, economic, educational, and religious. The expressed policy of the Japanese government in these districts is to make all members of the indigenous populations into standardized Japanese subjects, both legally and psychologically. The passage from the pen of Mr. Horie which we cited earlier in the discussion as an expression of the missionary enthusiasm of contemporary Shinto speaks of the give-and-take of ordinary intercourse between incoming Japanese and the older populations. Any sound and mutually acceptable acculturation process would demand this as a primary necessity. It must be free exchange, not one-sided penetration and displacement. If Shinto really includes a humanitarianism that is effective in transfusing "self-interested internationalism" with good will, then all concerned must have like access to making contribution to the new whole, and personality, both individual and collective, must be respected. The experience of Japanese-dominated people has brought them deep misgivings on this score, not to say bitter resentment. Japan has talked valiantly about freeing the Eastern peoples from Western imperialism, about

Asia for the Asiatics, about a new order in the Far East that will bring opportunity and contentment to all. Those who have questioned this avowed benevolence have been accused of insincerity and misunderstanding.

If we apply a standard of judgment which tests this much-heralded altruism by fruits rather than by words, then aspects of the Japanese venture in overseas expansion come to light which on the ethical side amount to an invasion of personality no better than Western imperialism at its worst. Asiatic peoples themselves have sometimes declared that, much as they hated occidental dominion, they hated and feared Japanese dominion more. This is the explanation of the bitter resistance of China to the armies of Japan. For China the only possible basis of a new order of mutual co-operation in the Far East is the elimination of all imperialism, Western and Japanese alike.

The Japanese policy of cultural assimilation in Formosa includes the displacement of the old Chinese language by the exclusive use of Japanese in the schools and all ordinary organs of publication as part of a program for the eventual elimination of vernacular everywhere, the prohibition of the Chinese national dress, and the interdiction of the worship of Chinese idols, accompanied by rigid requirements for participation in Shinto ceremonies and the erection of Shinto god-shelves in the homes. The nationalization of Korea follows the same pattern of inner penetration. Its avowed purpose is to effect psychological as well as institutional identity with Japanese domestic standards. Every Korean is to become a safe Japanese subject both spiritually and legally. Apart from economic discrimination and severe police and military control, the program, already largely accomplished, includes the substitution of the Japanese language for Korean in education and publication, the requirement that Koreans give up their former clan and family names and take Japanese names, the abandonment of the indigenous religious practices in favor of the worship of the Japanese "ancestors," and "a Shinto shrine in every town and village." Acceptance of rigorous conformity in these directions is taken as the measure of Korean sincerity toward Japanese benevolence. It is futile to talk of humanitarianism and righteousness and the mutual give-and-take of a free internationalism in the face of this kind of wholesale subordination of the souls of a conquered people. The Japanese conviction of themselves as a superior race and their state as a divinely ordained and peerless institution leaves no room for anything other than subserviency on the part of the peoples brought under their dominion.

Here the question arises: Is not the Westernization of the Far East, including the penetration of Christian propaganda, merely a unilateral acculturation process which attempts a full assimilation to nonoriental norms? We have already seen that Japanese nationalism has formulated its strongest protest against Christianity exactly on these grounds. It is possible to rest the issue with the quality of genuine universalism that inheres in the world expansion of Christianity, dissociated from the Western economic and political imperialism by which it has been compromised, as compared with the inversion of universalism manifested in Shinto-military expansion. The right of the Japanese to protect their cultural and state life within their own national boundaries by whatever means may seem necessary is one thing. The attempt through military and political duress to force other peoples to relinquish their own culture and assimilate that of the Japanese under the name of universalism is quite another. What Japan claims for herself as her chief national interest is deliberately denied to others.

The third influence that negates the fruition of potential universalism resides in the fact that, in spite of constant governmental proclamations to the contrary, Shinto is to all intents and purposes the state religion of the Japanese empire. It rises and falls with the destiny of a special form of state structure; its fate is bound up completely with that of the Japanese nation; it is the emotional concentration of an unusually intense nationalism. The reasons for its official protection and utilization in the overseas expansion of Japan are to be found in the determination of the Japanese rulers to employ the unique resources of its ceremonies and beliefs as a means of political control. If, from the point of view of those in power, this involves any benevolence or universalism, it is due to the fact that they are convinced that Shinto is fit for world-wide acceptance because it embodies political ideas and gives support to state institutions that have absolute validity. To be effective this must completely ignore the rights of self-determination on the part of other peoples. The terms of acceptance are set by military conquerors and enforced with the powers of police offices. Under the circumstances genuine universalism could become a positive force in Shinto only by some sort of inner revolution comparable to that which broke up the hardened shell of Jewish nationalism and set the spirit of Christianity free.

State Shinto as it stands today, saturated with nationalistic self-interest, made incredible by mythological crudity, and devoted to the suppression of freedom, can be propagated among intelligent men only by the use of force, and it is to force that the final appeal is made whenever the issue of resistance to Japanese penetration has become acute. The story of Japanese colonial policy in Korea fully attests this fact. Here the interests of political unification have resulted in requirements of Shinto conformity even more severe than those in Japan proper. This has extended even to the prohibition of the right to discuss whether or not State Shinto is a religion. In 1936, when the storm over the shrines was breaking in Korea, the chief of the home office of the South Heian province of Korea issued a statement reading:

As a matter of fact the shrines are public agencies whereby the ancestors of the Imperial Family and people who have rendered distinguished service to the state are enshrined, and where the subjects of the state may offer true reverence and commemorate their meritorious deeds forever. Thus the fundamental idea differs from that of religion. That is to say, from ancient times down to the present the shrines have been national institutions expressive of the very center and essence of our national structure. Thus they have an existence totally distinct from religion, and worship at the shrines is an act of patriotism and loyalty, the basic moral virtues of our nation.

Schools, whether or not they are founded by governmental or private agencies, and regardless of whether or not they are supported by religious groups, all without exception have their primary significance in the cultivation of national character. It is, accordingly, entirely proper that educational institutions which are charged with the important duty of developing Japanese subjects, should carry out worship at the shrines for educational reasons. It is on no grounds permissible that school principals and teachers who unite their educational functions with those of religious propagandists, should confuse religion and education and be deficient in an understanding of the system of laws and ordinances which the state has established because of the requirements of national education, and oppose educational orders and fail to perform worship at the shrines.

In the matter of the national interpretation of the shrines and of national necessity all people, both from the point of view of their relation as subjects of the Empire and from that of the education of the people of the nation, should yield obedience. Such things as the advocacy of the individualistic and arbitrary interpretation that the shrines are religious in nature and in particular the opposition to orders concerning educational administration are not to be permitted.[13]

This order, and many others like it, precipitated a crisis for Christianity in Korea, resulting in the closing of numerous schools and in the withdrawal from the country of many foreign representatives of Christian organizations. The net result for Korean Christianity itself was full accommodation to the Shinto political standards. It is outside the interests of our discussion to enter into the details of this situation. We are concerned here with the emergence in this particular colonial area of impressive evidence of the subservience of Shinto policy to national political influences. Acquaintance with State Shinto should have led us to expect nothing else. The fact that the interests of

national expansion completely dominate the formation of
religious policy leaves absolutely no room for the free manifestation of whatever "ethical spark of universalism" may
lie hidden in Shinto. In the hands of its official directors,
Shinto can expand into new territories only as an agency of
political and military control. This requires a systematic
subordination of non-Japanese peoples such as nullifies all
pretense to universalism. For peoples so placed the essence
of their sincerity becomes obedience to rulers; the give-
and-take of social intercourse becomes an assimilation that
displaces the older culture by the Japanese; the Shinto
benevolence that is extended to them becomes a political
regimentation that effects conformity by police authority.

As might be expected in view of the time elements involved, the number of new shrines as yet established in this
extension of control into overseas territories is relatively
small as compared with the prolific developments which
we have already noted for Japan proper. Prospects of considerable future expansion must be recognized, however,
when we take into consideration the expressed intentions
of the Japanese authorities. In carrying out its program
for the psychological unification of non-Japanese peoples
under the sanctions of State Shinto, the imperial government has had to overcome the same conditions of heterogeneity that have come under observation at an earlier point
in the discussion.

Until very recent times matters of jurisdiction over
shrines abroad have been without adequately centralized
supervision, and in spite of tendencies toward the exclusive
selection of the sun-goddess and the spirit of Emperor
Meiji as deities, manifested especially in Korea, the shrines
have differed much among themselves not only in the *kami*
worshiped but also in such other details as ceremonies and
style of architecture.

In recognition of this situation the bureau of shrines of
the Department of Home Affairs, which has final charge of

the activities of State Shinto, whether at home or abroad, in the year 1938 adopted a policy intended to bring unification into the procedures of overseas shrines. After a study of the problem by a special commission of the government, the following regulations were drawn up with the approval of the army and the navy and the indorsement of the various administrative agencies in direct charge of the relations with the territories concerned:

1. Amaterasu Ōmikami shall be enshrined and worshiped as the chief deity.
2. In general the sanctuary shall be constructed in Japanese *gongen* style [a special combination of Buddhist and Shinto architectural features], but embodying new features suitable to climate and locality.
3. Priests shall be Japanese Shintoists and at the same time men who possess an understanding of national polity. For this purpose a training agency shall be newly established in collaboration with the National Association of Shinto Priests and with the Japanese Classical Literature Research Institute.[14]

During the year 1939, beginnings were made in carrying out the decision embodied in these regulations concerning the special preparation of priests. In the summer of this year a course of instruction for the training of priests for overseas service was opened by the Japanese Classical Literature Research Institute in Tokyo. At the same time the national Department of Education established facilities for the training of schoolteachers designated for service in newly opened lands in the functions of Shinto priests, with the idea that in case of need they could supplement their educational activities by acting as ritualists of the state cult. All these adjustments are significant of the scope and methods of Japanese politico-religious policy in relation to world expansion.

For an authoritative statement of the purposes that underlie the extension of State Shinto to new territories we are provided with an official declaration made in connection with the transfer of the spirit of Amaterasu Omikami to suzerainty over Manchukuo in the summer of 1940. On

July 15 of this year a sanctuary called the Manchukuo Foundation Shrine was dedicated to the great goddess of Ise in the capital city of Hsinking. Emperor Kangte conducted the ceremonies. After the close of the rites an imperial rescript was issued which says:

Out of his own profound experience and conviction, Emperor Kangte has decided to enshrine the spirit of Amaterasu-Ōmikami in the new national shrine of Manchukuo and to pray for the welfare of Manchurians through the providence of the Sun Goddess. As an auxiliary of the shrine, a shrine dedicated to the memory of those who died for the founding of Manchukuo also will be established.

The creation of this Foundation Shrine will serve to consolidate all the more the guiding spirit of Manchukuo, which aims at co-operation among the five races of the state, and to show to the nation that Manchukuo has imported from Japan the "Way Intact from the Age of the Gods," known as *Kannagara no Michi*, and that it should go in this Way as far as the national spirit is concerned. The Emperor also makes it known that the ethical virtues of Manchukuo must be based on loyalty and filial piety.[15]

At the same time a Shinto Shrine Board for Manchukuo was established, with Lieutenant General Toranosuke Hashimoto, vice-president of the Manchukuo Privy Council, at its head. The magnitude of the state ceremonies that accompanied this designation of Amaterasu Omikami to authority over new lands is suggested by the fact that they were commemorated to the nation by the proclamation of a general amnesty, involving the reduction of criminal sentences and the restoration of civil rights and affecting, all told, some 170,000 people. All this is consistent with that Shinto conviction mentioned earlier in the discussion that every shrine to the sun-goddess is an altar to the imperial throne.

The attempt to come to the conclusion of the whole matter leaves the student of Far Eastern affairs with the sense of groping on the borderland of uncertainty. The story which we have tried to tell of the conflict of forces in modern Japan—reactionary nationalism over against cosmopolitanism; suppression, regimentation, and misrepresentation over against freedom and the rights of personality; boastful racialism over against a universalism that fulfils the unity of humanity and the dignity of human reason— all this leaves us with the conviction that a cultural reformation, not to say a political revolution, is long overdue in Japan. There is evidence that, in spite of the apparent success of outward standardization and in spite of the enforced silence of intelligent and upright leadership on important issues, the best Japanese minds are full of painful misgivings regarding the extent to which reason, altruism, sincerity (to name the virtue which Shinto likes to proclaim), and honest respect for historical fact enter into the purposes of those who control the national destiny. The authorities are interested in Shinto for a crusade, one that is economic, political, and strategic. Shinto is a tool for the consummation of state policy.

The best Japanese leadership, Buddhist and Christian alike, knows these things well enough. But when that leadership speaks openly, it speaks, as does religious leadership everywhere when caught in the trap of power politics, with a strange double tongue. In the course of his discussion of contemporary Japanese Buddhism and the problems of Shinto nationalism on which we have had occasion to draw at an earlier stage in our study, Dr. Takakusu records how the late Count Gotō, one of the great liberals of modern Japan, once said "with a sigh," "The Japanese have the Japanese Spirit but they do not have the World Spirit."[16] Reading between the lines, one is tempted to believe that the venerable Buddhist scholar who borrowed these words also shared in the sigh.

In another place Dr. Takakusu tells the story of the visit of a Chinese envoy to Japan and the address which the latter gave before a gathering of Japanese businessmen. In it he spoke of how economic considerations had dominated recent Sino-Japanese communications to the exclusion of everything else and expressed the hope that Buddhist activities might be restored to the important position which they once held in the intercourse of the two countries. To this the businessmen are reported to have replied, "We do not see the least need of it; we will keep our relations purely economic."[17]

Yet in spite of this heartening recognition of the inadequacies of the Japanese spirit and the serious defects in Japanese relations with China, it takes Dr. Takakusu only a few lines to get back on the approved track of a superior Japanese nationalism. The last sentence of his discussion is: "After all there is nothing for us to rely on except the strength of the culture of the blood."[18] Dr. Takakusu makes it plain that he means Japanese blood.

These incidents are a parable of the position of religious universalism in Japan today. This universalism has compromised and accommodated itself until it seems almost to have sold its soul to the state. In so doing, it has suffered much. Yet it has not altogether died. The time may yet come when this suppressed power, brought to a realization of the true nature of Japanese expansion and an understanding of the effective purposes of the state, will assert itself in a mighty upheaval in which the old order with its obsolete, coercive sanctions will go down forever and a new and truly modern Japan arise.

NOTES

1. As this goes to press, the armed forces of Japan are in control of all of the eastern seaboard of China, the Philippines, the Malay States, Burma, the Netherlands Indies, and hold Rabaul in New Britain. From east to west on the Equator their domination extends along one-fourth of the circumference of the earth.

2. Hideo Horie, "Kaigai ni okeru Jinja Mondai" ("The Shinto Shrine Problem Overseas"), *Shūkyō Nenkan* ("Yearbook of Religion") (Tokyo, 1939), p. 145.

3. *Ibid.*, p. 146.

4. Cited in Genchi Katō. "A Trait of the Religious Character of the Japanese People in Close Connection with Their Institutional Life, as Illustrated by Shinto: A Study of the National Faith of the Japanese," *Young East*, VII, No. 4 (1938), 7.

5. *Ibid.*

6. *Ibid.*, p. 6.

7. *Ibid.*, p. 8.

8. *Tenri Kyō Kōyō* ("An Outline of Tenri Kyō") (Tamba Ichi, 1929), pp. 246–47.

9. A well-known writer on Japanese history and poetry who flourished in the Tokugawa period.

10. A famous scholar of the late eighteenth and early nineteenth centuries.

11. *Kokutai no Hongi* ("The Fundamental Principles of the National Structure") (Tokyo, 1937), pp. 59–60.

12. Miura Fujisaku, *Kokutai no Hongi Seikai* ("A Commentary on 'The Fundamental Principles of the National Structure'") (Tokyo, 1937), p. 179.

13. *Jinja Fusampai Mondai ni Tsuite* ("Concerning the Refusal To Participate in Worship at the Shrines") (South Heian Province, Korea, 1936).

14. *Jiji Nenkan* ("Jiji Yearbook") (Tokyo, January, 1939), p. 402.

15. *Japan Advertiser*, July 16, 1940.

16. Junjirō Takakusu, *The New Japanism and the Buddhist View on Nationality* (Tokyo, 1938), p. 33.

17. *Ibid.*, pp. 41–42.

18. *Ibid.*, p. 42.

CHAPTER VII

THE NEW SHINTO

ON TUESDAY, August 14, 1945, the President of the United States of America announced that Japan had agreed to surrender on the basis of the declaration drawn up at Potsdam the latter part of the previous month. On August 28 the first air-borne units of the American occupation army landed at Atsugi, not far from Yokohama. On Sunday, September 2, the Japanese government formally surrendered to representatives of the United Nations in epoch-making ceremonies carried out aboard the United States battleship "Missouri" in Tokyo Bay. The swiftness with which these momentous events unfolded was matched only by the profundity of the change which they presaged for Japan. The social and political upheaval which Japan so sorely needed and which for so long she had been unable to accomplish by her own efforts was now launched at the order of a conquering power.

The directives that were issued from the offices of the Supreme Commander of the Allied Powers in Tokyo for the control and reconstruction of Japan reached into every phase of her public and private life. The secret police system which had long held the Japanese people in the tyranny of its "thought control" was abolished, and the whole vicious network of political and military regimentation was broken up. At the same time the number of civilian police was decreased, and police methods were modernized. Far-reaching agrarian reforms were instituted. The old absentee landlord and farm-tenancy systems were dissolved, and rural co-operatives were revived or expanded. Finance was reformed, and orders were issued for curbing the monopolistic family trusts. Restrictions on labor organization were removed. Political prisoners were liberated. Civil, religious, and political liberty was proclaimed. Freedom of speech, and of press and of assembly, was established. Even the propagation of communism, which had long been illegal, was thereby permitted. Public office and influence were purged of all who had had part in leading Japan into war. Ultra-nationalistic, terrorist, and militaristic organizations were abolished. The military pension system which, if continued, might have invited the perpetuation of a form of army influence, was dissolved. The national educational system was reorganized, and militaristic and ultra-nationalistic teaching was eliminated from the schools. Textbooks were purged or re-written. The electoral franchise was extended to women, and the voting age was lowered to twenty-one. Indicative of the magnitude of the last-mentioned change is the fact that the new Diet which was returned in the general election of April 10, 1946, included thirty-nine women. The dignity of woman in social life was further enhanced by the abolition of licensed prostitution, which had been a source of public revenue all through modern Japanese history. Finally, a new constitution was drafted, founded on the extraordinary declaration that sovereignty rested in the will of the people.

Drastic as these innovations were, none was more revolutionary than that called for in the directive for the disestablishment of State Shinto issued on December 15, 1945. In its most significant provision this order says:

The sponsorship, support, perpetuation, control, and dissemination of Shinto by Japanese national, prefectural, or local governments, or by public officials, subordinates, and employes acting in their official capacity are prohibited and will cease immediately.

All financial support from public funds and all official affiliation with Shinto and Shinto shrines are prohibited and will cease immediately.[1]

Even more far-reaching in its implications was the emperor's renunciation of divinity that was announced in a

New Year's Day rescript only two weeks after the publication of the directive calling for the disestablishment of State Shinto. Referring to the traditional belief in imperial divinity which had been exploited so ruthlessly in Japan's program of militaristic unification, the emperor said:

The ties between Us and Our people have always stood upon mutual trust and affection. They do not depend upon mere legends and myths. They are not predicated upon the false conception that the emperor is divine and that the Japanese people are superior to other races and are fated to rule the world.[2]

With these great changes, Shinto as the state religion of Japan ceased to exist. Did it cease to exist as a national faith? Was it so weakened by the sharp reverses of its fortunes that it had lost all importance in the total life of the nation? The answer to these questions must be found in the study of the debit and credit pages of the record—in balancing what had been abolished against what had been preserved of the old regime as significant for the future.

First and foremost, the Japanese state had lost its superhuman basis of authority. It could no longer sanctify its proclamations by the claim that they were derived from an imperial personage who was in unique rapport with the spirits of the divine ancestors. The emperor himself had renounced the idea that he was some sort of special medium of supernatural infallibility.

Throughout their long history no greater change than this had ever come to the Japanese people. For two thousand years the ultimate authority by which government had imposed its will on the nation had rested on sanctions that transcended the right of subjects to criticize or to resist. The Japanese state had been not merely a secular entity. It had been a sacred church as well, and, like other churches, it was founded on the arrogation that in the last analysis the validity of its decisions was superhuman or supernatural. The state had claimed the authority to impose unquestionable obligation. It could not do this without trying to establish the fiction that over it hovered a special source of final truth. For the Japanese system of things, this existed in the person of the emperor, in whom resided an inherited sacredness which made his will irresistible.

No question regarding the postwar reconstruction of Japan was more vigorously and variously debated in America than that of the proper fate of the emperor. Opinions ranged from that favoring the forcible elimination of the emperor system as the main cause of Japan's dereliction to that claiming the need of protecting the imperial throne as the institution most essential to the orderly reconstruction of the nation. On the one hand, prosecution and punishment of the emperor as Japan's chief war criminal were called for. On the other, he was either exonerated as the enlightened opponent of Japan's aggressive militarism or relegated to unimportance by the assertion that he was less a war criminal than "a figurehead and a fraud perpetrated on the Japanese people."

It will be recalled that, in his renunciation of divinity, Hirohito had stated that the ties between the throne and the nation had always stood on mutual trust and affection and not on mere myth and legend. This must be understood as tantamount to an offer to modernize the tennoate by removing the anachronisms associated with its operations and, by so doing, to enter a bid for its retention, whatever political and social changes the nation might be forced to undergo.

If we can assume that Hirohito was speaking for the entire imperial dynasty of which he was a part, then his claims regarding the nature of the ties between sovereign and subjects were a tremendous idealization of history— claims which over and over again had been contradicted with a definiteness that could be controlled, from the governmental point of view, only by suppression and misrepresentation. Yet not all the ties were the creation of statecraft. Some were part of ingrained ways of thinking and acting that had persisted out of an ancient past.

There were three bonds between the throne and the people that were chiefly exploited by the ruling oligarchy. They were sacredness, benevolence, and power or authority. The three were so tightly interwoven by skilful governmental fingers that the manifestation of one was the manifestation of all. Sacredness was a means to power through religious qualifications; benevolence was a way to the same end through moral qualifications; authority, that is, power exercised by virtue of legal, moral, and religious capacities, was the goal of all.

Just as in the matter of the final disposition of the entire emperor system, so also in the discussion of the sacredness or divinity of the emperor, American attitudes showed a great variety of comprehension and emphasis. At the one extreme the *Tennō* was called the greatest god of Shinto and the main inspiration of a false worship that had spawned the most dangerous fanaticism on earth. In the other direction, any tendencies to become alarmed over the dangers of religious attachments between the Japanese throne and the people were allayed by the assertion that they were entirely the creation of modern politico-religious manipulation and would disappear of themselves when the artificial props of militarism were knocked away. According to this latter point of view, the so-called "divinity" of the emperor was something that had been improvised by nineteenth-century Japanese militarism in order to meet the demands of unification in the time of national crisis.

It is true that the modern nationalistic revival witnessed the creation of complicated governmental agencies for the control and dissemination of State Shinto so obviously contrived and so thoroughly unknown in the preceding Tokugawa era of Japanese history that even an authority on Japanese culture of the standing of Basil Hall Chamberlain was constrained to write about the situation as "The Invention of a New Religion." In its total aspect, however, the so-called "invention" was more a revival and a restoration than it was the development of something entirely new. It was an effort to provide modern Shinto with equipment and influence comparable to what it had possessed in the "golden age" prior to eclipse by Buddhism.

It is true again that the coercive measures frequently adopted by government offices, such as the forcing of god-shelves and talismans from the shrines on the homes of the nation, the requirement of participation in the ceremonies of Shinto as a token of loyalty, and the demand of assent to official propaganda, however mythological and unhistorical it might be, were all "manufactured." In the same category must be placed the multitude of burdensome conventions by which the subordination of the masses to the emperor was consummated.

Some of these conventions represented the survival of ancient taboos that protected the early priest-kings or persons of exalted position from the contamination of the common herd, and the latter on their part from the awesomeness of the *kami*-filled man of mysterious greatness. Some were shrewdly designed to inconvenience the subjects, under the influence of a well-known principle of oriental social behavior which holds that prestige is enhanced in proportion as others are hindered, embarrassed, humiliated, or insulted. The principle is not unknown elsewhere, but in Japan it approached the status of a fine art, especially in the emperor-subject relationship. Some of the conventions were undoubtedly the manifestations of a fear lest the person of the emperor might be subjected to actual physical violence or other indignity if he were permitted to come too near to his people. Some were the expression of normal social etiquette, strongly influenced by Confucian ceremonialism.

Elaborate language conventions that made use of a bewildering multiplicity of special honorifics emphasized the augustness of the *Tennō* and the vastness of his separation from ordinary mortals. The emperor's personal name was a legally protected monopoly. There could be only one Hirohito in all the world. The royal journeyings called for especially rigid ceremonial protection and emphasis. Whole countrysides through which the imperial cortege was to move were ostentatiously cleaned and disinfected under police supervision, houses were washed and fumigated, highways and bridges repaired, even new roads built, all to make the royal procession safe—and impressive. All looking down on the emperor from any superior position as from upper windows or from tramcars was prohibited.

Every Shinto shrine in the land furthered the same end of the ceremonial subordination of the masses to the sovereign. Members of the royal family had special privileges of approach to the gods. They were required to dismount from vehicles only when at the very entrance to the inner inclosure of the sanctuary; ordinary subjects had to walk, sometimes long distances, from the entrance to the outer inclosure.

Detailed regulations stipulated that the portraits of the emperor bestowed on the schools should receive the same ceremonial treatment as the person of His Majesty himself. Specially constructed repositories modeled on the architecture of the shrines or rooms dedicated exclusively to the purpose within the school buildings housed these precious objects. Teachers charged with the duty of protecting the portraits with their lives were on duty day and night. Well-authenticated stories of school principals who had perished while attempting to rescue the sacred likeness from school fires attest the grimness which this trust at times attained. On those special occasions when the portrait was brought forth for the reverence of mass obeisance, the ceremonies took on an elaboration that approached the climax of ritualistic subordination of participants.

Bowing before the gates of the imperial palace and distant salutation from all parts of the empire accomplished a like result. The same official motive was apparent in the treatment of imperial rescripts, especially the Imperial Rescript on Education. When the latter document was read before student assemblies, its ethical import took second place to punctiliousness and solemnity of procedure. By every possible ceremonial device the sacredness of the imperial person was impressively dramatized.

The discussion comes to a head when we turn to the question of the sense in which the emperor was regarded as a god. Is it legitimate to describe him as "the greatest god of Shinto"? If it is asked whether by this is meant the chief recipient of worship at the state shrines, then the answer must be an emphatic negative. In this sense he was never a god, since the living emperor was never the object of state enshrinement at any sanctuary, large or small. The study of Shinto ceremonies past and present will quickly dispel any tendency to believe that the living *Tennō* was ever supplicated as a supernatural god. The subordination of the emperor to the national deities is a definite aspect of Shinto. His part in the rites shows essentially the same kind of dependence on the gods as that of the humblest of his subjects.

Yet, we know that, in apparent contradiction to all this, the Japanese government definitely cultivated the idea that the emperor was *kami*, that is, sacred, and surrounded him with a protective ritualism which was more appropriate to the treatment of a god than a man. In view of the revolutionary change that came to Japanese ideology and law alike in the wake of the surrender at the close of World War II, it is important that we try to make clear to ourselves just what this meant.

On the basis of extensive evidence which cannot be introduced here, there are substantial reasons for concluding that the psychological roots of the *kami* concept in Japa-

nese culture are identical with those of the *mana* symbol,
so well known to students of human social origins as the
marvelous power or "occult force" which preliterate man
ascribed to objects which stimulated in him emotions of
wonder and awe. This occult power or "sacredness" was
resident in the man of special cunning or skill or wisdom,
or in the person of majestic mien or high authority, just
as it was in the roar of the thunder or the flash of the lightning.

This made the tribal chiefs of early Japanese culture the
manifestations of a mysterious "virtue" through the mediation of which the approved objectives of society were safeguarded and brought to fruition. These personages, and
later—as unification under a single dominant clan head
was consummated—the emperor, became the main avenue
along which the luck-giving power of the supernatural
flowed into human affairs. This was true of the conception
of the function of the reigning emperor. It was because of
Hirohito's "virtue" that his armies won victories in the
early stages of the Pacific war. The need of preserving the
purity and continuity of this virtue, and at the same time
of protecting ordinary mortals from a too violent exposure
to it, gave birth to a vast number of taboos which isolated
the emperor from his people. As the great Motoori said
long ago, this made the *Tennō* a "distant-*kami*." Some of
these taboos became actual laws written into state documents, even into the constitution of 1889; more of them
survived in the elaborate ceremonialism which separated
ruler and subjects and, at the same time, bound them together.

All this did not raise the emperor to the full status of an
enshrined god; but it made him a partaker in the essence
of the gods, a demigod, an offspring of the gods who was
always infallible in his revelation of the will of the gods.

We may summarize this section of the discussion by repeating, in relation to the Japanese insistence that their

emperor was *kami*, what R. R. Marett has so penetratingly
said about the significance of the *mana* symbol elsewhere—
that it was the authority behind the taboo wherewith the
inviolable right to rule on the part of the governing class
was enforced.[3] Seen in this perspective, it appears that the
conception that the emperor was *kami* is something very
old, even primitive, in Japanese tradition, not something
"manufactured" by recent politico-military utilitarianism.

The bond of sacredness by which the attempt was made
to tie the emotional life of the nation to the imperial throne
was closely intertwined with the idea of benevolence. A
main area of emphasis in the national life was the dis-
interested and even sacrificial goodness of the *Tennō*. This
was one of the chief means of official thought control. At
its most exaggerated level of interpretation the righteousness of the emperor was made the source of all the creative
love in the life of the people; viewed in its most realistic
light, it was the pious covering under which absolute authority sought to win for itself a hold on the deepest affections of the nation.

The propaganda pattern was so often repeated that it
became an easily identifiable stereotype. The successive
generations of emperors always loved and provided for
their subjects precisely as a good father cared for his children. As the sun in heaven shed its rays over all the world,
so the boundless benevolence of the emperor extended to
all his people. The mercy of the emperor reached everywhere within the land, and his righteousness shone beyond
the seas.

The Japanese nation was a single great race-family pre-
sided over by the father-emperor. While all were subjects
of the *Tennō*, the vast majority were at the same time his
actual blood-relations. The nation had a one-tribe origin.
At the center of the tribe was the imperial family, and at
the head of all was the emperor. Thus, while the people
revered the emperor as sacred or *kami*, they clung to him

and depended on him as their father. This is what they meant when they said that, in their system of national values, loyalty and filial piety were one and the same thing. In the last analysis the emperor, as the great father of all, owned both the land and the people and was obligated to make paternal provision for them. The whole nation was embodied in the person of the ruler. Furthermore, since the state was in reality a family, it followed that the right of headship must be hereditary in the royal line.

Since all the constructive forces of the national achievement stemmed from the ruler, it followed that the highest manifestation of virtue open to a Japanese was to respond to this imperial fatherliness with the morality of a good child, that is, obedient gratitude. This theme was idealized extravagantly and repeated endlessly in the national education. History was exploited with zeal and fabricated without conscience to demonstrate that throughout their long past the people had always revealed a matchless loyalty to their emperors. This was not the mere duty-feeling of the Gentiles; it was a unique devotion that only the Japanese understood. Subjects were taught to profess that they loved their emperor above all else on earth. Corresponding to the emperor's fatherly love for his children, it was the delight of the subjects to call themselves his babes —his *aka-chan* or "little red ones." In response to the question, "Whom do you love more than all others on earth?" the school child was taught to reply, "The emperor."

That this kind of conditioning, systematically carried on throughout the life-span of the individual, brought good returns in the widespread acceptance of the emperor system was made plain in the unpopularity of proposals to abolish the tennoate in the reconstruction period that followed immediately upon Japan's surrender. The truth is that most Japanese were able to think only in terms of a world view which had the emperor system at its center. In the spring elections of 1946 only the small Communist party demanded the elimination of the monarchy.

The two bonds between the emperor and his subjects which we have just examined were but auxiliary strands,of the main fastening, which was power. The whole thrust of State Shinto was directed toward the sanctification of authority. To all intents and purposes the third article of the constitution of 1889 declared this fact when it said that the emperor was sacred and inviolable. He was inviolable because he was sacred. The same purpose inspired the cultivation of the idea of imperial goodness. Japanese writers have often held Chinese statecraft up to ridicule for making a pretense of benevolence for the sake of power. This is exactly what the Japanese brand of political manipulation did, and on a scale unknown in China or anywhere else.

Sooner or later, everything in Japanese state ideology came around to the idea of a quality of infallibility lodged in the imperial will. Complete goodness and inherited sacredness were important in so far as they gave reinforcement to the authority of the imperial mandate. Regardless of what he might do or say in his private life, in matters of state the emperor could make no mistakes and could do no wrong. In this realm he represented all that was good and perfect. In this respect there was an important difference between the Japanese conception of divine imperial sovereignty and the European theory of the divine right of kings. According to the latter, outraged subjects could offer prayers to Almighty God that an evil-doing monarch would be led to mend his ways. The Japanese scheme offered no such recourse—because it was not needed. Japanese subjects prayed to the national gods on behalf of the emperor, but never that his wrongdoing should be forgiven and corrected. In his public relations the emperor was sinless and infallible. He functioned through the state but was always above it. If error appeared in national business, it was because his ministers and subjects had either misunderstood or misused his commands. Officers of the state had to take complete responsibility, not he. It was a sacrilege to attribute error and wrongdoing to the emperor or to subject his person to derogatory comment. He was always good and always right.

The significance to Japanese ideology of the proclamation of "a single dynasty unbroken for ages eternal" becomes apparent at this point. This declaration, which is the first article of the constitution of 1889, had three important values to the ruling oligarchy. In the first place, it was the chief support of the claim that the sovereign right was a sacred trust that had been inherited from the imperial ancestors and was not owned by the state, that is, the people. In the second place, the belief in the unbroken royal line and its corollary of inherited right to rule—for all who could accept it—made revolution and even peaceful revision of the fundamental nature of the state impossible, since a god-line could not be broken. Finally, it guaranteed "the eternity," that is, the continuity of the nation.

The one condition that the Japanese government tried to attach to the acceptance of the Potsdam ultimatum was the understanding that this declaration did not constitute a demand that prejudiced the prerogatives of the emperor as sovereign ruler. This condition was not merely the registration of Japan's desire to keep up a show of authority over against that of the Allied powers and thus save face. It was only partly that. It was also the expression of a deep-seated conviction that the continuation of the emperor system was necessary for the prevention of chaos within Japan.

The surprising ease with which the Allied powers were able to establish control over Japan was due in no small measure to their recognition of this important fact. The experts on Japanese affairs who formulated the policies knew very well that a people so thoroughly indoctrinated as were the Japanese in the teaching that the "eternity of the throne" was necessary to the "eternity of the state" could not be directed or organized in any other practicable way than under the emperor.

Apart from the ideological and ceremonial bonds by which the authority of the emperor was attached to the emotions of the nation, there were two other important "ties" that contributed to royal power, one economic, the other legal.

The subject of the wealth of the imperial family was not easily opened for discussion among the Japanese people during the absolutist regime. Respect for taboo carried over into this area and inhibited both initiative in investigation and opportunity to secure information. There are reasons for believing that data regarding royal economic resources were deliberately withheld from public knowledge. On the other hand, the emperor's simplicity and even his frugality of life, his generosity, and his gifts to charity and public welfare were emphasized. Stories of the poverty of rulers of other days, like that of the emperor who was reduced to the extremity of selling specimens of the imperial calligraphy in order to buy food, were often repeated.

The Meiji emperor came to the throne in 1867 a relatively poor man, but, by the time his reign closed in 1912, the wisdom of his ministers had laid the foundations of an economic supremacy which later made the imperial family the richest in Japan. In resources of lands and buildings and in business investments of all sorts the security of the emperor and his immediate relatives was pre-eminent. In this fundamental aspect of the relations of the *Tennō* and his people, the ties that connected them, far from being those of mutual trust and affection, were the operations of ordinary capitalistic exploitation, differing not at all from those of the feared and hated *Zaibatsu*, or family trusts.

It is outside the purposes of our discussion to go into the details of the legal manifestation of imperial authority in the Japanese political structure. We are interested primarily in the emotional and ceremonial aspects of the matter. It must be acknowledged, however, that the proper definition of *Tennō* is in terms of legal authority. In this respect his powers under the old regime were far more substantial than is generally recognized by Westerners. Under the articles of the constitution of 1889 and those of Imperial House Law, he was the supreme ruler of the empire and the repository of hereditary sovereignty in the male line. In addition to the exclusive right of initiating constitutional revision, he exercised legislative rights with the consent of the Diet. When this body was not in session, he could promulgate imperial ordinances in the place of law, subject to Diet approval later. It was within his jurisdiction to determine the organization of the various branches of government and to fix the salaries of all civil and military officers, along with the terms of their tenure of position. He was the supreme commander of the armed forces, and in him was vested the power to declare war, make peace, and conclude treaties.

As far as the relations of ordinary subjects were concerned, this vast power was mediated through complicated bureaucratic offices and courts of justice, along with much police and military regimentation, that were no better and no worse than the mediation of legal authority in other directions. As a matter of fact, "mutual trust and affection" was a subsidiary aspect of the situation.

The ties that bound the throne and the people together, that is, the nature of the mediation of authority in the Japanese state, are thus seen to have been very complex. If, in one direction, social and political organization appeared to gain in stability through the tendency to reverence the taboos and conventions thrown about the sovereign because he was "sacred," in another direction, the development of self-respecting personality on the part of ordinary people was seriously damaged. The overemphasis on ceremonialism and fiction produced artificiality, make-believe, and even hypocrisy in the national character. If, again, the systematic cultivation of the idea of imperial benevolence promoted subordination to the emperor's divine right to rule, the continuation of the relationship was possible only because it was accompanied by a regimentation that gave practically no opportunity for the development of effective public opinion and sound historical criticism.

The chief effect of the disestablishment of Shinto and the emperor's renunciation of divinity may be described, then, as the secularization of the state. This was the culmination of everything. It marked the end of the Japanese phase of the long struggle that has been going on throughout world-wide human culture for centuries past to release government from involvement with organized supernaturalism. Seen in this light, the development which we have been following takes on truly epic proportions. It is the major event in Japanese history—a transition from superhuman political sanctions to the status set forth in the inspiring words of the Preamble of the new constitution promulgated by the emperor on November 3, 1946:

> We, the Japanese people, acting through our duly elected representatives in the National Diet, determined that we shall secure for ourselves and our posterity the fruits of peaceful cooperation with all nations and the blessings of liberty throughout this land, and resolved that never again shall we be visited with the horrors of war through the action of government, do proclaim the sovereignty of the people's will and do ordain and establish this Constitution, founded upon the universal principle that government is a sacred trust the authority of which is derived from the people, the powers of which are exercised by the representatives of the people, and the benefits of which are enjoyed by the people.[4]

The emperor system itself gained great advantages from this change. The only conditions on which it could possibly survive in a world of intelligent, self-respecting men and women had been met. The sovereign had been set free, to move as a man among fellow-citizens and to win the right to rule on his merits. The events that followed the great change showed him striving almost pathetically to establish himself before the nation in a relationship of friendship and sanity. Legally the emperor had become "the symbol of the state," devoid of powers relating to government and completely under the direction of the Diet. His vast fortune was subjected to the same processes of inventory and redistribution as that accorded other family trusts.

We have examined thus far the traditional basis of authority in the Japanese state and the effect of the disestablishment of Shinto and the emperor's renunciation of divinity on this situation. It remains to consider the manner in which the directive of disestablishment removed the right of the officials to make participation in Shinto ceremonies and beliefs a standard of loyalty to the state.

By cutting the lines of all governmental affiliation with worship at the shrines, the power to compel the nation to make obeisance before the altars of the "ancestral deities" was abolished. In addition, all "physical symbols of State Shinto" in public buildings, which meant mainly small shrines and god-shelves, were ordered removed. Public money could no longer be diverted to the support of the shrines and their ceremonies. At the same time, by special proclamation, all Japanese were released from "any compulsion to believe or to profess to believe in Shinto." Public education and all official propaganda were freed of Shinto teaching. Textbooks used in the schools were ordered purged of all Shinto-inspired nationalism. Teaching staffs were screened to eliminate all partisans of militaristic and ultra-nationalistic ideologies. These new conditions had far-reaching implications. For the first time in her entire modern history, Japan had complete religious freedom.

Exactly what were the Japanese people compelled to believe, or to profess to believe, regarding the national cult?

The need of raising the question is augmented by the fact that no small amount of obfuscation of the issue with which it deals has been propagated in the American press, even since the disestablishment of State Shinto. Writers who have had introduction as authorities on Japanese affairs have aided and abetted this confusion.[5]

The situation is not clarified merely by repeating the assertion—made so constantly by Japanese government officials prior to the surrender—that State Shinto made no credal demands whatsoever upon its adherents. Their argument was very definite and, backed up as it was by the physical authority of the state, was generally conclusive. State Shinto was proclaimed to be without formal creed or official doctrine. Therefore, it was not a religion; its ceremonies had a purely civil or political meaning. Therefore, participation in the rites of the state cult did not contravene the freedom of religious belief guaranteed in the written constitution of 1889. Therefore, all Japanese subjects, regardless of private religious affiliations or convictions, must accept the duty of supporting State Shinto.

The whole series of propositions just reviewed is a texture of half-truths mixed with misunderstanding and outright misrepresentation. The fact that the participant in the state ceremonies was not obliged to make verbal attestation of acceptance of special creed and doctrine regarding the objects of worship altered in no way the basic condition that underlying the entire system were certain well-known forms of belief which he could not repudiate without endangering his entire status as a "good Japanese." The government itself sponsored these forms as the essential features of nationalism on the ideological side, and they could not be denied or resisted openly without meeting strong censure, public and private, and in some cases punishment by the police.

Central to the belief forms which all Japanese subjects were obliged to accept without question was the Ama-

terasu myth. We know that the national propaganda exalted this ancient sun-goddess above all other personages and
that the main purpose of educational policy, especially in
the lower grades of instruction, was to predispose the national character to the unquestioning acceptance of the
idea that the emperor's rights of sovereignty were intimately associated with the worship of this deity.

The means by which this was accomplished involved
assent on the part of all to certain propositions which, if
not stated in an explicit creed, were nevertheless definitely
proclaimed in the official definition of the structure of the
state and were implicit in the entire nationalistic nexus.
They are:

1. The emperor is the supreme head of the nation.
2. His right to rule is a family monopoly, handed on from generation
to generation in the royal line.
3. This right to rule was originally instituted by the sun-goddess in
a "divine edict," written into the text of the *Nihongi*. In this respect, at
least, this document becomes a sacred scripture as definitely as the Old
Testament is a sacred scripture to the Jews.
4. The sun-goddess is the supreme being in the scheme of Japanese
loyalties.
5. By cultivating the veneration of the sun-goddess, the acceptance
of the superhuman basis of the emperor's right to rule is reinforced.

At no point did the new conditions created by the disestablishment of State Shinto contribute more whole-
somely to a great clearing of the air than in the blowing-
away of the fog of the Amaterasu myth. It has to be admitted, however, that, when Hirohito announced that the
ties between himself and his subjects did not depend on
mere legends and myths, there was a strong probability
that he did not recognize the Amaterasu myth for what it
was in actual fact. It is fairly certain that the new education will have to work for a long time at the roots of Japanese conviction before there is a widespread capacity to
distinguish between history and mythology. At the same
time it is possible to undervalue the potentialities of Japa-

nese scholarship in this field and the response of the nation to it. The military defeat of Japan was at the same time the defeat of the traditionalists and the *goyō-gakusha*—scholar-purveyors to the Imperial Household—under whose aegis an impossible anachronism had been kept at the center of the political structure. The new order meant the elimination of an extraordinary claim on credulity and the opening of an opportunity for scientific scholarship (which still existed in Japan in spite of the suppressions of the old regime) to re-write the history of the nation and, in so doing, to introduce sanity into its entire cultural design—political, educational, and religious.

NOTES

1. *New York Times*, December 16, 1945. Cf. below, Appendix A, p. 000.
2. *New York Times*, January 1, 1946. Cf. below, Appendix B, p. 000.
3. R. R. Marett, "The Conception of Mana," *Transactions of the Third International Congress for the History of Religions* (Oxford), I (1908), 46–57.
4. *Mainichi Shimbun* ("Daily News"), November 4, 1946.
5. See *Newsweek*, January 14, 1946, p. 46.

CHAPTER VIII

PERMANENT VALUES

THE liberal creed for Japan is a challenge to all who believe in the possibility of a world community founded on universal justice and rationality. While seeking catholicity, it does not demand uniformity. It repudiates the narrow provincialism that finds other people trustworthy only in proportion as they are standardized in terms of one's own institutions and ideologies. It cherishes the expectation that out of cultural variety may come the enrichment of all. The creed says:

> We believe in the power of every race and every nation to create from its own cultural resources something good for itself and for the whole world. That is the liberal creed. . . . . It is the responsibility of all in authority to find out how much can be allowed rather than how much can be forbidden. That is the meaning of liberalism.[1]

With these words the commission of prominent Americans who visited Japan in the spring of 1946 prefaced their report to the Supreme Commander of the Allied Powers in Tokyo, covering recommendations for the reconstruction of the nation's educational affairs. The recognition of the existence of permanent values in Japanese culture which the creed sets forth is reinforced by the statements with which General Douglas MacArthur began his account of the Japanese general elections held in April of the same year. Behind the general's words the reader will be able to discern a conviction that the only enduring solution of the problems of Japanese reformation lies in the capacity of the people themselves to achieve democratic self-direction —essentially the same faith in the potentialities of Japanese culture as that expressed in the proclamation of the educators.

194

Pure democracy is inherently a spiritual quality which voluntarily must spring from the determined will of the people. It thus, if it is to become firmly rooted, may not be imposed upon a people by force, trickery, or coercion—nor is it a quality for barter or trade.[2]

These two remarkable declarations, coming as they do from the representatives of the nation that had most to do with the military defeat of Japan, serve to emphasize the impression that the future of that country, in so far as it is related to the attitudes and determinations of the American government and people, is to be left open to the guidance of the principles of liberalism, that is, to broad human sympathy, respect for personality, and belief that all peoples regardless of race, creed, or circumstances are identical in their capacities for intelligent and upright conduct. They give support to the conclusion that the fate of Shinto in a world of free men will depend in a large measure on whether or not it has within itself the possibilities of permanent contribution to a cosmopolitan society.

Reports that reached America immediately after the disestablishment gave evidence of a considerable falling-off of attendance at the Shinto shrines. Can this trend—if such it may be called—be expected to continue until the former state religion is reduced to impotence, its sanctuaries in ruins or turned to new uses, its priesthood disbanded, and its followers attached to new loyalties? Most important of all for the part of the American people in the settlement, should the goal of the complete overthrow of everything that State Shinto stood for be made the direct objective of policy toward Japan?

Now and then voices have been raised in America which answer these questions in a strong affirmative. The ultra-nationalistic policies which State Shinto fostered—the world rule of the emperor, Japanese racial superiority, the exaggeration of national peculiarities, preoccupation with Japanese culture, jealous exclusion of cosmopolitanism, the superiority of the Japanese state structure over all others, political absolutism founded on supernaturalism and mythology, the negation of democracy by the complete subordination of personality, and the subjection of conquered peoples to the national gods of Japan—all these characteristics are so utterly at variance with the principles on which true universalism must be founded that there is no room for tolerance toward State Shinto. If this is all that it has to offer in the way of cultural resource either for the Japanese people or for the world, then Shinto is fit only for repudiation and must be approached as the enemy of civilization and destroyed root and branch.[3] From this point of view it is as dangerous and ill advised to advocate the retention of any part of Shinto as it would be to favor the rehabilitation of naziism or fascism.

Over against this stands the wisdom of first investigating the possibility of a Shinto contribution to a sane, normal, and legitimate Japanese nationalism. Is it feasible or desirable that Shinto should be eliminated completely from Japanese society? It is particularly worthy of remembrance in this connection that the directive of disestablishment issued by the Allied supreme command did not risk any such wholesale and certain alienation of the co-operation of the Japanese people as would have followed the adoption of a policy of iconoclasm toward their national gods. Those who held the future of Japan in their hands remembered that Shinto was never a political party and that it was not merely a political philosophy—although it included that—but a religion, a sacred cultural heritage embodied in a community which had been rendered peculiarly sensitive by adversity.

Shinto was eliminated as a state religion but was not abolished as a national faith. No shrines were closed. The emperor was left free to take part in the worship of the former state sanctuaries as a private person. The same was true of all officials of the government, whether national, prefectural, or local. Under certain conditions, financial

donations to the national shrines from the Imperial Household Department were permitted. While it is true that ordinary subjects could no longer be forced into support of
the national religion, yet each was left to participate to the
limit of his own choice.

The old bureau of shrines of the Department of Home
Affairs, which was the major administrative agency by
which a favored status for State Shinto had been maintained, was abolished. The Religious Corporations Ordinances were amended so as to be applicable to the Shinto
shrines,[4] which meant the provision of legal arrangements
for the treatment of the former state cult as a privately
supported sect. For this is exactly what it had now become—another sect, thrown out into the national life
without discriminations against it or special favor to encourage it, to find a place entirely on its own merits.
Though deprived of the special legal privileges of the old
regime, it still had much left: extensive properties, sanctuaries, festivals, rituals, priesthood, literature, a long history, the prestige of former rank, and a large group of adherents whose loyalty could be counted on to become effective in proportion as those who had been held in line by
external compulsion withdrew. As for organization, there
remained to it whatever it saw fit to work out for itself
under the provisions of general law.

To what extent does the presence of these assets give assurance of a contribution to the future good of Japan or
to that of the wider international society? Has national
Shinto any qualifications as a good-will religion? These
questions may be examined from the points of view of potentialities as an ethics, a ritual, and a system of thought.

Whenever Japanese writers have attempted to appraise
the worth of their culture in its broadest aspects, they have
been prone to speak in terms of moral characteristics. The
tendency is so strong that even political documents are
likely to take on the complexion of hortatory ethics. Mag-

nificent tradition—the appeal to which makes up the well-known nationalistic pattern everywhere—has been created and guarded through the workings of the Japanese spirit. Shinto has been defined as a racial psychology that has persisted throughout the vicissitudes of the entire national story. Japan has produced a superior and enduring culture because of the contribution of a special type of "Japanese man"—a man furnished with a genius for acculturation, yet peculiarly endowed with the power of remaining "forever Japanese."

Can we identify this man? Not easily. So-called "racial psychology," particularly as it concerns the study of moral characteristics, seems to be singularly elusive of scientific treatment. It is difficult to steer a straight course in a sea as full of driftwood as that which we encounter when we approach Japan, one which is so agitated by the conflicting tides of self-adulation and prejudice, one which is still swept by the hatreds of the storm of war. Even when we say that "by their fruits ye shall know them," consistent objectivity is difficult, for there are many kinds of fruit.

Foreign critics of Japan have also sometimes announced their discovery of a characteristic Japanese man. His moral disposition has been depicted as sadistic, treacherous, and dominated by the worship of power. This has made him sycophantic toward those who control him and brutal toward those whom he himself controls. From the point of view of this kind of analysis, the dominant postwar attitude of the Japanese people is represented as one of suppressed bitterness and revenge. They are declared to have begun already a psychological and diplomatic offensive against the democratic powers of the West, designed to beguile their conquerors into a weak sentimentality in which their inhumanity will be forgotten and they will be assisted to get on their feet once more. To respect their cultural independence at this stage of the game is to play into the hands of trickery.[5]

Both of these views must be.repudiated. It is no more possible to find a persistent psychological endowment that makes a certain group of oriental people "forever Japanese" than it is to discover one that makes certain dark-skinned people "forever Negro," or certain aggregations of Westerners "forever American" or "forever British." The problem of change in moral characteristics must be approached from the standpoint of the flexibility of human nature, the certainty that its fundamental ways of reacting have a world-wide identity and the relation of these things to alterable environment—social, political, economic, and even geographical.

The chief defects of the ethical basis of Japanese life under the old regime appeared in the tendency to refer responsibility for programs of social melioration and education to governmental offices, and this corresponded to a notable deficiency in opportunity for developing effective public opinion. Shinto in the past fostered the perpetuation of these defects by upholding in precept and dramatic representation an extreme dependence on supernatural authority, and this weakened the sense of personal responsibility. As far as the influence of the shrines went, Shinto was very little interested in the inculcation of the ordinary, every-day, man-to-man virtures. The schools devoted great attention to these matters, but not the state cult.

While speaking in this manner, we do not overlook the fact that a certain amount of ethical symbolism is always present at the important festivals of the shrines in the form of the Three Sacred Treasures of Shinto—the mirror, the sword, and the stone necklace. All shrines of significance provide themselves with these emblems, and on occasions that call for a full array of ceremonial objects they are elevated on poles at the main approaches to the sanctuary —the mirror and the necklace together on the right as one faces the altars, the sword on the left. The moral qualities attached to them are various. The mirror has been made to

stand for wisdom, integrity, purity, and righteousness; the
sword for valor, sagacity, justice, and firmness; the jewels
for benevolence, gentleness, affection, and obedience. The
student of the history of East Asia may find Buddhist and
Confucian influences in a tendency to arrange these
virtues into triads. The best known is a restatement of the
Confucian grouping of wisdom, courage, and benevolence.

The ethical value of the Three Sacred Treasures is modified in two ways. One is the mechanical conception of their
operation. Ceremony never quite outgrows its magical
origins. Always there lurks behind the rite the shadow of
an ancient savage practice, an old confidence that in the
ceremonial paraphernalia and hocus-pocus themselves
there lives a vital, creative force. In the beginning the
Three Sacred Treasures were powerful magic—powerful
enough to call back the sun after prolonged obscuration—
and even today the level of virtue in human society is
raised merely by lifting them aloft on poles.

The other modifying influence lies in the fact that any
ordinary ethical significance that the three objects might
have is dominated by their place in the transfer of the authority of the throne at the time of the accession of a new
ruler. In this connection the official explanation is that they
symbolize the emperor's right to rule. Imperial House Law
of the present requires that, immediately on the death of
a *Tennō*, his successor be invested with the Three Sacred
Treasures of the imperial family. In origin they were
mighty regalia, talismans by which the *mana* of the dynasty was carried across the break of death. In Japanese
history the one who has them in his possession is the authentic sovereign. So intense are the emotions of awe and
reverence with which they are protected that one is in-
clined to believe that even in the present their meaning
partakes more of the old magical coloring than it does of
the symbolic. In the dark days just before the acceptance
of the Potsdam ultimatum, when it was plain that Japan

had finally arrived at the end of an age, the emperor called in his chief advisers and promised to guard the Three Sacred Treasures with his life.

When in 1940, Henry Pu-yi, the puppet emperor of Manchuria, visited the imperial court of Tokyo, he was presented with a mirror and a sword, two of the three holy objects, at the hands of the Japanese emperor. Six years later, when testifying before the International Military Tribunal in Tokyo, Mr. Pu-yi recalled the incident with the statement that it marked the greatest humiliation of his life.[6] In saying this, he indicated that he had not misunderstood the presentation. It meant that he was receiving an incomplete investiture of office—the stone necklace was absent—from the hands of his overlord, the emperor of Japan. He was recognizing the right of the Japanese to rule over Manchuria. It is the presence of this kind of political symbolism in the Three Sacred Treasures that complicates their use as imagery to reinforce the teaching of ordinary social ethics in Shinto.

In connection with the examination of the possibilities of ethical reconstruction in the national faith, the most significant fact to keep in mind is the fundamental one of military defeat. The arbitrament of war has thrust Japan into an era of unprecedented change and released suppressed forces of progress. Important aspects of the mental and moral climate have been transformed overnight. Much of the basis of the old nationalism to which Shinto gave supernatural sanction is gone. The artifice that the source of truth is in the proclamation of divine imperial authority is broken beyond repair. The idea that the state is a mystical body held together by the sentiment of awe is giving place to the conception of a unity to be achieved through the co-operation of morally responsible individuals. It is difficult to see how Japanese nationalism will ever again be able to make much use of the old slogans of a sacred soil that has never been defiled by the footsteps of a foreign enemy, a nation that has never brooked a foreign insult or been defeated in a foreign war, a people unique in loyalty or a state that is peerless in its structure.

Into this world of new opportunity the "average Japanese" brings a capacity for hard work and thrift that has been nurtured by long experience in the school of poverty. He brings a resiliency and fatalism that enable him to face calamity with equanimity. He brings aesthetic discernment and skill in working with his hands, love of grace and simplicity, attachment to local scenes, intimacy with nature, high intelligence and alertness, and pride in national achievement. His domestic and neighborhood virtues are those of mankind everywhere. His minimum definition of the "good life" would certainly include freedom from want and from fear. The inculcation of conventionality and docility was vastly overemphasized under the old regime, but these are not defects entirely. Recast by opportunity to participate in public enterprise on the basis of free private judgment of worth, they signify a capacity to follow wise leadership.

These are not special Shinto characteristics any more than the moral qualities that underlie Western culture are exclusively Christian. But it seems incontestable that if national Shinto is to make a contribution either to the good of Japan or to the world, it must find means of supporting them. It is possible that Shinto will be passed by as entirely irrelevant to the ongoing stream of Japanese life. Religions generally die that way. The remarkable growth of the Social Democratic party in postwar Japan suggests that the most aggressive organization for a new social order lies entirely outside religious arrangements. National Shinto, in so far as it has a future at all, may become merely an esoteric cult for the preservation of an antiquated classicism, devoted to ancient records and old rites. But this does not seem probable. State Shinto always had a strong national conscience; it is hard to believe that it will not have a strong social conscience.

The center of the issue of the ethical possibilities of national Shinto lies in the range of its support of world peace. In this matter we may accept the verdict of those who have affirmed that the Japanese people, if left to their own choice, will never want to go to war again. There is more danger that they will be cultivated as a war potential for assistance to one side or the other in a conflict of the great powers than that they themselves will seek to force their national will on others by means of military might. "Only the common people," says a recent Japanese writer, "know the bitterness of war."[7] The bitterness of the draught they have had to drink is too deep, their resentment against deception at the hands of their former military masters too strong, their sense of the need of turning all the resources they can muster into rehabilitation too discriminating, their consciousness of dependence on normal world fellowship too urgent, to afford grounds for serious apprehension in this matter.

In spite of the fact that the declaration of the purpose to bring "the whole world under one roof" was prostituted by Japanese militarism to the ends of a ruthless conquest of other peoples, it was always represented to the nation as an ideal of benevolence. It was to bring in the reign of peace and brotherhood over all the earth. In order to make its claims acceptable, militarism had to exploit the capacities of good will which the Japanese masses shared with the common people of the world everywhere as members of the human race.

Japanese sources have appealed to a certain passage in the Imperial Rescript on Education for evidence that this, the most important ethical document of pre-war Japan, exhorts to internationalism. In the official English translation the passage reads, "Extend your benevolence to all." The Japanese text says, *Hakuai shū ni oyoboshi*, "Extend benevolence to the multitude," that is, to people outside the narrower circle of family and immediate friends. The commentary prepared by the national Department of Education for the use of teachers in primary schools says: "It is important to have a heart of benevolence toward everybody and without distinction of degree of intimacy or proximity, to exert this influence widely. When this takes place, the peace of the world is realized and human life prospers in happiness and tranquility."[8] Other commentaries say that the Imperial Rescript on Education in this respect recognizes Japanese moral obligations to the human race and claims of a world-wide humanitarianism.

Japanese literature may not abound to overflowing in the expression of sentiments like these, but they are not absent from the total picture. It is certain that the *hakkō ichi-u* command and the passage from the Imperial Rescript on Education that we have just noted, along with similar statements from elsewhere that could be cited, will offer reinforcement to a desire for peace only to the extent that the conditions of peace—economic and political—are conceived as lying within the reach of serious effort. Without the assurance of a world organization for peace in which the Japanese people are permitted to participate as free members on a full parity with other nations, resentment and frustration, degradation and despair, cynicism and double-dealing, will only deepen among them. The demon of war, expelled from their house, will make companions of seven other evil spirits and return to bedevil the people. Every experienced educator knows this. The fate of man depends on the extent to which it becomes effective world opinion.

It is as essential for a nation as it is for an individual to have a sense of significance and achievement. Every people lives by a conviction of benevolent destiny. The growth of the "world spirit" among the Japanese—to recall the words of Count Gotō mentioned earlier in the discussion—will be in direct proportion to the cultural and economic reciprocity they meet with in associations on a world level. There is even a possibility that they will seek meaning and leadership as a "holy nation" in a special sense, that is, as a people who have forever renounced war.

Whether or not Shinto becomes a positive source of something good for the Japanese people depends in part on the shape of the world situation. Shinto may be expected to respond to its dominant human environment as well as to its local surroundings. The opposite contingency, that of Shinto becoming a veritable Cave of Adullam for all sorts of nationalistic plotting and revenge, exists, but it deserves serious consideration only to the extent that international relations themselves move in the direction of intrigue and darkness.

The ceremonial importance of national Shinto in its new status as a privately supported cultus has to be considered in the light of the services it rendered in this respect as a state religion. One of these is its commemorative function on behalf of those who have died for emperor and fatherland. The future of the great Yasukuni Shrine to the nation's war dead, on Kudan Hill in Tokyo, is the most sensitive area of a delicate problem. There are peculiar elements in the means that Japan has taken to honor her fallen heroes. There is no special Tomb to the Unknown Soldier. In a sense there are no unknown soldiers, for all are enshrined and their names recorded among the *kami*.

The difficulties that arise here are twofold. One lies in the fact that the commemoration includes definite presuppositions regarding the spirits of the dead. The state once shared in these presuppositions, and its priests offered prayers to the enshrined spirits for the protection of military enterprises. In the old regime this was no problem to the majority of the people, but a respectable minority either abstained from the rites or participated under protest on the grounds that definite deification was involved and that some of the spirits had been of inferior moral character when they lived on earth.

The second difficulty arises because the enshrinements are overloaded on the side of the glorification of the military ideal. Scattered throughout the land are a number of important sanctuaries where individual heroes other than those included in the mass enrolments of the Yasukuni Shrine are commemorated. In almost all cases the underlying reasons for the dedications are the same—the reward of those who died fighting for the imperial dynasty and the stimulation of patriotic military service.

Merely to hand the institutions set apart for these ends over to sectarian enterprise does not solve the basic problems. As long as national Shinto remains a privately supported sect, the worship of the spirits of the dead, in and of itself, is not a difficulty. The martial ideal is, however. If these military shrines are to be kept open—and it is not easy to see how they can be closed without violating the principle of religious freedom for which the Allied powers stand—the enshrinements should be broadened to include the commemoration of all who have rendered especially meritorious service in ordinary civilian life, and the *norito*, or ritualistic prayers used in the rites, should either be eliminated entirely or be recast to include a larger recognition of the concerns of peace.

On the other hand, it is no part of the proper operation of a conquering power to deny to a defeated enemy the right to carry out ceremonies in honor of its war dead, even though the cause for which they died is believed to have been a mistaken one. It is not sufficient to leave these rites to a private religious sect. They have a national importance; they are affectionately regarded as part of the magnificent tradition, probably its most tender part, and to close them to national celebration is only to feed the flame of resentment and bitterness.

The extensive arrangements which Shinto provided for

directing the activities of the emperor into religious rituals
have been interpreted as a clever device for keeping the
royal hands out of mischief. They also served to set a good
example for the people. The authorities took great pains to
remind the nation that the *Tennō* was scrupulous in his
attention to the gods. His processions to the Grand Imperial Shrine of Ise as well as his occasional visits to other
sanctuaries were accompanied by much pomp and ceremony. His participation in the services of the three Shinto
shrines within the palace inclosure at Tokyo was publicized
in much detail. All this supposedly served to increase popular dependence on the gods, to strengthen the system of
sanctions by which the authority of the emperor was maintained, and to emphasize the fact of Japan's self-sufficiency
in ceremonial tradition.

In the new order of things the emperor is given the right
to carry on his former ritualistic activities as a private person. The difficulty of preserving a clear and consistent distinction between purely individual functions and participation in an official capacity on the part of a person of such
importance hardly requires pointing out. Theoretically, if
the emperor continues to maintain a personal affiliation
with Shinto, his part in the ceremonies is interpretable in
a manner similar to that of the attendance of the President of the United States of America at the church of some
particular denomination. But, even in the case of the latter, public and private differentiation of function is not
rigid. The presidential inauguration ceremonies are, at the
very center of their meaning, Christian rites which make
use of the Bible and an oath in the name of the Christian
God.

This public association with traditional religious forms
is even more conspicuous in the enthronement ceremonies
of the Japanese emperor. Half the elaborate rites carried
out on this occasion are Chinese in origin; half are pure
Shinto. In the latter the emperor, in his capacity as high

priest of the nation, holds midnight communion with the gods of early Japanese worship and receives into his own body the Food Spirit by which the sustenance of the nation is assured. The ceremonies revive the procedure of the kingship succession of ancient Japan. For complexity and richness of parts and for suggestiveness to anthropological research they are probably unique among the enthronement ceremonies of history. They are part of the rightful cultural heritage of the nation. They cannot be forced into molds of mere private or sectarian meaning.

Japanese legal holidays are twelve in number. In the pre-surrender regime seven of them were specifically designated as festivals of the state cult. They comprised a worship on January 3 of each year of the ancestors who founded the nation, a festival of the vernal equinox, a worship of the spirit of the first emperor in April, a festival of the autumnal equinox, the presentation of first-fruits to the gods in October, a harvest thanksgiving festival in November, and the worship of the father of the reigning emperor at the end of December. All were commemorated by services at the imperial court, at the shrines, and in the schools.

Under the conditions of the disestablishment of Shinto, the festivals remain as legal holidays but without religious significance in so far as official participation on the part of public agencies and personnel of all sorts, including schools, is concerned. The opportunity for religious ceremonies remains in much the same sense as the celebration of Christmas and Thanksgiving Day is open to the churches of America. The change in Japanese holiday observance is not so much of an invasion of culture as it might appear to be at first glance. While the roots of some of the festivals go far down into the nation's past, the actual holiday calendar itself is a very recent achievement. It was not until March 4, 1927, that it was fixed as outlined above.

The consideration of Shinto's survival value as a system of thought arrives at an area of unusual sensitiveness in ancestor worship. From this point of view, Japanese writers have frequently viewed with alarm the story of the progress of Christianity in the West and have given expression to the fear that the veneration of their own forefathers would be "smothered by an invasion of monotheism." The determination of Japanese culture to resist fundamental change here has been emphasized repeatedly. Is there, then, any permanent value in Japanese ancestor worship?

The question is largely answered when we remember that Shinto is not and never was pure ancestor worship. This does not alter the fact, however, that the voices of officials of the government often united with those of scholars and priests to declare that essential Shinto was the veneration of those who had contributed meritorious service to the state. Shrines to old nature-gods, comparable to Wodin and Thor in the Western tradition, were meticulously designated "tombs." The sanctuary of the sun-goddess at Ise was not a religious edifice in the ordinary sense of the term but a splendid mausoleum where an ancient "empress" who founded the state was venerated. Japan was proclaimed to the world as "the classical land of necrolatry or the worship of the spirits of the dead and of ancestor worship."[9]

All this was disseminated vigorously abroad and yielded results so substantial that the truth never caught up with the propaganda and perhaps never will. Beginning with the idealizations of Lafcadio Hearn and extending to the very present, Shinto has been represented to the American people in the form of the worship of heroes and the veneration of the dead.

The stakes of the rulers of Japan in this misrepresentation were large. Shinto, promulgated as ancestor worship, and accepted as such by a people who were denied opportunity to learn otherwise, gave special dignity and authenticity to the requirement that all should participate in its ceremonies and beliefs. It was a perpetual challenge to the living that their devotion should measure up to the standards of an idealized past. It offered attractive rewards of continued remembrance after death to those who met its demands. Gratitude to ancestors and the perpetuation of "the beautiful customs of loyalty and filial piety," binding past and present, were cultivated as a great seedbed out of which grew conformity and subordination. "Ancestor worship" was an important means of keeping Japanese society static and safe against the inoculation of "foreign individualism."

The fact of the matter is that State Shinto was not interested in ancestor worship as such at all. It was primarily devoted to the concentration of public sentiment on a certain type of national polity. It was really the worship of the state in a particularly dangerous absolutistic form. The reduction of this situation to a level at which it becomes assimilable with a culture that has world-wide validity is far from being at root a simple matter of the change of the intolerance of Christian monotheism to an attitude of tolerance. It requires that an area of the national life that has been nurtured in darkness be thrown open to the light of scientific research. Most of all, it requires a fundamental change in the nature of the state itself. Before Shinto can claim respectability as ancestor worship, it has to produce the legitimate marks of the thing it claims. Always the Shinto argument has moved in a great circular begging of the question. The state religion had to be ancestor worship, otherwise Amaterasu Omikami was not an ancestress, and the foundations of the emperor's right to rule were straw and stubble. Since, therefore, Amaterasu Omikami was a true ancestress, Shinto was ancestor worship.

There is an inheritance in the Japanese family system, however, in which the worship of ancestors, or at least the veneration of the dead, has an authenticity and a genuine cultural significance that cannot be set aside. The lines here lead back to Confucianism, not Shinto. Regardless of this fact, however, there seems little doubt that the Japanese are conscious of a historical depth to the family perspective not common in America. The Japanese family is not merely an aggregation of people present in physical form on earth at any given time. Belief in the continued existence of the dead in the spirit world is deep, and, even where it is absent, custom is strong. The spirits of the dead must be honored by symbolic presentations of food and drink—once they were fed that way. They must be kept informed of important happenings among those left on earth, especially of births and marriages. They are present at the family council and, ever watchful from the spirit world, stand by ready to help in the crises of precarious mundane affairs. These aspects of belief in the powers and needs of the family dead are in no danger of violation at the hands of Western culture on the religious side. If they are washed away, it will be by a wave of secularism to which Japan herself has contributed.

Other phases of Shinto's significance as a system of thought need not detain us long. The capacity of the human mind to rationalize inherited beliefs is apparently unlimited. All theology shows the influence of this talent for reorientation. The process has been conspicuous in Shinto history. Reflecting Buddhist contacts, Shinto thinkers have at times declared that the unifying principle beneath all the external diversity of their god-world was pantheism; under Christian influence they have discovered the germs of monotheism in their classical literature. Development toward either a pantheistic or a theistic world-view is a possibility in proportion as one or the other of these two great religious systems gains ascendancy. In the one case, the members of the old polytheistic pantheon become merely local appearances of the Great Life of the Universe. It was a Shinto-Buddhist syncretist of the Tokugawa period who declared: "All the Heavenly and Earthly

Deities, the Ancestral Deities, the Mountain Deities and the Sea Deities are nothing but different manifestations of the Fundamentally True One [that is, of Mahavairocana, the Absolute Buddha]."[10]

In the other case, the rank and file of the gods are simply neglected and finally disappear. All that is left is God under a Japanese name and a certain number of Japanese saints. As we already know, many Shinto-Christian syncretists have announced that the first god mentioned in the *Kojiki* is none other than the Lord of the Universe and the Maker of the World of Christian faith. The effect of closer contact with other religions on the organization of Shinto thought, brought about by the disestablishment, will probably be considerable.

Unbroken and enduring continuity is the idea toward which Japanese nationalism reaches out when it contemplates the worth of its Shinto tradition. This is the primary quality of the national faith noted by Dr. Genchi Katō in an account of its cultural significance which he has drawn up. In Shinto survives the oldest institutional life of the Japanese people—older even than the emperor system. In spite of all the changes of fortune that have come to it, Shinto still lives on, while all the old tribal and communal religions of the West have passed away. In Shinto appears a unique tenacity, which is the registration, through the conviction of faith and the drama of ritual, of the existence of an indestructible vitality enfolded within the national life. The Japanese people are possessed by a powerful determination to keep Shinto alive and significant. Its will to live is as strong as is the will to live on the part of the nation itself. It may change, but it will not die. The Shinto emphasis on absolute sincerity has as much ethico-religious significance to the world as has the principle of universal love that once became incarnate along the shores of Lake Galilee or the theme of unconditional benevolence which once came to life in the valley of the

Ganges.[11] Other Japanese writers have given expression to a like idealism.

After reviewing the record of the use that was made of Shinto to force conformity on the members of conquered nations and the Japanese people alike, and with the knowledge of how officialdom degraded the meaning of sincerity into an unquestioning acceptance of governmental orders, the Western critic may be forgiven when he raises the suspicion that this eulogy is a strong affirmation of the possession of something that secretly and perhaps subconsciously is felt as a lack. No one who really knows the Japanese people, however, will admit that the story of their sincerity in all its parts rings untrue to universal ideals. When in the thirteenth century the priests of the Outer Shrine of Ise wrote in the *Shintō Gobusho:* "That which pleases the gods is virtue and sincerity and not any number of material offerings," they spoke for the entire human race.

Shinto in the past gave its blessing to whatever was regarded as having utmost importance in the general social and national experience. It will continue to do so in the future. Everything depends on the nature of what is believed to have utmost importance. This is a factor that is subject to change. The Western world is much concerned with the purpose that the Japanese conviction of what is significant shall include in its dominant pattern a respect for individual personality and a social and political nexus woven from the free co-operation of morally responsible men and women. This is the meaning of real democracy. The measure of Japan's participation in it depends directly on the extent to which she is given a vital stake in genuine democracy on a world level.

NOTES

1. *Report of the United States Education Mission to Japan, Submitted to the Supreme Commander for the Allied Powers, Tokyo, March 30, 1946* (Washington, D.C.: United States Government Printing Office, 1946), pp. 4–5.

2. *Department of State Bulletin, June 27, 1946* (Washington, D.C., 1946), p. 1067.

3. See Robert O. Ballou, *Shinto, the Unconquered Enemy* (New York, 1945), p. 79.

4. *Department of State Bulletin, May 12, 1946* (Washington, D.C., 1946), p. 807.

5. See Channing Liem, "The Re-education of Japan," *Forum*, November, 1945, pp. 193–97.

6. *New York Times*, August 20, 1946.

7. Shūmei Ogawa, *Nippon Nisen Roppyaku Nen Shi* ("Two Thousand Six Hundred Years of Japanese History") (Tokyo, 1939), p. 436.

8. *Jinjō Shōgaku Shūshinsho: Kyōshiyō* ("Textbook of Ethics for Ordinary Primary Schools: Teachers' Manual"), VI (Tokyo, 1939), 231.

9. Genchi Katō, *A Study of Shintō: The Religion of the Japanese Nation* (Tokyo, 1926), p. 51.

10. From the writings of Minamoto-no-Yoshiyasu (cited and translated in *ibid.*, p. 136).

11. *Ibid.*, pp. 200, 213–14.

APPENDIX A

DIRECTIVE FOR THE DISESTABLISHMENT OF STATE SHINTO

ORDERS FROM THE SUPREME COMMANDER FOR THE ALLIED POWERS TO THE JAPANESE GOVERNMENT

15 December 1945

MEMORANDUM FOR: IMPERIAL JAPANESE GOVERNMENT

THROUGH : Central Liaison Office, Tokyo

SUBJECT : Abolition of Governmental Sponsorship, Support, Perpetuation, Control, and Dissemination of State Shinto (*Kokka Shintō, Jinja Shintō*)

1. In order to free the Japanese people from direct or indirect compulsion to believe or profess to believe in a religion or cult officially designated by the state, and

In order to lift from the Japanese people the burden of compulsory financial support of an ideology which has contributed to their war guilt, defeat, suffering, privation, and present deplorable condition, and

In order to prevent recurrence of the perversion of Shinto theory and beliefs into militaristic and ultra-nationalistic propaganda designed to delude the Japanese people and lead them into wars of aggression, and

In order to assist the Japanese people in a rededication of their national life to building a new Japan based upon ideals of perpetual peace and democracy,

It is hereby directed that:

a. The sponsorship, support, perpetuation, control, and dissemination of Shinto by the Japanese national, prefectural, and local governments, or by public officials, subordinates, and employees acting in their official capacity are prohibited and will cease immediately.

b. All financial support from public funds and all official affiliation with Shinto and Shinto shrines are prohibited and will cease immediately.

> (1) While no financial support from public funds will be extended to shrines located on public reservations or parks, this prohibition will not be construed to preclude the Japanese Government from continuing to support the areas on which such shrines are located.

(2) Private financial support of all Shinto shrines which have been previously supported in whole or in part by public funds will be permitted, provided such private support is entirely voluntary and is in no way derived from forced or involuntary contributions.

c. All propagation and dissemination of militaristic and ultranationalistic ideology in Shinto doctrines, practices, rites, ceremonies, or observances, as well as in the doctrines, practices, rites, ceremonies, and observances of any other religion, faith, sect, creed, or philosophy, are prohibited and will cease immediately.

d. The Religious Functions Order relating to the Grand Shrine of Ise and the Religious Functions Order relating to State and other Shrines will be annulled.

e. The Shrine Board (*Jingi-in*) of the Ministry of Home Affairs will be abolished, and its present functions, duties, and administrative obligations will not be assumed by any other governmental or tax-supported agency.

f. All public educational institutions whose primary function is either the investigation and dissemination of Shinto or the training of a Shinto priesthood will be abolished and their physical properties diverted to other uses. Their present functions, duties, and administrative obligations will not be assumed by any other governmental or tax-supported agency.

g. Private educational institutions for the investigation and dissemination of Shinto and for the training of priesthood for Shinto will be permitted and will operate with the same privileges and be subject to the same controls and restrictions as any other private educational institution having no affiliation with the government; in no case, however, will they receive support from public funds, and in no case will they propagate and disseminate militaristic and ultra-nationalistic ideology.

h. The dissemination of Shinto doctrines in any form and by any means in any educational institution supported wholly or in part by public funds is prohibited and will cease immediately.

(1) All teachers' manuals and text-books now in use in any educational institution supported wholly or in part by public funds will be censored, and all Shinto doctrine will be deleted. No teachers' manual or text-book which is published in the future for use in such institutions will contain any Shinto doctrine.

(2) No visits to Shinto shrines and no rites, practices, or ceremonies associated with Shinto will be conducted or sponsored by any educational institution supported wholly or in part by public funds.

i. Circulation by the government of "The Fundamental Principles of the National Structure" (*Kokutai no Hongi*), "The Way of the

Subject" (*Shinmin no Michi*), and all similar official volumes, commentaries, interpretations, or instructions on Shinto is prohibited.

j. The use in official writings of the terms "Greater East Asia War" (*Dai Toa Senso*), "The Whole World under One Roof" (*Hakko Ichi-u*), and all other terms whose connotation in Japanese is inextricably connected with State Shinto, militarism, and ultra-nationalism is prohibited and will cease immediately.

k. God-shelves (*kamidana*) and all other physical symbols of State Shinto in any office, school, institution, organization, or structure supported wholly or in part by public funds are prohibited and will be removed immediately.

l. No official, subordinate, employee, student, citizen, or resident of Japan will be discriminated against because of his failure to profess and believe in or participate in any practice, rite, ceremony, or observance of State Shinto or of any other religion.

m. No official of the national, prefectural, or local government, acting in his public capacity, will visit any shrine to report his assumption of office, to report on conditions of government, or to participate as a representative of government in any ceremony or observance.

2. *a.* The purpose of this directive is to separate religion from the state, to prevent misuse of religion for political ends, and to put all religions, faiths, and creeds upon exactly the same legal basis, entitled to precisely the same opportunities and protection. It forbids affiliation with the government and the propagation and dissemination of militaristic and ultra-nationalistic ideology not only to Shinto but to the followers of all religions, faiths, sects, creeds, or philosophies.

b. The provisions of this directive will apply with equal force to all rites, practices, ceremonies, observances, beliefs, teachings, mythology, legends, philosophy, shrines, and physical symbols associated with Shinto.

c. The term State Shinto within the meaning of this directive will refer to that branch of Shinto (*Kokka Shinto* or *Jinja Shinto*) which by official acts of the Japanese Government has been differentiated from the religion of Sect Shinto (*Shuha Shinto* or *Kyoha Shinto*) and has been classified as a nonreligious national cult commonly known as State Shinto, National Shinto, or Shrine Shinto.

d. The term Sect Shinto (*Shuha Shinto* or *Kyoha Shinto*) will refer to that branch of Shinto (composed of 13 recognized sects) which by popular belief, legal commentary, and the official acts of the Japanese Government has been recognized to be a religion.

e. Pursuant to the terms of Article I of the Basic Directive on "Removal of Restrictions on Political, Civil, and Religious Liberties" issued on 4 October 1945 by the Supreme Commander for the Allied Powers in which the Japanese people were assured complete religious freedom,

(1) Sect Shinto will enjoy the same protection as any other religion.

(2) Shrine Shinto, after having been divorced from the state and divested of its militaristic and ultra-nationalistic elements, will be recognized as a religion if its adherents so desire and will be granted the same protection as any other religion in so far as it may in fact be the philosophy or religion of Japanese individuals.

f. Militaristic and ultra-nationalistic ideology, as used in this directive, embraces those teachings, beliefs, and theories, which advocate or justify a mission on the part of Japan to extend its rule over other nations and peoples by reason of:

(1) The doctrine that the Emperor of Japan is superior to the heads of other states because of ancestry, descent, or special origin.

(2) The doctrine that the people of Japan are superior to the people of other lands because of ancestry, descent, or special origin.

(3) The doctrine that the islands of Japan are superior to other lands because of divine or special origin.

(4) Any other doctrine which tends to delude the Japanese people into embarking upon wars of aggression or to glorify the use of force as an instrument for the settlement of disputes with other peoples.

3. The Imperial Japanese Government will submit a comprehensive report to this Headquarters not later than 15 March 1946 describing in detail all action taken to comply with all provisions of this directive.

4. All officials, subordinates, and employees of the Japanese national, prefectural, and local governments, all teachers and education officials, and all citizens and residents of Japan will be held personally accountable for compliance with the spirit as well as the letter of all provisions of this directive.

FOR THE SUPREME COMMANDER:

[*Signed*]   H. W. ALLEN,
Colonel, A.G.D.,
Asst. Adjutant General.

[NOTE.—The above is a transcription of an original received from the Civil Affairs Division of the War Department, Washington, D.C. I am responsible for the title that appears at the heading of this order—"Directive for the Disestablishment of State Shinto." Everything else is the official text.—D. C. H.]

APPENDIX B

IMPERIAL RESCRIPT ON THE RECON-
STRUCTION OF NEW JAPAN

[NOTE BY TRANSLATOR.—The following rescript was promulgated on January 1, 1946. It is chiefly noteworthy for the fact that it contains the passage in which the Japanese emperor makes renunciation of divinity. The translation is made from the *Tokyo Asahi Shimbun* for January 1, 1946.—D. C. H.]

IMPERIAL EDICT

Facing now a new year, we recall how, at the beginning of the Meiji Era, Emperor Meiji deigned to hand down the Charter Oath in Five Articles as the policy of the state.

He declared:

1. Conference shall be inaugurated widely, and all things shall be settled by public discussion.
2. Upper and lower classes shall be of one mind, and governmental administration shall be carried out vigorously.
3. Each and every person, in one and the same manner, beginning with the civil and military authorities and extending to all the masses, shall have opportunity to realize his aspirations, that the human spirit be not frustrated.
4. The evil practices of former times shall be broken down, and everything shall be founded on the just and equitable principles of nature.
5. Knowledge shall be sought throughout the world, that the foundations of imperial rule may be strengthened.

His Majesty's wishes were impartial and just. What can we add to them? We herewith renew the oath and resolve on the promotion of the welfare of the nation. At all costs we must pattern our actions according to the spirit of the Charter Oath, we must leave behind the evil practices of former years, we must foster the will of the people, raise up government and people, and carry through in the spirit of peace, we must enrich education and strengthen the foundations of culture, and thus undertake the advancement of the life of the people and the establishment of a new Japan.

Cities and towns, large and small, that have sustained the ravages of war, the sufferings of an afflicted people, the stagnation of industry, the lack of food, the growing trend of unemployment—all this wounds the heart. Yet we doubt not that if our countrymen [*waga kokumin*], by squarely facing the ordeals of the present and by firmly resolving to seek civilization through peace, bring this resolution to good issue, then not only for our country but also for all mankind a bright future will open up.

Moreover, we know that the spirit of love of home and the spirit of love of country are especially strong in our nation. Now in truth is the time for expanding this and for putting forth sacrificial efforts for the consummation of the love of mankind. When we reflect on the results of the long-continued war which has ended in our defeat [*haiboku*], we fear that there is danger that our people find the situation hard to bear and that they sink to the depths of discouragement. As the winds of adversity gradually heighten, there is peril in the weakening of moral principles and the marked confusion of thought that they bring.

We stand together with you our countrymen. Our gains and losses have ever been one. We desire that our woe and weal should be shared. The bonds between us and our countrymen have been tied together from first to last by mutual trust and affection. They do not originate in mere myth and legend. They do not have their basis in the fictitious ideas that the emperor is manifest god [*akitsu mikami*] and that the Japanese people are a race superior to other races and therefore destined to rule the world.

In order to alleviate the trials and sufferings of the people, my government will exhaust all means for devising every kind of plan and program. At the same time, it is our wish that our countrymen should trample disaster underfoot and rise above it, and that they should go forward bravely in making good the suffering of the present and in building up industry and civilization. In the development of the characteristics of tolerance and mutual forgiveness, in mutual dependence and assistance, in the unity of the civil life of our country—in these things there is well revealed the true worth of our supreme tradition, for which we are not ashamed. We doubt not that herein is the reason why in truth our countrymen can make a tremendous contribution to the happiness and progress of mankind.

Plans for the year are made at the beginning of the year. We earnestly desire that our countrymen, on whom we rely, may have the same purpose as ourselves, that we personally take warning and that we personally take heart in order that we may bring to fulfilment this great task.

[*Imperial Sign Manual, Imperial Seal*]   January 1, 1946

[*Countersigned by*

    The Prime Minister
    Other Cabinet Ministers]

INDEX

Allied Powers, in Japan, 174, 194

Amaterasu Omikami, 5, 6, 9, 10, 11, 25; ancestress of Japanese emperor, 60-62, 210; in Christian syncretism, 114, 117; cosmic significance of, 63-64; founder of Japanese state, 17, 61; function of, in national unification, 65; myth of, in state education, 192-93; recent interpretations of, 60-65; worship of, at Ise, 54-65

Ame-no-Minakanushi-no-Kami("Lord of the Center of Heaven"), as evidence of early Shinto monotheism, 112-16

Ancestor worship, 7, 10; abolition of state support of, 190; national protection by ancestral spirits, 13-19; place in new Shinto, 209-12; required in Imperial Rescript on Education, 81-82; union of, with nature worship, 62-63

Anesaki, Masaharu, 48

Antiforeignism in Japan, 76-78, 88-91

Arai, Sekizen, 149

Araki, General Sadao, 11

Army, Japanese: agent of benevolent destiny, 23; inviolability of, 23-24; seat of antiforeignism, 90-91

Assimilation, Japanese policy of, as related to conquered peoples, 163-65

Aston, W. G., 20

Authority, of emperor, 185-87

Benevolence, of Japanese emperor, 183-84

Buddhism: acceptance of Shrine worship, 131-32; and art, 141; attacked by Shinto and Confucianism, 125-28; characteristics of, in relation to nationalism, 136-38; contribution of, to national emergency, 132-33; contribution of great priests of, to national welfare, 138-40; criticism of Shinto by, 129-31; doctrine of state of, 143-46; education, 128, 141; harmony with recent science and philosophy, 142; introduction of, into Japan, 59, 124; and Japanese nationalism, 124-51; moral influence of, 141-42; and pacifism, 146-49; social welfare work of, modern, 140-41; syncretism with Shinto, 211-12; and war, 148-51

Bushidō: and Christianity, 102-7; and sincerity, 159

Ceremonies, in new Shinto, 205-8

Chamberlain, Basil Hall, 113, 178

Charter Oath of Emperor Meiji, 74-75, 219

Christianity, Japanese: acceptance of Shinto shrine worship by, 96-101; accommodation by, to Shinto doctrine, 110-22; adjustments of, to Shinto nationalism, 70-93; 95-122; and Bushidō, 102-7; as the center of the problem of nationalistic unification, 93; ethical apologetic for, 101-7; and meaning of kami, 117-22; periods of growth and repudiation of, 75-93; repeal of edicts against, 71-72; statistics of, 95; surrender of initiative by, 95; suspected by the army, 91-93; syncretism with Shinto thought, 211-12; and war, 108-10

Communist party, in Japan, 185

Confucianism in Japan: characteristics of, 76; in Imperial Rescript on Education, 79; opposition to Buddhism by, 126-27; and Three Sacred Treasures, 200

Constitution of 1889, 7, 182, 185, 186,